D1525708

TO CHANGE THEM FOREVER

To Change Them Forever

Indian Education at the
Rainy Mountain Boarding School, 1893–1920

by Clyde Ellis

UNIVERSITY OF OKLAHOMA PRESS
NORMAN AND LONDON

This book is published with the generous assistance of The McCasland Foundation, Duncan, Oklahoma.

Book design by Bill Cason

Chapter 1 is reprinted from the *American Indian Culture and Research Journal*, volume 18, number 3, 1994. Chapter 3 is copyright 1994, reprinted from *The Chronicles of Oklahoma* (Oklahoma City: Oklahoma Historical Society, 1994).

Ellis, Clyde, 1958–
     To change them forever : Indian education at the Rainy
Mountain Boarding School, 1893–1920 / by Clyde Ellis.
          p.   cm.
     Includes bibliographical references and index.
     ISBN 0–8061–2825–9 (alk. paper)
     1. Kiowa Indians—Education.   2. Rainy Mountain Boarding
School. 3. Kiowa Indians—Cultural assimilation.   4. Indians of
North America—Education.   5. Indians of North America—
Cultural assimilation.   I. Title.
E99.K5E45   1996
370′.89974—dc20   95–45423
                                                              CIP

The paper in this book meets the guidelines for permanence and durability of the Committee on Production Guidelines for Book Longevity of the Council on Library Resources, Inc. ∞

Copyright © 1996 by the University of Oklahoma Press, Norman, Publishing Division of the University. All rights reserved. Manufactured in the U.S.A.

1   2   3   4   5   6   7   8   9   10

To

HARRY AND JESSIE TOFPI

and

PARKER MCKENZIE

Contents

Illustrations

Photographs

Maps

Preface

There are on the way to Rainy Mountain many landmarks,
many journeys in the one.
—N. SCOTT MOMADAY

ON A CLEAR, WINDY AFTERNOON IN AUGUST 1990, NINETY-TWO-
year-old Parker McKenzie, a Kiowa Indian from Mountain
View, Oklahoma, pointed to the ramshackle remains of the
Rainy Mountain Boarding School and said, "That was where I
got my start." The ruins to which he pointed lay in the center
of what had once been the campus of a reservation boarding
school where between 1893 and 1920 hundreds of young Kiowas
underwent what the U.S. government hoped would be a transforming experience. Here, in a remote corner of the sprawling
Kiowa-Comanche-Apache Reservation in southwestern Oklahoma, government teachers struggled for nearly three decades
to make the vision of a new Indian race a reality. Crowded into
the school's dormitories and classrooms, Kiowa children toiled
to become the sort of civilized, competent citizens whom the
government hoped would be culturally indistinguishable from
the whites who surrounded them.

The price of their transformation was the forfeiture of what
made them Indian. Youngsters like McKenzie were to emerge
permanently transformed; the school's immediate goal was to
prevent them from "going back to the blanket," a term of deri-

sion applied to backsliders who could not resist the temptation of returning to native ways. The long-term hope was that, guided by the liberating experience of the school, children would serve their communities as beacons of change and examples of proper living. It was a grand plan, for schooling meant more than simply inculcating Indian children with white education: it was to be the definitive moment in the metamorphosis of a people. Writing to the commissioner of Indian affairs in 1899, Rainy Mountain Superintendent Cora Dunn spoke bluntly of the school's mission: "Our purpose," she wrote, "is to change them forever."[1]

As part of the nationwide system of government-sponsored reservation boarding schools, Rainy Mountain functioned as a laboratory of change and transformation in which Indian youth would discover and copy forms of behavior and culture. The idea was not new. Speaking to the 1895 Lake Mohonk Conference, United States Commissioner of Indian Education Dr. W. N. Hailmann preached a philosophy that reached back to the age of Jefferson. The message combined Jefferson's vision of peaceful reform with the need to find a solution to the late nineteenth century's Indian Problem. The answer, said Hailmann, was the school. "Give us your children," he implored Indian parents. "We will give them letters and make them acquainted with the printed page. . . . With these comes the great emancipation, and the school shall give you that."[2] To those who designed it, such a policy seemed practical, rational, and permanent.

Policy makers and reformers alike envisioned a truly transformed Indian population—that is, one culturally indistinguishable from its Anglo-Saxon, Protestant (usually) model. Observers generally agreed that little if anything in Indian culture was worth saving and deemed schooling both prudent and humane in the campaign to save the Indians from their own barbarous habits. Indeed, the alternatives were stark, for the choice seemed to lie between the extremes of the uplifting experience of schools and the gospel and the extinction that many believed to be the fate of all backward races. For the most part policy makers settled on a program of civilizing the tribes, which meant exposing them to the rudiments of the Christian faith, to habits of industry and Anglo-American agriculture, and to the discipline and self-discovery of the schoolroom. And, above all, it meant saving them from what most observers considered a blighted existence, devoid of law or morals and lacking Christian truth. Slowly and steadily the classroom would remold generations of Indian youth into a new race. Dedicated to a peaceful war of assimilation, U.S. government officials sincerely believed, as one Indian agent explained it, that the "constant dripping of the water . . . wears away the hardest stone." Like the proverbial drop of water, schools would systematically wear away the hardest cultural stones. Thus armed with the skills and knowledge necessary to forge new lives, reformers said, Indian students would not only be Americanized, but would also become the models for the complete transformation of a people.[3]

An ambitious but flawed plan, Indian education usually sounded better in theory than it was in fact. Despite the rhetorical flourishes of the Bureau of Indian Affairs, the program never had the support necessary to accomplish its huge goals, and it never produced the degree of change that reformers and policy makers envisioned. Although they depended on education to bring Indians into the American mainstream, government officials rarely proved willing to build schools in sufficient numbers or to allocate sufficient funds. This was especially true on the reservations, where schools represented the front line of the forced assimilation campaign. The failure to compel every Indian child to spend a decade immersed in American culture had enormous implications, for it doomed to failure the government's hopes for civilizing the tribes according to Anglo-American values. This failure in turn enabled Indians to maintain their cultural identity in varying degree on reservations throughout the country.

Despite education's importance in the campaign to transform Indians, Indian schools (especially those on the reservations) have received relatively little attention. Major off-reservation schools such as Carlisle and Phoenix have attracted notice, but reservation schools have not. This is unfortunate, for reservation boarding schools represented the critical link in the government's civilizing program. What is more, they were a clear example of how the campaign to change Indians foundered on the shoals of politics and expedience. Because the schools lay at the center of the campaign for forced assimilation, notes Willard Rollings, yet failed of their purpose, their role in the campaign deserves much deeper study.[4]

Recent contributions to the field have begun to do this. Significantly, most of these works go beyond simple discussions of policy and recognize the need to place Indian education in broader historical and cultural contexts. Margaret Szasz and Frederick Hoxie, for example, joined their discussions of education policy to larger intellectual and political currents. In his important book on policy making between 1880 and 1920, Hoxie maintains that science, politics, and popular culture each had a profound influence that led ultimately to dramatic changes in Indian education policy at the turn of the century. Szasz's two volumes on the history of Indian education discuss the subject in greater detail than ever before.[5]

Added to these are more and better studies of Indian education that have brought the Indian schools under closer scrutiny. Sally McBeth's work on boarding schools in southwestern Oklahoma skillfully combined oral accounts with historical narrative to produce a more sophisticated understanding of schooling's cultural consequences. Placing students at the center of her discussion, McBeth's book suggested important new ideas about whether the schools effectively assimilated students and raised issues that helped to initiate this study. Henrietta Mann's study of Cheyenne-Arapaho schooling between 1871 and 1982 took a similar approach. By using oral histories collected from former students, Mann presented perspectives often overlooked in policy-based studies.[6]

By the late 1980s, Adams, Szasz, Hoxie, McBeth, and Mann,

among others, pointed the way to significant new approaches for examining Indian education. The 1988 publication of Robert Trennert's work on the Phoenix Indian School showed the influence of these works, especially in the book's sections on student life. Trennert's was the first in a steadily growing collection of studies that placed great emphasis on oral histories and long-neglected memoirs. Basil Johnston's work on Canadian boarding schools, Devon Mihesuah's study of the Cherokee Female Seminary, K. Tsianina Lomawaima's remarkable discussion of Chilocco, and Michael Coleman's book on Indian schooling from 1850 to 1930 all attest to the interest in Indian schools and the issues of assimilation and cultural change that characterized them. Coleman's work is especially important on this count. It reminds us of the survival of literally hundreds of memoirs and autobiographical accounts that have all too often been overshadowed but that illustrate the richest sources available on the Indian schools.[7]

This study examines education on the Kiowa-Comanche-Apache Reservation in western Oklahoma during the critical period of the late nineteenth and early twentieth centuries. It explores how in reality the government's agenda of forced assimilation worked in a reservation boarding school. Created in 1867 by the Treaty of Medicine Lodge Creek, the Kiowa-Comanche-Apache Reservation represented what Robert Utley once described as the "severest test" of the government's civilizing agenda.[8] The Kiowas and Comanches who epitomized Utley's description were among the last of the region's tribes to accept reservation life, and even after agreeing to it they proved to be a difficult, sometimes recalcitrant lot. Determined to settle and civilize them according to Anglo-American notions of work and culture, the U.S. government promised a school and teacher for every thirty school-aged children, of whom there were about six hundred at the Kiowa-Comanche Agency. Convinced of the urgency of introducing these tribes to Christianity, farming, thrift, discipline, and notions of private property, the government promised extensive support for such endeavors. Indeed, said observers, here was a laboratory in which to test the effectiveness of the campaign of forced assimilation spearheaded by the schools.

I explore boarding school education in the broad context of the reservation era, roughly 1870 to 1920, in an attempt to link Rainy Mountain and the Kiowa people to larger forces and issues that affected Indian education. Chapter 1 summarizes the policy decisions and developments that created the Indian school system during the nineteenth century. Chapter 2 introduces the Kiowa-Comanche Agency and examines the early history of schooling under the reservation's difficult circumstances. Chapter 3 turns directly to Rainy Mountain School and discusses its early years. Chapter 4 focuses on student life at the school and rests heavily on interviews and conversations with former students from the Rainy Mountain, Riverside, and Fort Sill boarding schools. Chapter 5 examines the changing attitudes inside the Indian Office during the Progressive Era— changes that marked a reordering of policy aims in general and of the Indian schools in particular. Chapters 6 and 7 assess the school's last ten years and its closing. Chapter 8 considers Rainy Mountain's legacy in the Kiowa community.

To understand a school like Rainy Mountain is to open a window on the lives of the Kiowa children who went there and in turn to explore the fate of a people. In the words of N. Scott Momaday, it is an intellectual and historical journey "intricate with motion and meaning; and it is made with the whole memory, that experience of the mind which is legendary as well as historical, personal as well as cultural." "Personal as well as cultural": that is an apt description of the journey begun by Parker McKenzie and hundreds of his kinsmen in the fastness of a reservation boarding school one hundred years ago. Momaday says that in the time before such places existed, the Kiowas "had conceived a good idea of themselves; they had dared to imagine and determine who they were."[9] This book is about how that good idea was challenged, and about how it survived.

Of those who helped make this study possible, none are more

important than the Indian people who agreed to share their personal histories with me. This book is evidence of the fact that Indian people have a great deal to tell and that they have something to say that is worth hearing.

I cannot fully express my thanks to Harry and Jessie Tofpi and to Ron and Jennie Bemo. Their willingness to take my wife and me into their lives has taught us much about the richness and vitality of contemporary Indian life. I am deeply indebted to Harry for his willingness to share with me the most precious knowledge of all: an understanding of how he and so many others survived the rigors of boarding school life and why they fought so hard to remember who they are. To the Bemos, who took us into their home and family, fed us, and looked after us, I wish to acknowledge a debt that can never be accurately described or adequately repaid.

Parker McKenzie's memories of Rainy Mountain School gave me rare insights into the life he led there as a student ninety years ago. His remarkable collection of documents and his unparalleled knowledge of the Kiowa-Comanche Agency helped me understand the schools more thoroughly than I otherwise could have done. His willingness to discuss those subjects and to visit the campus with me on several occasions proved to be invaluable both personally and intellectually.

Numerous other people agreed to speak about their experiences or about those of their relatives. In doing so, most of them did not submit to formal interviews but offered valuable insights during informal conversations and visits. Many of them have asked that they not be identified or cited in the text, but I wish to acknowledge publicly their contributions to this study.

Professor L. G. Moses of Oklahoma State University helped form and strengthen my ideas about Indian education in the dissertation from which this manuscript has evolved. His sharp editorial skills, his understanding of American Indian history, and his friendship have greatly enhanced this study. Professor W. David Baird, the Howard W. White Professor of History at

Pepperdine University, was instrumental in my early doctoral
training and provided the impetus for this study while it lay
in its early stages. Paul Bischoff, Donald Brown, Richard Rohrs,
and Michael Smith of Oklahoma State University read this
manuscript in earlier forms and offered criticisms that strength-
ened it enormously. Professor Robert Trennert of Arizona State
University read the entire manuscript at an early stage and
offered suggestions that were incisive and challenging. Luke E.
Lassiter of the University of North Carolina at Chapel Hill,
James B. Ellis, Sr., of the University of Nevada at Reno, Robert
P. Slater, and Bryan Smithey each read portions of this manuscript and offered sound advice and good ideas. Dr. and Mrs.
David Salay gave me the use of their home in Edmond, Okla-
homa, during the summer of 1990 and enabled me to work in
Oklahoma during the most critical stage of my early research.

I take particular pleasure in acknowledging the Oklahoma
Historical Society's Indian Archives Division. I thank Director
William Welge, who suggested Rainy Mountain as a topic and
then eagerly assisted my research; Judith Michener, whose unstinting assistance at the archives hastened my work and vastly
improved my all too limited knowledge of the society's hold-
ings; and photoarchivist Chester Cowen, who guided me
through the society's voluminous photographic archives. In
addition, staff members at the National Archives in Washington, D.C., and at the University of Oklahoma's Western History
Collections pointed the way to important collections and documents. Significant financial assistance came through the Town-
send Dissertation Fellowship awarded to me in 1989 by the
Department of History at Oklahoma State University.

At the University of Oklahoma Press, John Drayton, editor-
in-chief, and Mildred Logan, my in-house editor, were generous
and encouraging through every phase of the project. Noel Par-
sons copy edited the manuscript with both precision and a light
touch, qualities that all authors ought to appreciate. Collectively they have made this experience rewarding and exhilarat-
ing, and I thank them for it.

Finally, my wife Mary has endured this project longer than she should have had to and has been unfailingly supportive during the months required to finish it—except when the muffler fell off the car. Caught between the dilemma of finishing off a chapter or repairing the car so that she could avoid the baleful stares of fellow motorists, I was quickly convinced that there *are* things in this world that exceed a manuscript in importance. Her editorial skills and sense of good history have made all of this worthwhile.

TO CHANGE THEM FOREVER

1

"It Is a Remedy for Barbarism"
The Creation of the Indian School System

ALTHOUGH THE U.S. GOVERNMENT'S CIVILIZING AGENDA EM-
braced a variety of means, none was more important, or prob-
lematic, than education. It alone promised a systematic, uniform standard against which progress could be measured.
Schools could be built anywhere and everywhere, they could
be opened to students of all ages, they could accommodate both
boys and girls, and they could act as the most powerful engine
of all in the cultural transformation that policy makers devised
for Indians. Most importantly, education targeted children. Vul-
nerable to change and least able to resist it, at least in theory,
children represented the logical targets of a policy designed to
erase one culture and replace it with another. Education, as
Robert Utley has observed, "represented the most dangerous
of all attacks on basic Indian values, the one most likely to
succeed in the end because it aimed at the children, who had
known little if any of the old reservation life."[1]

During the nineteenth century policy makers understood the
advantages of such a policy and eagerly pursued it. A popular
maxim of the post–Civil War era held that educating children,
not feeding adults, constituted the government's truest policy
objective. Commissioner of Indian Affairs Edward Smith caught
the mood in 1873 by boldly suggesting that "any plan for civilization which does not provide for training the young is short
sighted and expensive. . . . Four or five years of this appliance
of civilization cures [sic] one-half of the barbarism of the Indian
tribe permanently." Success, of course, meant more than liter-

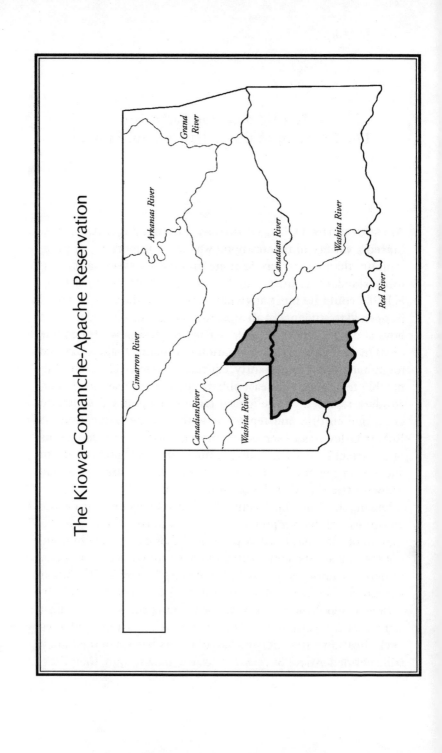

The Kiowa-Comanche-Apache Reservation

ate school children; it meant an end to the confusing and confounding Indian Problem. This was the most important test of all, for until the schools erased all traces of native culture, the campaign remained unfinished. The classroom promised to prepare the way for a new kind of Indian, one who would not be identified with any kind of problem. It was slow, frustrating work, but no other approach, in Frederick Hoxie's opinion, could so marvelously achieve the task of "molding people anew."[2]

This kind of thinking appeared early in the colonial era, became a centerpiece of Indian policy by the early eighteenth century, and dominated policy making for much of the next one hundred years. Accepting the challenge to extend the fruits of civilization to its Indian wards, the U.S. government constructed a set of policy objectives in the late eighteenth century that survived virtually unchanged into the early twentieth century. Leading figures like Thomas Jefferson, Thomas L. McKenney, Cyrus Kingsbury, and Jedidiah Morse laid the foundations for a civilizing program that rested on the twin pillars of church and school. Describing such a program "as not only a dictate of humanity, and a duty enjoined by the Gospel, but an act of justice," Kingsbury observed that an Indian school system would "impart to them that knowledge which is calculated to make them useful citizens, and pious Christians." Though the decades to come would batter such thinking, no other approach eclipsed it until the early twentieth century. "Among the responsible and respected public figures in the first decades of United States developments," notes historian Paul Prucha, "there was a reasonable consensus that was the underpinning of official policy toward the Indians." And that "reasonable consensus" meant civilizing and assimilating Indians, not killing them.[3] Settle them, school them, above all teach them to farm, and the issue would resolve itself. As for the remnant that resisted, time would eventually rid the country of those who refused the new order of things.

The fledgling Indian school system established during the

first third of the nineteenth century became extraordinarily
significant in the post–Civil War years. Indeed, its role in the
campaign to transform the tribes, especially on the Great Plains,
was unquestioned by that time. Commenting on the situation
as it appeared in 1866, Commissioner of Indian Affairs Dennis
Cooley asserted that education was virtually "the only means
of saving any considerable portion of the race from the life and
death of [the] heathen."[4] Cooley's observation, made in the
wake of the opening of the trans-Mississippi West, underscored
the urgency of a civilizing agenda that came to rest on education. Moreover, the government's self-professed intention to
save and civilize the nation's Indians helped to ensure the survival of the Indian school system.

By the 1870s, then, the time had come to make good on the
promise of civilizing the Indians. Policy makers in Washington
agreed that education pointed the way to the quickest, most
enduring success. With the reservation system and much bally-
hooed Peace Policy in place, the task of erasing the Indian
Problem began in earnest. Now, said government officials, it
would build enough schools to educate every eligible Indian
child in the country. Supporters lined up enthusiastically behind the campaign. Commissioner of Indian Affairs Ezra Hayt
observed in 1879 that "Indian children are as bright and teach-
able as average white children of the same ages."[5] Hampton
Institute Superintendent General S. C. Armstrong assured the
National Educational Association in 1884 that schooling for
the Indian was proper, necessary, and realistic: "Wherever I go
I find this question, Does it pay? . . . We say this: that there is
no difficulty in educating Indians. . . . The work for these races,
the Indian and the Negro, is the most stimulating and hopeful
of any on this continent, for the reason that those to whom
light is first offered receive it with an earnestness." Of some
seventy students at Carlisle and Hampton, reported Armstrong,
only seven, in his words, had "gone back to the blanket." Not
even the best white schools, he reminded his audience, could
claim a 90 percent success rate. A. L. Riggs of the Santee Normal

School struck an even more emphatic note when he said "I take it that the question of the possibility of educating Indians is settled; that no more discussion is needed."[6]

Others offered similarly optimistic hopes for the Indian schools. In one of his most famous statements, Thomas Jefferson Morgan, the architect of the Indian school system, said in 1892 that no "insuperable obstacles" existed to prevent the successful education and absorption of Indian children. A roundtable discussion on Indian education at the 1895 annual meeting of the National Education Association led one participant to affirm that the Indian pupil "is just as capable as any white pupil I have ever had." When queried as to whether or not the "intellectual faculties of the Indian are essentially different from those of the white race," Richard Pratt, the famous Carlisle School founder and superintendent, answered that he did not think they were.[7]

A widespread belief in the possibilities of achieving a substantial degree of change marked the era. Friends of the Indian insisted that the tribes suffered only from inferior circumstances, not from deficient capacities. Pratt assured his listeners that Indians were not intellectually inferior; their flaw was an environmental one that, because it produced no law or religion in the Western mold, left native peoples culturally thwarted. The surest route to success, therefore, lay in altering the conditions in which Indians lived and matured.

Reformers believed deeply in the humanity, and ability, of Indian students and in the correctness of the campaign to elevate them. Thomas Jefferson Morgan believed that the transformation could be handled with relative ease. "The task is not by any means an herculean one," he observed. "The entire Indian school population is less than that of Rhode Island. The government of the United States . . . has at its command unlimited means, and can undertake and complete this work without feeling it to be in any degree a burden." What the plan required, Morgan said, was "wise direction." In 1885 Commissioner of Indian Affairs Hiram Price assured his audience that

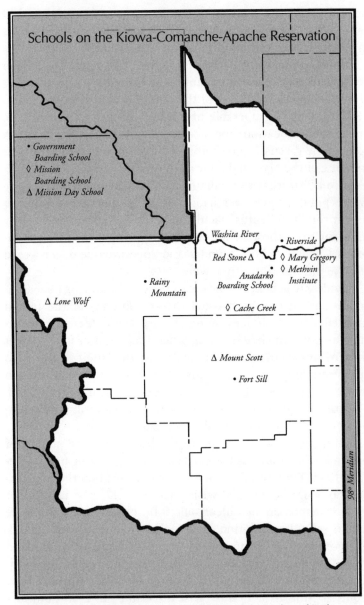

Schools on the Kiowa-Comanche-Apache Reservation

• Government
  Boarding School
◊ Mission
  Boarding School
Δ Mission Day School

Washita River
• Riverside
Red Stone Δ
◊ Mary Gregory
◊ Methvin
Anadarko   Institute
Boarding School
• Rainy
  Mountain
Δ Lone Wolf
◊ Cache Creek

Δ Mount Scott
• Fort Sill

98° Meridian

Adapted from George Posey Wild, "History of Education of Plains Indians of Southwest Oklahoma Since The Civil War. " Ph.D. dissertation, University of Oklahoma, 1941: p. 256.

"It is cheaper to give them education . . . than it is to fight them. . . . Since experience and practical demonstration has [sic] taught us that the Indian is easily educated, and that he is, like the Anglo-Saxon, a progressive being, capable of the highest mental and moral development, it is the policy of the friends of civilization . . . to extend to him the advantages of education as rapidly as possible."[8]

Combining their optimism with evangelical fervor, reformers and so-called friends of the Indian predicted sweeping success in the schools. U.S. Commissioner of Education William T. Harris observed in 1889 that "the new education for our American Indians as it has been founded in recent years by devoted men and women, undertakes to solve the problem of civilizing them by a radical system of education not merely in books, nor merely in religious ceremonies, but in matters of clothing, personal cleanliness, matters of dietary [sic], and especially in habits of industry."[9]

Pratt put the matter more bluntly. "I am a Baptist," he said, "because I believe in immersing the Indians in our civilization and when we get them under holding them there until they are thoroughly soaked."[10] Once soaked, Pratt assured his audiences, Indians would never return to the blanket. The process was benevolent by the standards of the day, it was less expensive than the dole (or combat), it fit nicely with the nation's assumptions about its Christian duties, and, best of all, it seemed practical.

Essays and commentaries from the post–Civil War years are replete with descriptions of Indians as unfortunate, simple, or backward. Yet these adjectives suggested permeable conditions, circumstances that could be changed by the forceful application of training and discipline. Moreover, Indians could be transformed into more than workers; Pratt and Morgan insisted they become part of mainstream society. Ironically, the most difficult barrier to such a transformation was not the fear that the Indians could not attain the goals set by the government, but that whites might not embrace them if they did. Indians were not the problem, said Hampton Superintendent S. C. Armstrong, for they had the capacity to make the adjustment. "The trouble," he noted with prophetic candor, "is with the white people."[11]

Spurred on by U. S. Grant's famous Peace Policy, momentum for a comprehensive Indian education system emerged during Carl Schurz's tenure as secretary of the interior (1877–81). An outspoken reform advocate and an enthusiastic supporter of a nationwide reservation school system, Schurz outlined his ideas at the beginning of his tenure. The program included much that reformers already embraced: exclusive use of the English language, compulsory education laws, an extensive system of boarding schools, manual and industrial training for the boys, domestic training for the girls, and religious training for all. Moreover, instead of dallying, Schurz urged the government to commit significant funds to such a program and to accept the burden of doing so for at least the next decade and a half.[12]

In 1880, Schurz decried the disgraceful lack of support for education on many reservations and noted that the commissioner's report for the same year described the "utterly insufficient . . . means at the disposal of the department." The report went on to state that in 1880 fully "15,000 Indians at seventeen agencies have no treaty school funds whatever." Surely the importance of having at least one boarding school at each agency "need not be argued," especially when a mere fifteen of sixty-six agencies had adequate schooling facilities. Echoing Schurz's call for action, the commissioner's report concluded that "the necessity for increased and increasing appropriations . . . is manifest and urgent."[13]

Schurz was not alone. By far the most important advocate of Indian schools was Thomas Jefferson Morgan, whom Father Prucha has described as "the first significant national figure in the history of American Indian education." Beginning with Morgan's appointment as commissioner of Indian affairs in June 1889, Indian education became the chief tool in the government's civilizing program. In Morgan, moreover, the Indian

Office found a strong-willed and ambitious leader. An ordained Baptist minister and professional educator, he brought administrative experience and a reformer's zeal to the Indian Office. Announcing in 1889 that the "anomalous position heretofore occupied by the Indians in this country cannot much longer be maintained," Morgan introduced a program that he promised would "turn the American Indian into the Indian American."[14] Speaking that year to the Lake Mohonk Conference of Friends of the Indian, Morgan outlined his philosophy of Indian education:

> When we speak of the education of the Indian, we mean that comprehensive system of training and instruction which will convert them into American citizens. . . . Education is the medium through which the rising generation of Indians are to be brought into fraternal and harmonious relationships with their white fellow-citizens, and with them enjoy the sweets of refined homes, the delight of social intercourse, the emoluments of commerce and trade, the advantages of travel, together with the pleasures that come from literature, science, and philosophy, and the solace and stimulus afforded by a true religion.

Admitting that "this civilization may not be the best possible," Morgan nonetheless believed that it was the best the Indians would get. "They cannot escape it," he concluded, "and must either conform to it or be crushed by it."[15]

Morgan promised nothing less than a new future to those who accepted the program. "Nothing . . . is so distinctly a product of the soil as is the American school system," he wrote. Under its shadow "race distinctions give way to national characteristics," Morgan continued, and produce generations who honor the same institutions, celebrate the same heritage, and worship the same God.[16] It all seemed so obvious, and so practical.

In 1891, Morgan issued a ten-point plan for an Indian school system that represented what he called "a settled Indian policy." First, the Indian school system must be comprehensive and must offer the fullest educational opportunities to the largest possible number of students. "Nothing less than universal education should be attempted," he insisted in a separate opinion. The absence of such a system, he warned, left Indians "doomed either to destruction or to hopeless degradation." Universal education, moreover, should conform to the course of study used in public schools, which was where Indian students should ultimately complete their studies. Thus, not only would they educate and elevate native youngsters, but Indian schools would also provide the solid foundation from which those children could make the leap into the mainstream. Emphasizing more than literacy and discipline, the classroom would be a conduit through which children would pass on their way to being completely absorbed. Education was not some neutral enterprise; it was a way to conduct a peaceful war on Indian children.[17]

Second, Morgan demanded "definiteness of aim." The lack of such clarity had produced "confusion in the public mind as to precisely what the Government is aiming to accomplish." In reality the goal was unmistakably clear: "to incorporate the Indians into the national life . . . as Americans . . . enjoying all the privileges and sharing the burden of American citizenship. . . . [This] should be inculcated as a fundamental doctrine in every Indian school." The problem, of course, was finding a way to achieve such lofty goals. One way was to be clear and consistent in the creation and application of standards, thus the ten-point plan. Another was to ensure that Indians understood "that their future lies largely in their own hands." Accepting this responsibility meant prosperity and happiness; neglecting it meant being "swept aside or crushed by the irresistible tide of civilization, which has no place for drones, no sympathy with idleness, and no rations for the improvident."

Points three and four addressed the plan's administrative structure. Dismayed by the chaotic bureaucracy of the Indian Service, Morgan called for "clearness of outline" and reminded his audience that "we cannot gather grapes from thistles nor figs from thorns." Because Indians were a backward race, he said, the situation demanded clear, well-thought-out policies.

Fortitude and careful direction could close "the dreary chasm of a thousand years of tedious evolution," but bureaucratic wrangling would continue to cause the indirection and hand-wringing typical of the Indian Service. But such clarity must also include flexibility, something that Morgan defined loosely as the adaptation of means to ends. Acknowledging that not all Indians were alike, and that single-minded policies could not work equally well in all places, the commissioner advocated specific goals and plans according to immediate circumstances.

Fifth, Morgan addressed what he called justice. For him this did not mean protecting Indian rights, but reflected instead the paternalism that had long influenced the Indian Office. When Morgan spoke of justice, he spoke in terms of accepting the obligation to do right by his wards. "We do not ask that they concede anything of real value to themselves," he wrote, "but only that for their highest welfare they abandon their tribal organizations . . . and accept in lieu thereof American citizen-ship." Of course, such pronouncements reached to the heart of paternalism by defining "real value" as nonexistent in native culture. After all, as one of Morgan's successors observed in 1899, "the well-known inferiority of the great mass of Indians in religion, intelligence, morals, and home life" simply necessi-tated taking the children so that they might be guided "to the proper channel."[18]

This meant that resistance justified coercion. The matter of justice was clear to Morgan; he had the responsibility of ensur-ing that Indian children received useful educations. Indians, on the other hand, were responsible for accepting the opportunity. Morgan wrote to the secretary of the interior on the matter:

I do not believe that . . . people, who, for the most part, speak no English, live in squalor and degradation, make little progress from year to year, who are a perpetual source of expense of the Govern-ment , . . a hindrance to civilization and a clog on our progress, have any right to forcibly keep their children out of school to grow up . . . a race of barbarians and semi-savages. We owe it to these children to prevent, forcibly if need be, so great and appalling a calamity from befalling them.[19]

Morgan underscored this idea in point six by announcing that the government had certain obligations it could not shirk. Like most of his colleagues, Morgan believed he had the right and obligation to require parents to enroll their children and to administer severe punishment to those who resisted. He brooked no dissent on this issue and used it often as an illustration of how important it was for the government to stand firm in its resolve. If his plans were followed to the letter, he said, the bulk of Indian children would soon be in school and thus well on their way to transforming an entire race. "Two or three years I think will suffice," he wrote optimistically in 1890, "when all Indian youth of school age . . . can be put in school."[20]

Insisting that such powers "belong unmistakably to the prerogatives of the National Government," Morgan pleaded only for what he called "a reasonable opportunity . . . whereby [Indian] children can be lifted onto a plane where they will have an equal chance." There could be no discussion of the matter; as with so much of what Morgan espoused, his absolute sense of moral and cultural superiority made any alternative untenable. He responded to his critics by reminding them that he was being firm for the good of the Indians, who did not understand what was in their best interests anyway. Any other course was sure to produce well-deserved failure. And to those Indians who might be tempted to stand in the way of progress, Morgan issued a stern warning: "If after this reasonable preparation, they are unable or unwilling to sustain themselves, they must go to the wall. It will be survival of the fittest."

Despite the unyielding nature of Morgan's rhetoric, point seven demanded humanity in all that the Indian Service did. "For the sake of the history we are making as a Christian nation," he wrote, "we should treat them not only justly and humanely, but with as much generosity as is consistent with their highest welfare. This we are doing." Future generations might find Morgan's moral posturing hypocritical or even dishonest. Still, when viewed in the historical context of the late nineteenth century and of the values that determined race relations at the time, Morgan's philosophy reflected a relatively humane solution.

Eighth, the commissioner demanded "radicalness," which he defined as taking his plan at full value and implementing it completely:

> If we purpose [sic] to educate Indian children, let us educate them all. If we look to the schools as one of the chief factors of the great transformation, why not establish at once enough to embrace the entire body of available Indian youth? . . . If there could be gathered by the end of 1893 . . . nearly all of the Indian children and they be kept there for ten years, the work would be substantially accomplished; for . . there would grow up a generation of English speaking Indians, accustomed to the ways of civilized life. . . . Forever after [they will be] the . . . dominant force among them.

Radical application meant radical change. Get them in school, he said, and keep them there. Erase completely any vestige of their culture, inculcate in them American values and ideas, and then release them to an independent life.

Finally, Morgan insisted on two mutually dependent ideas that tied the campaign together—stability and time. One without the other doomed the system to failure. Stability meant trained professionals in the schools, administrative competence, able leadership, and a bureau that was politically and personally above reproach. Chafing at the mediocrity that afflicted so much of his bureau, Morgan called for higher standards and cautioned against caving in to easy, short-term fixes. It might take a full decade for the effort to succeed, he said (Schurz had predicted at least fifteen years), but nothing short of a long-term vision would do. Given enough time, he argued, education would "bring the young Indians into a right relationship with the age in which they live, and put into their hands the tools by which they may gain for themselves food and clothing and build for themselves homes."

Like Jefferson before him, Morgan hoped that Indians would come willingly to the schools. In the end, he believed that Indian students themselves would realize that their new way of life could far exceed anything that the old life had to offer, and that they should eagerly embrace it. Failure to achieve the goals he set for himself and the Indians would mean nothing less than a moral disgrace. Ignoring the imperative to save the Indians, noted the Lake Mohonk conferees in 1885, was nothing less than the continuation of "the National dishonor of supporting ignorant and barbaric peoples in the heart of a Christian civilization."[21] It was this devotion to the transformation of a people that created schools like Rainy Mountain and took the crusading zeal of Thomas Morgan out to the remote corners of the nation's reservations.

Morgan's successors also expressed faith in educating Indians, although they eventually began to challenge his demand that schools receive top priority in the government's civilizing program. Yet even when the schools began to lose steam, the government's official policy remained entrenched in Morgan's rhetoric. One need look no further than the bureau's annual reports, which suggested no end to the opportunities and possibilities in Indian schools. Each year the solution to the Indian Problem edged closer as more and more Indian children came under the influence of the classroom. In 1895, for example, in a passage that reflected the unbounded optimism of official Washington, Commissioner Daniel M. Browning reported that the tribes recognized that "the old order of things has passed away . . . and that only by educating his children can the Indian compete with the white man in the struggle for life. . . . The most effective means for this end are those exerted through a wise educational plan." Three years later, Commissioner William A. Jones was even more emphatic: "Education is the greatest factor in solving the future status of the Indian. . . . No parent, whether red or white, has a moral or legal right to stand in the way of his child's advancement in life; no nation has a similar right to permit a portion of its embryo citizens to grow up in ignorance and . . . vice." And in 1900, Dr. W. N. Hailmann observed that education made the Indian "ethically a better individual," who was "more persevering, more persistent, more thoughtful."[22]

Schools pointed the way toward a self-supporting Indian population and an end to both the reservation system and government services for Indians. In 1899, Commissioner Jones observed: "It is essential that the education of the present generation of young Indians . . . prepare them to take and properly appreciate their share of the common land belonging to themselves and parents. . . . The entire educational system . . . is therefore predicated upon the final abolishment of the anomalous Indian reservation system. " Two years later the Indian Office solemnly reported that "education and civilization are practically synonymous" and that the schools were "doing a great work in preparing the way for emancipation from reservation life."[23]

The urgency with which administrators spoke reflected stark alternatives. "There is no one who has been a close observer of Indian history," wrote Commissioner Hiram Price in 1881, "who is not well satisfied that one of two things must eventually take place, to wit, either civilization or extinction."[24] Twenty-two years later the official opinion had not changed. "There are only two phases of the Indian question," wrote Commissioner Francis Leupp in 1903: "One, that the American Indian shall remain in the country as a . . . study for the ethnologist, a toy for the tourist, a vagrant at the mercy of the state, and a continual pensioner upon the bounty of the people; the other that he shall be educated to work, live and act as a reputable, moral citizen, and thus become a self-supporting, useful member of society. . . . To educate the Indian . . . therefore, is to preserve him from extinction.[25]

Regarding their work as the most morally urgent exercise ever undertaken by a civilized people, reformers looked time and again to the common school as the source of enduring change. Speaking in 1901 to the Board of Indian Commissioners,

Annie Beecher Scoville, a teacher in the Indian schools, summed up the prevailing wisdom of the era as neatly as any government report ever did:

> If there is an idol that the American people have, it is the school. What gold is to the miser, the schoolhouse is to the Yankee. If you don't believe it, go out to Pine Ridge, where there are seven thousand Sioux on eight million acres of land . . . and find planted . . . thirty-two school houses, standing there as a testimony to our belief in education. . . . It is a remedy for barbarism, we think, and so we give the dose. . . . The school is the slow match. . . . It will blow up the old life, and of its shattered pieces [we] will make good citizens.[26]

The rhetorical and philosophical utterings of education leaders, however optimistic they were, would only work if a school system capable of enforcing such goals actually existed. In the post–Civil War era reformers clamored for action but had little clear sense of direction. In 1886, for example, Frances S. Sparhawk applauded the government's determination to see that "something satisfactory ought to be made out of the Indian Question," but went on to say that "thus far the trumpet has given a very uncertain sound."[27]

How was Miss Scoville's dose of humanity to be administered? The answer, of course, was to be found in the Indian schools. Modify them to fit the needs of western tribes, expand the reservation idea that removal had created in the 1830s, and the entire question could be tidily and humanely addressed. And that is what occurred. By the end of the 1870s the pieces fell into place. During the 1880s and 1890s an unprecedented explosion of building took place on reservations throughout the nation as the government rushed to drive the wedge of education into the heart of Indian country. The Rainy Mountain School, as well as the Fort Sill School and the Riverside School on the Kiowa-Comanche-Apache Reservation, may be correctly labeled the fruit of such efforts.[28]

Morgan proposed a four-tiered collection of schools that roughly resembled the American common school system. At the bottom were reservation day schools within easy distance of reservation communities; those day schools were akin to the primary schools young whites attended. With an average capacity of thirty pupils, the day school introduced Indian youngsters to white values and institutions and served in Commissioner William Jones's words as "an object lesson to the Indians who daily visit it." Often located in fairly remote areas with only modest facilities, the day school taught rudimentary skills in domestic arts, hygiene, and discipline. "These schools bring a portion of the 'white man' civilization to the home of the Indian," observed the commissioner in 1898. "As a rule, industrial training on a small scale is adopted for boys . . . whereas girls are taught in a simple way the adornment of the home and the purity of home life. Unconsciously the little one bears with her back to the rude tepee . . . some small portion of the civilization with which she is in contact."[29]

Day schools served as the foundation for the boarding school, where, as one commissioner loftily suggested, "the superstructure" of education was added. Because they took "the little ones from the very heart of barbarism," noted Commissioner D. M. Browning in 1895, "these schools perform serious work in the educational plan." Importantly, day schools aimed not just at children, but at parents as well. Calling such schools "the gradual uplifter of the tribe," Sister Macaria Murphy reminded her audience in 1901 that the schools meant "the hand of progress has been here!" Lessons imparted to children were intended to extend to parents so that those exposed to the day schools might find it more difficult to undo their effects. "The day school is as much an educator of the father and mother as of the child," noted Browning in 1896, and could be counted on to help convince parents of the necessity of putting their children into school. This was so, believed C. C. Covey of the Pine Ridge Indian School, because "the day school comes nearer the home and heart of an Indian than any boarding school; he sees his children go to school every morning, dirty perhaps, but when they return of an evening they are neat and clean—this must exert a great influence for good at home."[30]

Although less expensive and more numerous than other types of Indian schools, day schools gave way wherever possible to the reservation boarding school, arguably the single most important type of school in the system. They were the bedrock of the government's assimilation program, and Morgan promoted them tirelessly, calling them "the gateway out from the reservation." According to him, they taught Indian children the one value that barbarism could not stand: "the marvelous secret of diligence." Although the government would eventually emphasize off-reservation schools such as Carlisle, Chilocco, and Phoenix, those schools enrolled a relatively small percentage of the overall school-age population. The majority of children spent their entire educational careers in reservation boarding schools; thus, such schools performed a particularly important role in breaking the habits of camp life and tribal identity. "Mere day schools upon the Indian reservations have . . . proved insufficient," Schurz wrote in 1880, because they did not remove pupils from the influence of their home surroundings. "To this end boarding schools are required. . . . In fact, it is just as necessary to teach Indian children how to live as how to read and write."[31]

The emphasis on environment resonated deeply with reformers. Convinced that lifting Indian children up from savagery required a complete change of physical and cultural surroundings, reformers believed that the boarding school represented the best avenue for such change. As Bruce David Forbes has observed:

> Indeed, the claim that Indian students were learning just what whites learned had far-reaching implications. More than simply offering an education in certain subjects, the boarding school lifted young people out of native contexts and immersed them in white American culture. The intention was to raise godly, civilized, educated children, with all the implications that those words carried. The goals were difficult to achieve if the child remained in touch with old ways and life-styles; the separation of the boarding school made children more educable in new patterns.[32]

Boarding schools kept students closely supervised for an average of ten months a year and thus controlled them to a degree not possible in the day schools. And like the day schools, boarding school lessons served a two-fold purpose. One was to provide students with the discipline and training they would need to lead successful lives. The reservation boarding school, said Commissioner William A. Jones in 1899, "presents daily object lessons . . . and forms a stepping stone from camp conditions to home life. . . . Within its walls boys and girls are taught the charms and advantages of civilization, presented ideals for emulation, and a desire [is] awakened for a more moral and profitable existence."[33]

A second objective identified the boarding school as a role model for the reservation community it served. Like day schools, an important part of the boarding school program lay in its ability to influence entire communities. "The agency boarding school," wrote Morgan in 1881, "is the object lesson for the reservation."[34] The more parents knew about the boarding school, administrators reasoned, the better. Rather than operating beyond the reach of parents, therefore, reservation boarding schools often encouraged visitation and were usually not deliberately segregated from the rest of the community except in times of illness or emergency. In that way, parents could see for themselves the effects of schooling. If it overwhelmed them, so much the better, for then administrators would have less to fear from parents who might be tempted to undo what their children were learning. There was also always the possibility that parents might actually accept what the schools did. The Kiowas, for example, showed great enthusiasm for Rainy Mountain and in time came to consider it a critical part of their tribe's continued success. Parents eagerly visited the campus, and overall the Kiowa community took great pride in the school.

Parental support and interest no doubt contributed to better relations and increased enrollments, which were exactly what the Indian Office wanted. Commissioner Browning wrote in 1896 that "the Indian as a rule looks upon the reservation school as peculiarly his own, and by a wise system of visitation on the part of the parents is kept in touch with the older Indians. These schools are the backbone of the Indian education system, and their influence in uplifting the tribal life . . . is wonderful." Two years later Commissioner William A. Jones was equally emphatic: "These institutions present themselves to him as an object lesson of the power and influence of the General Government; they appeal to him through his children, and awaken any smoldering sentiments for the betterment of his and their condition."[35]

The importance attached to boarding schools is revealed by the annual statistics of the Indian Office for the years 1877 to 1911. In 1877 the government supervised only 48 boarding schools, and the total budget for Indian education was a mere $20,000, a sum that also supported 102 day schools. A decade later 117 boarding schools enrolled 8,020 pupils, and the budget had increased to $1,211,415. By 1897, 15,026 students attended 145 boarding schools, and total appropriations had more than doubled to $2,517,265. In another decade the numbers were 173 boarding schools, 21,848 students, and a budget of $3,925,830. Until the 1910s, when the government began to retrench and boarding schools fell out of favor, the trend was generally toward growth. This environment produced Rainy Mountain, and the school's entire history ran through the decades when the government heralded boarding schools as the most important key to civilizing young Indians.[36]

In addition to government-sponsored schools, private and church-supported schools played important roles in the reservation school system. Among other things, the Peace Policy initiated an intense competition among groups determined to obtain, and cling to, some piece of the education pie. Mission schools, religious day schools and boarding schools, and various privately funded efforts all found their way into the agencies. At the Kiowa-Comanche-Apache Reservation, for example, church-related efforts were fairly common after the 1870s. Although it is true that such schools were often small and operated at great disadvantages, they cannot be ignored. The Indian Office actively recruited such schools, entered into contracts with them, and relied on them to achieve the same results hoped for in government schools. Nevertheless, the rigors and limitations of operating such schools usually conspired to sharply reduce their effectiveness.[37]

The great bulk of Indian children who received any education in the late nineteenth and early twentieth centuries got it in reservation schools. But most schools also produced students who showed promise of greater accomplishment. For those relatively few, off-reservation boarding schools offered better training and the opportunity to experience first-hand, even if in limited fashion, the outside world. The off-reservation boarding school, reported Commissioner Browning in 1895, "should stand in relation to the regular Government school as the college to the high school. . . . The brightest and most efficient higher grade pupils are recommended by school superintendents . . . in the nature of a promotion." Richard Henry Pratt was the architect and leading advocate of off-reservation boarding schools. After trying out his ideas at Fort Marion and later at Hampton Institute in Virginia, Pratt received permission in 1879 to open a boarding school for Indians at the abandoned army barracks in Carlisle, Pennsylvania. Carlisle was the first of more than two dozen such schools scattered across the country by the turn of the century. Off-reservation boarding schools emphasized industrial and domestic training, but at levels higher than their reservation counterparts. Instruction was better, facilities were generally superior to anything found on reservations, and students were the best the other schools had to offer.[38]

Because off-reservation boarding schools were usually located close to what one commissioner called "civilized centers," they could expose students to the realities of the outside world. "Their principal advantages lie in contiguity to white civilization and in bringing together at one place Indian children of diverse tribes," wrote the commissioner in 1902. These advantages are of great benefit, and round out the education begun in the reservation day and boarding schools." The outing program, for example, placed students with white families and businesses in the community. Such students, reasoned confident administrators, would never go back to the blanket. The outing program represented in practice what the entire school experiment meant in theory: the total immersion of students into white culture and communities.[39]

Yet even with schools like Carlisle and Phoenix aggressively using the outing program, only a fragment of the total Indian school population had regular and systematic contact with the outside world in ways that would hasten and improve the assimilation of Indian children. Clearly, the answer to mainstreaming Indian children lay not with segregated Indian schools, but with public schools. Accordingly, the Indian Office introduced ambitious plans in the 1890s to transfer large numbers of Indian children to local public school systems. In making those transfers government could gradually reduce the expense of maintaining a separate Indian school system and accomplish the goals of assimilation more quickly and efficiently. Morgan considered transfer to the public system the logical conclusion to reservation education and hoped to see the day when Indian children attended only public schools. Such schools would do for Indians "what they are so successfully doing for all the other races in this country," said Morgan: "assimilate them."[40] This plan was consistent with the larger vision of liquidating tribal domains, closing reservations, ard ending government services to the tribes as soon as possible. Once reservation schools were gone (and the day was coming, announced the bureau), Indian children would have no choice but to attend public schools.

In theory the plan was reasonably sound. In reality, it operated poorly in most school districts. Although bureau statistics suggest a monumental shift in policy after the 1910s, the shift was illusory. Local school districts proved reluctant in most cases to accept Indian children, even when required by law to do so. As a result, the plan to transfer large numbers of Indian children to public schools rarely succeeded. By 1899 nearly a decade of effort had netted contracts with only thirty-six public schools throughout the entire country. Space was available for 359 pupils, but only 167 were in attendance. "Theoretically the placing of Indian youth in the public schools . . . is a most admirable expedient for breaking down prejudices," commented the commissioner in 1899. But the lamentable truth was that the government would still have to accept responsibility for laying the educational foundations for Indian children. Only a year earlier, in fact, the Indian Office admitted that the plan "does not appear to meet with much success" and reported a decrease of more than 100 Indian students in public schools. In 1905 the government reported a meager 84 pupils in only six schools, figures that showed a serious drop from less than a decade before, when forty-five schools had enrolled more than 400 students. And in 1911, Commissioner of Indian Affairs Robert G. Valentine admitted that it was not "the intention or desire of this Office to force the attendance of children in the public schools . . . in direct opposition to the manifest wishes of the people."[41]

As the experience of Rainy Mountain will show, such resistance was usually the result of local intransigence and outright Indian hating. Determined to keep Indian children out of schools for which their parents paid no taxes, for example, whites mounted campaigns in many communities to intimidate Indians or to deliberately deny them access to public facilities. Even when parents could show proof of citizenship, and when they could produce evidence of having paid local taxes, the sentiment remained unchanged. "It is remarkable . . . how friendly people are toward . . . Indian education, as long as we talk in the abstract," wrote one Californian in 1917. "But when we want them to take some Indian children into their own school, there are forty thousand ways of how not to do it."[42]

According to government reports, however, the situation

changed dramatically by 1910. "Progress is being made in the important work of more closely connecting the Indian schools with the public schools," asserted Commissioner Valentine in 1910. (This was the same commissioner, of course, who thought it unwise to act "in direct opposition to the manifest wishes of the people.") Valentine reminded his audience that, above all, public schools were "a definite means of promoting the assimilation of the Indians into American life." Two years later the commissioner described the process as "probably the most noticeable example of what is believed to be the 'final step' in the education of the Indian youth" and reported that out of 46,131 Indian children in school, 17,000, or nearly 30 percent, attended public schools. And in 1921 the Indian Office reported that the placing of Indian children in public schools met "with the heartiest cooperation" in the majority of states.[43]

Statistics appear to bear this out. Decade-long increments between 1890 and 1920, for example, show impressive improvements. In 1899 the Indian Office reported a total of 20,522 Indian students attending government-supported schools. Importantly, more than 16,000 of them attended reservation or off-reservation schools, and public schools enrolled only 167. By 1912 a decisive shift seemingly appeared. Of 46,131 Indian children enrolled in schools, 24,341 were in reservation or off-reservation schools, and, as noted earlier, 17,000, or nearly 30 percent, attended public schools. By 1921 the shift was even more dramatic. Of 62,764 Indian children enrolled in schools, fewer than 24,000 were in reservation or off-reservation Indian schools, and 33,250—more than 50 percent—attended public schools.[44]

These statistics should be read with suspicion, however. Government officials notoriously inflated such figures, and rarely did enrollment figures accurately reflect the number of children enrolled anyway. In reservation boarding schools, for example, it was unusual for the same children who enrolled in September to be there when school closed in June, or for them to attend regularly for the entire session. At Rainy Mountain only about half of those who enrolled each fall were present when the term ended; thus, the 150 or so students listed in September were not usually the same 150 there in June. Rainy Mountain's attendance records also show that the average attendance was often lower than the reported total enrollment. Average attendance statistics for the entire system reveal similar discrepancies. The total school-age population for 1920 has been estimated by Frederick Hoxie at 50,500, but government reports show that the total average attendance in government schools was only 23,248. Indeed, average total attendance showed no significant increases between 1902, when the rate stood at 24,120, and 1920, when it had declined to 23,248.[45] For that period it is unlikely that the percentage of children actually attending any kind of school ever exceeded 50 percent.

Dedicated in the late nineteenth century to building hundreds of schools as the spearhead in a campaign to transform the tribes, by the early twentieth century the Indian Office changed direction and sought instead to close as many schools as it could and force Indian children into public schools. Simultaneously, the Indian Office adopted a narrowly focused vision of assimilation that justified limiting educational opportunities. No longer laboratories of change, schools ultimately became simple way stations as students matured and prepared to enter a social and cultural environment in which they almost never gained full membership.

For boarding schools like Rainy Mountain this shift proved fatal. Unable to combat the changing philosophy of the Indian Office and unable to survive the retrenchment of the 1920s, reservation boarding schools were closed with increasing rapidity. The great experiment that had begun with Schurz and Morgan was largely over by the close of the 1920s. The bureau continued to operate schools, but their goals were low and their scope limited. While it lasted, however, the fervor for educational reform produced remarkable results. This was especially so for the Kiowas, to whom Rainy Mountain School was to become a beacon of hope.

"No More Incongruous Spectacle"
The Kiowas and Their Agency

IN THE MINDS OF MANY NINETEENTH-CENTURY AMERICANS THE vast austerity of the Southern Plains seemed so complete that the region deserved the epithet of Great American Desert. Like the Spanish who preceded them, many Americans in the mid-nineteenth century preferred to ponder the open plains from a safe distance. Those forced to cross them did so as quickly as possible, for the most desirable lands lay in California. To many overlanders, the boundaries of the West, to borrow Richard White's phrase, seemed to be walls and not doors. Behind the walls lay an uncertain combination of natives, environmental extremes, and enormous space. Better, perhaps, to leave it be.[1]

Experience proved otherwise. Beginning with the opening of Texas in the mid-1820s, in fact, the Southern Plains received more and more attention with each passing decade. By the 1850s overlanders knew that the Staked Plains of Texas, and the Cimarron Valley of western Indian Territory, were more valuable than had once been presumed. Despite hostile weather and difficult conditions, the region flourished when cattle interests and farmers began to settle there and to cultivate its resources. Far from being wasteland, the Southern Plains had natural pastures and an abundance of range and farmland. It was hard land, to be sure, but it was no desert. With a careful application of technology and capital, it could be transformed.

And yet transforming it was hardly that simple. Before American overlanders could settle the region, the government had to face up to the considerable task of controlling and pacifying the Indians who claimed it as their own. This meant coming to terms with the remarkably determined tribes that dominated the area between the Rio Grande and Platte rivers. Horse-mounted and occupying vast territories, tribes such as the Comanches, Kiowas, Southern Cheyennes, and Southern Arapahoes represented severe challenges to the Peace Policy and the reservation system. The Kiowas and their allies the Comanches comprised the vanguard of the resistance. Never numerous—together they numbered between four thousand and five thousand during the second half of the nineteenth century—they nevertheless constituted a significant threat to whites seeking to open the Southwest. Most of the region's tribes defied attempts to be collected on reservations until the late 1860s and early 1870s. And even then, they surrendered, as William T. Hagan has described the process, only by fits and turns.[2]

Alarmed by violent clashes on the Southern Plains, the U.S. government made a series of accords in the 1850s and 1860s with the region's tribes. Those negotiations failed one after another. Anxious to reach a conclusive settlement, the Peace Commission convened new discussions at Medicine Lodge Creek, Kansas, in the fall of 1867 with the region's most important tribes.[3] Three days of discussions produced a treaty containing the usual announcements of perpetual peace and friendship. The agreement established boundaries for a Kiowa-Comanche-Apache Reservation and guaranteed annuities for the next two decades. Plans for allotment (and inducements to encourage it) were included, and the typical rhetoric about education and civilization appeared. This was all standard fare.

Tribal leaders who listened to the negotiations, however, remained doubtful of the government's intentions. Hagan believes that Kiowa and Comanche skepticism was well founded. Despite its impressive promises, he concludes, the Medicine Lodge Treaty reflected not so much a plan to solve the Indian problem through peace and humanitarian reform as it did a desire to open the Kiowa-Comanche country to white settlement. In fact, the treaty's purpose was to clear Indians out of the way, not to worry at length about what should be done with them. It did not promote peace at all, but, concludes Hagan, was used to "give the stamp of legitimacy to United States efforts to concentrate the Indians and open the region to white exploitation." The government made promises that it would not keep, promises that according to Hagan it never intended to honor. Medicine Lodge was a specious document, and the civilizing program it outlined would prove that.[4]

At the heart of the program lay schools and teachers. "The necessity of education is admitted," noted the Medicine Lodge Treaty, and both sides agreed to abide by its stipulations. For their part, the tribes agreed to enroll all children between ages six and sixteen. The government agreed to supply a teacher and schoolhouse for every thirty school-age children, of whom there were between six hundred and one thousand, depending upon who was doing the counting. Concerned about the government's uneven performance to date, but heartened by the opportunity to bring more Indians under the influence of civilized institutions, reformers hoped that policy makers would embrace the cause. After all, the Indian Office has committed itself to a comprehensive Indian school system, had told the nation that education and civilization were synonymous, and had accepted the idea that educating children was the truest objective of policy. Schools, in the opinion of one scholar, "seemed like a holy experiment" whose time had come.[5] Over the next decade a handful of schools appeared on the reservation. But the fledgling system was falsely encouraging, a fact best revealed through a brief examination of the reservation in its formative years.

Control of the Kiowa-Comanche Agency passed to the Society of Friends in 1869 when responsibility for the Central Superintendency came to them under the Peace Policy.[6] In May 1869 a forty-seven-year-old Iowa farmer named Lawrie Tatum became the first Quaker agent for the tribes, an appointment he reportedly learned of through a newspaper story. A thoroughgoing Quaker whose temperament meshed perfectly with the humanitarian goals of the Peace Policy, Tatum faced an enormous task. Before him were more than six thousand Indians from ten tribes speaking nine languages and occupying an area the size of Connecticut. An earnest and eager agent, Tatum soon discovered that enlightened conduct—the key, he said, to solving the problem—was sadly out of step with the realities of the reservation. In Hagan's opinion "there was no more incongruous spectacle than that of a Quaker agent preaching the virtues of peace and agriculture to a plains warrior, treating this man . . . as a simple, misguided soul who could be brought to see the error of his ways by compassion and sweet reason."[7]

An omen appeared shortly after Tatum took office. An inspection of the agency left him convinced that it would need extraordinary increases in budgets and supplies to meet its obligations. On August 21, 1869, Tatum sent his revised estimates to the Indian Office, pointing out that he required no fewer than twenty-seven farmers and fourteen cooks for the current year to adequately meet the needs of the tribes. Moreover, he continued, those numbers would have to be increased to eighty and thirty, respectively, for the coming year. Tatum also requested twenty-five wagons, 160 mules, and 120 plows, all necessary to provide the "fostering and protecting care of the government."[8]

Tatum's requests exceeded two hundred thousand dollars— a figure far beyond anything authorized at Medicine Lodge and well beyond what the Indian Office could or would provide. The commissioner's response was coldly emphatic: the Medicine Lodge agreement guaranteed one farmer, not twenty-seven. When Tatum continued to push for larger budgets and greater support, Commissioner Francis A. Walker tersely reminded him in 1872 that "the United States have given them a noble reservation, and have provided amply for all their wants."[9]

Forced to make do with what little they had, Tatum and his successors forged ahead with the civilizing program. By transforming the tribesmen into farmers and stockmen, and by using the influence of schools, churches, and other Anglo-American institutions, agents hoped to lead the Indians as quickly as possible to new lives. It was a daunting task. As Hagan's analysis of the Comanche experience reveals, agents rarely gained control of the reservation and thus almost never forced tribesmen to toe the line. Despite their "semi-despotic powers," as Thomas Jefferson Morgan once put it, few agents ever managed to master the complexities of the reservation environment. Hagan, for example, has observed that "the typical agent learned to avoid trouble by not pushing the civilization program too hard and thus setting his Indians against him."[10] That being the case, it is not difficult to understand why the reservation experiment failed.

An 1870 report from Tatum confirms Hagan's analysis. Tatum concluded that annuity payments ironically represented an incentive to ignore agency policies. If the Indians behaved themselves, Tatum reasoned, they feared the reduction of such goods, because good behavior indicated progress on the path to civilization and self-sufficiency. In that case, the government would roll back supplies. "They repeatedly told me," wrote Tatum, "the only way to get a large amount [of supplies] was to go on the war path awhile, kill a few white people, steal a good many horses and mules, and then make a treaty, and they would get a large amount of presents and a liberal supply of goods for that fall."[11] Similar stories and accounts of failing programs were staples of subsequent reports.

This was so even when dedicated agents such as Tatum ran the agency. When less devoted souls took charge, the results were often devastating. Unfortunately, less devoted souls were rarely in short supply in the Indian Service. Long regarded as sinkholes of political patronage, the reservations, as Senator James M. Kyle concluded in 1894, attracted an unsavory lot who considered Indian work "a license to filch and rob the Indian for a period of several years." Several years earlier General Henry Heth observed that the Indian Office was little more than "the dumping ground for the sweepings of the political party that is in power." And Robert Utley cites an 1891 article by Herbert Welsh in which Welsh described a governor "who laughingly admitted that for party workers fit for nothing else, he usually found jobs in the Indian Service." It was little wonder that Carl Schurz once described "a thoroughly competent, honest, and devoted Indian agent" as "a rare jewel." As Robert Keller has observed, the workload, stress, and temptation of agency positions often proved too much. "For the weak and dishonest it was a wide-open opportunity for quick wealth; for the honest man it was an impossible job."[12]

Conditions at the Kiowa-Comanche Agency were consistent with such opinions. Agents and agency employees often turned out to be nothing more than political hacks without legitimate qualifications. One agent was a former lumberyard manager, for example. Another was a grocer. A third, despite the fact that he was, as Hagan notes, "innocent of any prior experience with Indians or the West," came with a reference that reported him "entirely free of bad habits (never drank liquor in his life)." Others, however, were not always as upstanding. Methodist missionary John Jasper Methvin, for example, once described agent J. Lee Hall as "a great man in ruins on account of drink." Matters improved after 1893 when army officers replaced civilians as agents. Until then a procession of malcontents, incompetents, and ill-suited appointees plagued the agency.[13]

Agencies attracted a colorful collection of job applicants who pulled every string, worked every angle, and slapped the back of every would-be supporter in sight. The Kiowa-Comanche Agency was no exception. Some applicants, like N. L. Purnell, were boldly solicitous. Writing to agent Charles Adams in March 1890, Purnell—a real estate agent from Dallas—stated that he was "wounded during the war and . . . I have a family of 7 children and wife. I understand farming," he continued, and added that he could certainly handle "the practical requirements of instructions to the Indians." In closing—just in case it mattered—Purnell let slip that he was the chairman of the Republican Executive Committee in the sixteenth ward for Dallas.[14]

In 1897, J. J. Barrett courteously inquired of Agent Frank

Baldwin if he, Baldwin, intended to remain in office for the coming year. If so, then Barrett—the vice-president of First National Bank in Montague, Texas—would not "press my application." Another job seeker explained that "I have been in hard luck for the past winter," and that "any assistans [sic] given me to make an honest living will be gratfully [sic] received and your confidence not misplaced." A third correspondent— whose sole qualification for agency work was his experience as a hotel owner—was so eager to get started that he offered to work for three months without a salary "to pay for the bother I have made." Others invoked different sorts of relationships. In 1903, for example, a Rainy Mountain employee wrote irritably to Agent James Randlett in reference to a transfer. "My request for your assistance was wholly on account of believing that I had a right to make such a request from a brother mason," she wrote.[15]

Part of the problem lay in the demands of the work, for the government's standards seemed to call for truly extraordinary individuals. One student of the Quaker era notes that agents, for example, were "expected to act in the capacity of governor, legislature, judge, sheriff, and accounting officer. Besides these duties he was theoretically responsible for hiring the many agency employees."[16] A November 1891 letter from the secretary of the interior to newly appointed Kiowa-Comanche Agent George D. Day clarified the situation:

> I am directed by the President to inform you that the office to which you are appointed is considered one of far more than ordinary importance . . . , [so] sobriety and integrity must mark the conduct of yourself and every one associated directly or indirectly with the Agency under your charge; that an improved condition in the affairs of the Agency will be expected within a reasonable time . . . ; that the education and proper training of the Indian children and the agricultural and other industrial pursuits of the adult Indians must receive your constant and careful attention, to the end that they may be advanced in the ways of civilization, and to the condition of self-support; and that your commission will be held with the express understanding that you will use your utmost endeavors to further these objects and purposes.[17]

Under the circumstances, this was a tall order. The lack of control meant that the tribes continued to raid with near impunity and to regard both the Medicine Lodge agreement and the reservation with so much disdain as to make a mockery of the Peace Policy. In 1870, Central Superintendent Enoch Hoag reported that the principal troubles in his region came from the Kiowas, Comanches, and Kiowa-Apaches, none of whom showed much interest in settling down to reservation life. Two years later the commissioner's office characterized those tribes as "wild and intractable. . . . Even the best of them have given small signs of improvement." Exasperated, the commissioner added that in light of continued raids and troublemaking, "the point has been reached where forbearance ceases to be a virtue." Most urgently needed, he wrote, was "a wholesome example which shall inspire fear and command obedience." Tatum confirmed Hoag's dreary evaluation by admitting that "the Kiowas and a few hands of the Comanches are uncontrollable by me."[18]

A half-dozen years after Medicine Lodge, little had changed on the reservation many considered an important test of the forced assimilation campaign. Government programs failed throughout the reservation: Schools languished, stock-raising programs fizzled, and attempts to get Kiowas and Comanches to farm met with limited success. Worse, with the agency often in the hands of political hacks, many Indians found it relatively easy to resist the civilizing programs or, at the very least, to accept them in ways and on terms that did not mean forfeiting their sense of cultural identity. In 1875, seven years after Medicine Lodge, Hoag reported that the number of Indians on the agency wearing citizen clothing stood at exactly eight. The number of houses occupied by Indians was eight. And the agency's only school enrolled just sixty of an estimated six hundred school-age children. (Matters improved very slowly in some parts of the reservation. A similar report filed twenty-seven years later indicated that in one district, seventy of ninety-three families interviewed still lived in tipis.)[19]

This was hardly the laboratory of change promised by Washington. Far from transforming the tribes, the reservation produced increasingly dependent Indians mired in poverty and subjected to one after another of the worst agents in the service. In 1871, Hoag concluded that although he believed that the Peace Policy was working (on what evidence he based such an assertion we may only guess), he added that "its beneficial results, in some instances, have been seriously crippled by want of promptness on the part of the Government."[20]

Nowhere was the want of promptness more keenly felt than in the schools. Like the rest of the reservation's programs, schooling met with indifference, poor support, and inadequate funding. Despite the lofty rhetoric of the Indian Office, the shocking lack of schools stood as testimony to the casual attitude of a government that liked to pride itself on a progressive approach to the Indian question. In truth, few examples more clearly illustrate the limitations of reform and the distance between rhetoric and reality.

Required by the Medicine Lodge Treaty to provide a school and teacher for every thirty school-age children on the reservation, the government failed from the beginning to meet its obligations. At no point in the agency's history were there sufficient facilities, and the Indian Office never came close to providing anything resembling enough schools for the children entitled to them. In 1870, for example (three full years after Medicine Lodge), Tatum reported that his agency had no schools—"there have been no funds either to build houses or sustain teachers"—and that he did not expect any in the foreseeable future. Tatum also expressed frustration at restrictions that required each new school to have thirty students before the next could be built. Many rural white districts in the region had schools with fewer than thirty students in them, he noted, yet added additional schools as they saw fit.[21]

Tatum waited nearly three years for the bureau to take action. Ironically, when the reservation's first school opened in 1871, it was not a government school at all, but a private effort supported by the Society of Friends. Between March 1871 and June 1873, Josiah and Elizabeth Butler, Ohio Quakers, ran a small boarding school near the agency at Fort Sill. Initially it attracted mostly Caddoes and Wichitas; Comanches and Kiowas did not attend it in significant numbers until three or four years later. During its first term Butler's school housed a total of twenty-four children, who attended class five days a week, four and one-half hours a day. Within two years enrollment leveled off at about three dozen students.

The Butlers introduced the children to rudimentary lessons in spelling, reading, and writing. Josiah's diary recounted the first day's triumphs:

> I read a psalm, explaining what it was. I then explained the use of the small bell. I got all in a class before Wilson's Chart No. 1, spelling cap, cat, dog, ox, hen, & c., the pictures of the same being expected. They articulated better than I had expected. . . . I gave them slates and they made fairly good figures. I kept them at it one hour and then dismissed until after dinner. I gave them an hour for noon, then an hour on slates and charts, an hour for recess and then another hour as before. . . . So ended the first day of school—memorable to both scholars and teacher. I feel thankful that we have at least made a beginning.[22]

Three days later Butler reported exuberantly that the children "know half of their letters and can spell cat, cap, dog, rat, red, boy, deer, pig, and fish and know what they mean." To complement their academic instruction, Elizabeth Butler taught sewing and domestic skills to the girls; her husband arranged work for the older boys at the agency sawmill on Saturdays for fifty cents each per day.[23]

Invited to see the school for himself, Tatum visited at the end of the first term and reported that the pupils "all showed marked progress for the length of time they have been studying." As for Butler, it was a modest beginning, but he saw great promise in the experiment, provided he could get help and support from the tribes and the agency. The school's first annual report carefully highlighted "the labor, anxiety, patience, and

forbearance . . . necessarily expended." It was hard work, continued the account, and the rewards were slim. Still, Butler
trusted God to lead him and closed by saying that he knew his
labor was not in vain.[24] It might not have been in vain, but it
was surely a lonely crusade; during the next six years there
were only two other schools at the agency.

Other schools opened, but none of them provided significant
help to Butler; in fact, most of them failed almost immediately.
An instructive example was that of Thomas C. Battey, an Iowa
Quaker who got along well with the Kiowas but who perhaps
underestimated the rigors he faced. During his journey to the
Wichita Agency in the fall of 1871, for example, Battey insisted
on walking the final twenty-three miles separated from his
traveling companions "when his conscience would not permit
him to listen any longer to their continuous swearing."[25] A
man who could not condone garden-variety swearing was not
likely to be comfortable when he ran up against the rough edges
of agency life.

Upon his arrival Battey assumed control of the Wichita
School (later renamed Riverside). One year later, after receiving
what he said was a sign from the Lord on March 30, 1872, he
announced plans to open a school out in the districts. (In addition to this inspiration, Kicking Bird, a prominent Kiowa, also
courted Battey.) Arriving in Kicking Bird's camp in December
1872, Battey opened his school on January 23, 1873, in a tent
divided into living quarters for himself and a classroom for his
pupils. By his own recollection, the Indians regarded the school
with some hesitation, and Battey found his hands full managing
simple conversation with children who did not speak English.
In her study of schooling on the reservation, Ida Moore commented that "as to the school, as is generally understood the
term, it did not seem to amount to much."[26] One former Riverside teacher was less gentle in her assessment: "Battey traveled
with the Kiowas for more than a year, but the school he tried
to hold in his tent was never very successful. Just about the
time he would get some scholars interested, either some old

Kiowas or some young Kiowas would enter the tent, laugh, or forcibly evict the students so that it was impossible to hold regular classes."[27]

Agent James Haworth offered a similarly dim appraisal in his annual report for 1873. "Thomas C. Battey has not been very successful in keeping up a school . . . among the Kiowas," he wrote, but Battey remained "much encouraged he will convince them to allow a regular school this fall and winter."[28] He was wrong.

In the meantime, the agency continued to rely on the Fort Sill School, which various Quakers administered following the departure of the Butlers in 1873. In a heartening development, Kiowas and Comanches enrolled their children for the first time in 1874. Agent Haworth's decision to create a school board composed of two men from each of the agency's tribes apparently spurred this event. Board membership changed frequently to ensure contact with as many leaders as possible and to spread the influence of those who supported the schools.[29]

The program seems to have produced improvements. Twenty Kiowa children enrolled at Fort Sill in 1875, for example, bringing the school's size to nearly sixty students. Ironically, this interest quickly pushed the school beyond its limits and contributed to the overcrowding that became chronic. Haworth complained to Washington that he could have had many more children in school if he had more schools and more teachers. As it was, he could accommodate only about sixty of more than six hundred school-age youngsters, and he turned dozens of children away every term. Some parents tried to pay for the privilege; one Kiowa chief reportedly offered a pony to get his child into the school. Despite the still crowded conditions and lack of facilities, Haworth went on to say "the clouds of trouble which were lowering around us . . . have happily about all passed away. . . . The interest of old and young in the school continued during the entire term; they are now very anxious to know when school will commence again. I would be glad if I could tell them soon."[30]

Between 1877 and 1880 agents reported that the schools filled to overflowing each term and that as a result young children were sent away with no hope of getting the education owed them. The situation was so bad that Indian agents began to lodge complaints with the agents, and Haworth noted in 1877 that "several of the Indians who have children in school have told me that they are very anxious for their children to get an education sufficient to become teachers among their own people." In 1880, Agent P.B. Hunt observed that "one favorable indication of improvement is what I believe to be a sincere desire upon the part of the parents to have their children educated in the schools." Compared to the agency's other tribes, the Kiowas, Hunt found, were "rather more earnest and decided in their efforts. . . . I am encouraged to remark that in a few years the Kiowas will be ahead of any of the tribes now under my charge." Fifteen years late one of Hunt's successors commented on "the imperative necessity of greater school accommodations. . . . There is scarcely one of the children that would not be brought in to school voluntarily by the parents if we had a place to put them."[31]

But other reports offset these announcements. "Agency schools have much to contend with," wrote Hunt in 1885. "So little has been accomplished by many of them that some persons have advocated that they be abandoned." Urged by the Indians to build more schools, Haworth offered a solution in 1877. He proposed dividing the agency into eight districts— one for the Kiowa-Apaches, three for the Kiowas, and four for the Comanches—with a school for each district. By building smaller schools the agency could save money and meet the needs of the large majority of children for whom there were no schools. Ironically, what he suggested resembled the Medicine Lodge Plans for multiple schools throughout the reservation. There is no evidence that his proposal received serious attention.[32]

Matters improved slightly by 1879. The consolidation of the

Wichita Agency with the Kiowa-Comanche Agency in 1878 meant more school-age children to worry about, but also provided an additional school. The Wichita School in Anadarko opened in August 1871 with a capacity of about one hundred students, most of whom were Caddoes and Wichitas. In addition, the agency ran the Kiowa School, a small school that had opened in the early 1880s on the south bank of the Washita River in Anadarko. (This school closed in 1896 after Rainy Mountain became the primary Kiowa school.) Agent Hunt announced plans to enlarge both Riverside and Fort Sill so that together they could accommodate three hundred pupils, nearly double the number then in attendance. Still, as he ruefully admitted, some five hundred other children—the majority of the reservation's school-age children—would lack classrooms.[33]

Without significant budget increases it was the best Hunt could do. In the meantime he improved the schools he had. In late 1879 a new building went up at Riverside; similar improvements to the Fort Sill School followed about a year later. In 1887, Washington approved a new school at Fort Sill for the Comanches. The deteriorating condition of the original campus and a reluctance to send their children to school with other Indians prompted the Comanches to insist on a separate facility. Agent J. Lee Hall supported the school because it could be used as a bargaining chip with the Comanches. It made sense to placate the tribe, he continued, because it was "by far the best material out of which to make good citizens." Construction began in 1890, and the school opened its doors in October 1892, when thirty-three Comanche girls enrolled. It reached its capacity of one hundred students one year later.[34]

Despite additional construction and improved facilities, the reservation's schools remained desperately overcrowded and poorly run. In 1884, for example, Riverside still suffered so badly from an 1882 fire that the main school building was near collapse. During the winter months, conceded the agent, "there was actual suffering" among the students. In 1885 the agent's official report made the embarrassing admission that on balance the schools had accomplished little of lasting value.[35]

Three years later matters remained miserably unresolved. Agent Eugene White complained that although the Kiowa-Comanche Agency was "very large and important . . . it would be hard to imagine one with fewer or less adequate facilities." He called the schools "greatly inadequate" and reported that the Fort Sill School was so badly in need of repair that it was scarcely habitable. Agent W. D. Myers continued the litany of complaints in 1889 by declaring the Kiowa School "a disgrace to the government that owns it." As evidence, he pointed to the sordid state of affairs at the school, whose superintendent had been dismissed for drunkenness and then inexplicably reappointed, a fact that Myers said had "wrecked it for the year." Worse, the Kiowas and Comanches refused to send their children to the same schools and demanded their own, separate, schools.[36]

As if the scarcity and quality of the schools did not pose serious enough problems, mediocre employees did. Located in remote areas, characterized by difficult conditions, and hobbled by low pay and long hours, reservation schools did not usually boast a large number of qualified, industrious employees. Indian Office guidelines did not make matters any easier. In 1891, for example, Commissioner Morgan reminded Kiowa-Comanche Agent Charles Adams to be mindful of budget appropriations when filling vacancies. "In fixing the compensation of the various employees," wrote Morgan, "you will bear in mind that . . . salaries should be as low as is compatible with efficient service." It was this sort of limitation that prompted the superintendent of Indian education to observe in 1883 that salaries were "too small, so small, in fact, that it is impossible to get the best talent unless a missionary spirit prompts the acceptance of less pay than can be obtained in civilization."[37]

Worse, until Civil Service requirements appeared in the 1890s, applicants needed no specific qualifications to serve in the schools, a policy that led to numerous troubles and headaches. Local licensing boards certified teachers; beyond this, there was often no assurance concerning the quality or ability of teachers and staff members. Agents could also legally appoint their wives, daughters, or sisters (but not their male relatives) to teaching positions, a situation that led in some cases to the worst nepotic abuses.

The government, however, did attempt to ensure that school employees exhibited moral and ethical qualities consistent with the work at hand. What the Indian Office requested and what it often got, however, were not always the same thing. In 1907, for example, Lloyd Click of Andersonville, Tennessee, accepted a teaching position at Rainy Mountain and shortly received the standard lecture about the rigorous demands of the service:

> Employees at Government boarding schools must understand when they accept the appointment that the conditions of life in an Indian boarding school differ from ordinary school or home life; that the work will be difficult and confining, with little opportunity for recreation or social pleasure; that long hours of service are required, and that every employee must be willing to work night or day if special emergencies arise; that the duties of an employee do not end at a given hour, but may be continued indefinitely.[38]

Click, it should be noted, did not last the year.

Despite the low pay (teachers earned $660 a year at Rainy Mountain, and other staff positions brought considerably lower salaries) and often terrible conditions ("This is a fairly desirable location" was how the Indian Office described Rainy Mountain to one applicant, but one employee countered by writing to a friend that "I am in hell"), applicants were not in short supply. In November 1871, for example, Cyrus Cook informed the regional superintendent for Indian education that he and his wife "seemed turned to the Indians. We are in sympathy with the travails of the Society of Friends," he continued, and wished to know their chances of working in the reservation's schools. "We are willing to labour as ability may be afforded among the

Indians," Cook wrote. "I was raised on a farm. . . . My wife
would be capable of assisting the women in housekeeping and
making garments. We would wish to know as soon as practi-
cable they [sic] mind about our going." Cook's wife, Phebe,
confessed that she was so determined to "go and labor among
the Red Men" that after delaying the decision she "could not
bear it any longer alone." Her husband, she added, was in full
accord on the matter and agreed that "the responsibility is
great. . . . I feel it is a great undertaking for us to make the
attempt to labor among the Indians."[39]

Agents even heard from international sources. In late 1879
Matthew Wahlstrom informed Agent P. B. Hunt that "owing
to a desire long cherished by our Swedish people to do something for the civilization and advancement of our aborigines, I
avail myself of this opportunity to inquire with you concerning
the state of things among the tribes." Wahlstrom was especially
interested in the "probability of a successful mission work . . .
as well as the tranquility and general state of affairs" in and
around Fort Sill, and revealed his intention to settle his family
of three somewhere in the region.[40]

Others wrote to inquire about opening missions and schools
("I love these Indians," said one man, "and know I desire above
everything to preach to them"), and some sent letters of reference ("He is an eccentric man, has seen a great deal of the
world, but I think him safe to trust anywhere" went one such
letter; "He is a good man, a good preacher, suited by the possession of 'horse sense' to the work given him," went another).
And still others requested instructions as to how, exactly, one
ought to go about opening a church on the reservation ("Will
you kindly inform me," asked one man, "[of] the necessary
steps in order to act in the name of the Lord Jesus for my people
in harmony with all national requirements?"). Yet it seemed
agencies always suffered from a lack of capable help. Like the
agents who supervised them, employees were a mixed lot at
best, a situation underscored by the Riverside superintendent,
who wryly observed in 1915 that the condition of any Indian

school was a compromise based on the hiring of "employees collected from the four ends of the earth."[41]

Several examples illustrate the situation. At the Kiowa School in Anadarko four men served as superintendent between 1885 and 1889. The first, although judged by an investigator for the Indian Rights Association to be "a nice well-meaning man; industrious, honest, and all that, and would make a good farmer, . . . has no faculty for managing a school." His successor was fired for drunkenness. The third stayed only a few months and, in the words of the Indian Office, left after using "objectionable and profane language to such an extent as to shock the female employees of the school." The fourth, a twenty-five-year-old Kansan, was removed in 1891 after one of his employees whipped two boys so savagely that the two plus a companion fled the agency, were caught in a winter storm, and froze to death. Following that episode, Agent George Day attempted unsuccessfully to have his brother appointed as superintendent at the school. The commissioner rebuffed him by replying that government regulations stated clearly that only the wife, daughter, or sister of an agent could be appointed as a schoolteacher. Day eventually managed to get his brother a position as the agency's issue clerk one year later. Other agencies suffered similar problems. Utley, for example, cites a reference in the 1889 Annual Report of the Board of Indian Commissioners to an "abandoned woman" running one Indian school, and a lunatic running another.[42]

Teachers proved equally uneven in quality. An 1887 report described two of the three teachers at the Kiowa School as plainly incompetent. The third, along with the matron and seamstress, were the "grains of salt which save this school from absolute stench." Nepotism was rampant, caused partly by the isolation of the agency and the difficulty in obtaining reliable help and partly by agents who knew they could appoint relatives with impunity. The staff of the Kiowa School in 1889 reflected this. The superintendent and one of the teachers were married, another teacher was a cousin to the superintendent's wife, the assistant matron and industrial teacher were married, and the cook was the matron's sister. It was no wonder that after evaluating the agency's school staff in 1885, one inspector described the schools as "asylum[s] for relatives and friends who cannot earn a support elsewhere."[43]

Indians Rights Association inspector C. C. Painter came away shocked at the indifference exhibited by teachers on the reservation:

> I was first introduced into the main room of the school where an Honorable Judge from Texas, who had deserted the bar and bench in behalf of these people, teaches the young Indians. . . . He is a little mite of a man—sallow, spiritless. He sat with one hand in his pocket; and about once a minute he would pronounce the word the pupil had been hung on since he pronounced the last. . . . He looked as if he had gotten out of his grave to find a 'chew of terbaccer.' I have never seen such a perfect picture of the old field schoolmaster. In another room presided the wife of the superintendent. . . . Both he and she had worked diligently, but so far had failed in this area as in everything else they had attempted in the way of teaching.[44]

As Painter's narrative suggests, schools attracted an odd assortment of employees. At Rainy Mountain, for example, a large number of widows, single women, and older men usually made up the work force. According to a 1902 pay roster, only two of the school's ten full-time female employees were married. Five were single and three were widows. And two of the three full-time male employees were Indians. Even though the government considered married couples a stabilizing influence in the boarding school environment, there were limits at a place like Rainy Mountain. In 1911, Rainy Mountain Superintendent James McGregor appealed to Agent Stecker for married couples to fill several positions but hastened to add that "I do not favor trying a newly married couple just out of school as the experiment is not a success at Rainy Mountain." Devotion and desire notwithstanding, marital bliss—even for newlyweds—was tough to maintain in a place as isolated as Rainy Mountain.[45]

Agencies also attempted to fill as many school positions as possible with local Indians, who were paid less than their white counterparts. Administrators typically hired Indians as laborers, cooks, assistant matrons, disciplinarians, school police, and laundresses and in other subordinate positions. Support staff in the schools almost always came from such sources, consistent with the government's desire to fill what it described as "small-salaried position[s] with . . . competent Indian[s]."[46]

Former students often eagerly took positions in the schools. At Riverside, Fort Sill, Anadarko, and Rainy Mountain former students and local residents regularly applied for jobs. In late 1899, Jennie Jackson, a twenty-year-old Kiowa, wrote to Agent James Randlett expressing interest in the assistant laundress job at Rainy Mountain. "I am a Kiowa girl," she wrote, "and belive [sic] that I am competent to carry out the duties of this position." Hired in January 1900 at $150 per year, Jackson had a short-lived career. The official record noted her release for "unwillingness to work" after only four weeks. Superintendent Cora Dunn described the situation somewhat more colorfully when she reported that Jennie and the laundress "did not quite agree as to the value of Jennie's services, which brought about an unpleasant feeling between them." At any rate, continued Dunn, she was hardly surprised. "Jennie is a true Kiowa," she wrote, "in that her zeal for work could not survive a grass payment."[47]

Dunn's attitude was fairly typical. She and her fellow superintendents often opined that Indian employees were even more unreliable and ill-trained than white staff members. Many administrators shared James McGregor's opinion that "it will never be profitable to the school nor to the Indian to employ a Kiowa as the visitors will consume the salary and beside [sic] bring horses around the school that have to be pastured and watered." At the time of his letter Rainy Mountain employed a grand total of three Kiowas (the policeman, the assistant seamstress, and the disciplinarian), and that seemed like plenty.[48]

A comparison with schools from other agencies across the nation reveals similar situations and complaints. The superintendent of the Fort Lapwai School in Idaho reported in 1892 that his school had no principal teacher for nearly three months and that a number of advanced Indian pupils had filled in for two months. Conditions were also uncomfortably crowded at the somewhat better positioned Haskell School in Lawrence, Kansas, where more than five hundred students and staff crowded onto a campus built for three hundred. In 1893 the Pine Ridge Agency reported "four complete changes in the corps of teachers and employees in two years" at the Oglala Boarding School. And at Wisconsin's La Pointe Agency, where an average of only 280 of 1,283 eligible children were even in school, the agent admitted to a particularly bad situation: "Physical comforts are not provided for the children and they suffer from want of proper food . . . and during the season of sugar-making, berry-picking, and rice-harvest, the children are taken [by their parents], otherwise they would starve."[49]

A flood of similar reports reached Washington the following year. From South Dakota's Crow Creek Agency, Fred Treon wrote: "The boarding school has been rather demoralized. Too many changes in employees have undoubtedly taken place. . . . One grade . . . had as many as four different teachers during the year just closed, and it is safe to say that the children know but little more than when they started in." The year 1894 found the superintendent of the Oneida School in Wisconsin in even worse shape. "Since September 1893," he wrote, "we have had eleven different persons in the classroom, six of them regular appointments and the others temporary."[50] Out on the Rosebud Agency, George Wright submitted an annual report that resembled what had been coming out of the Kiowa-Comanche Agency for years: "This agency (though one of the most important in the service) is still unprovided with a Government boarding school. . . . The question naturally presents itself to them [the Lakotas]: 'If so desirable, why not have one for our children on our own reserve.' This subject has had the attention of the

Department for the past *fourteen years.*"[51] Although it is possible to find glowing assessments and high marks for some schools, on balance the government's official record suggests that reservation schools suffered universally from overcrowding, high turnover rates, poor facilities, and tight budgets.

Private schools fared little better. Common on reservations across the country, mission schools and private academies appeared slowly at the Kiowa-Comanche Agency. They enrolled a relatively small number of pupils (agency records suggest combined enrollments of fewer than one hundred pupils) and often had brief life spans. An array of religious groups, including the Methodists, Baptists, Presbyterians, Episcopalians, Quakers, and Catholics, established schools on the reservation beginning in the 1880s.[52] In 1888, for example, the secretary of the interior notified the Indian Office of a request from the Board of Home Missions of the Presbyterian Church for 160 acres near Fort Sill to carry on "an Indian training school." Two years later Reverend S. V. Fait opened a church on the site and announced plans to build a boarding school the following year. In February 1893, Fait informed Commissioner Thomas J. Morgan that the Mary Gregory Memorial Mission School was ready to receive its first students. The school's first annual report advertised a twenty-student capacity but also revealed that average attendance during the eight-month term was a mere eight students. In fact, the school boasted more cattle and mules (ten) than students. By 1895 attendance rose to ten; in September of 1897, the year of its closing, enrollment finally reached twenty-one. Among the mission's staff was Joshua Given, who was Carlisle-educated, ordained by the Presbyterians, and son of the Kiowa chief Satank.[53]

The Methodists, Baptists, and Catholics were close behind. Supported by the Methodist Episcopal Church South and the Methodist Women's Board of Missions, the Reverend John Jasper Methvin opened the splendidly named Methvin Methodist Institute south of Anadarko in the fall of 1890. Methvin entered the fray with great enthusiasm, and by the spring of 1891 his school had sixteen Kiowas and five Comanches in class.[54] The Methvin Institute appears to have enjoyed the highest level of support among the agency's various mission schools, with the possible exception of Father Isidore Ricklin's Catholic boarding school at Saint Patrick's in Anadarko. Methvin was honest and forthright, and students remembered him as a true friend of the Kiowas. When asked about the school and its namesake, one former student said: "They don't whip us. They don't punish us. That's a good school. J. J. Methvin told the teachers and the employees, 'Don't be mean to the Kiowas. We're staying on their land and we treat them nice. Treat them nice. If they don't know the lesson, they'll learn it some day. Don't switch them and don't slap them, no. No. It's not right. . . .' Oh, it was so nice. Great man, J. J. Methvin."[55] The school finally closed in 1907 because of lack of financial support, the result, Methvin grieved, of a " 'vile misrepresentation' to the board by a greedy syndicate in Anadarko which wanted to obtain the Institute's property."[56]

Reverend W. W. Carithers of the Reformed Presbyterian Church opened Cache Creek Mission among the Apaches and Kiowa-Apaches at about the same time that Methvin began his school. Describing those tribes as desperately in need of education, Carithers informed Agent James Randlett that "there are a lot of children growing up in that section that are training for the penitentiary unless they are diverted from their present course." Cache Creek remained open until just after World War I. W. D. Lancaster, a Baptist missionary and one of Rainy Mountain's first employees, opened the Lone Wolf Mission with about a dozen pupils, most of them Kiowas, in September 1890 near the north fork of the Red River. The Kiowas liked the school, reported one observer, "because it is located among them. The Government school . . . and all the mission schools except one are . . . in a bunch near the agency at Anadarko."[57] Like most of the other small mission schools, however, Lone Wolf attracted few pupils and suffered from scanty support. It closed in 1910. In addition to these, the Catholics ran Saint Patrick's Catholic Mission in Anadarko between 1891 and 1911, after which the facility was leased to the government and known as the Anadarko Boarding School.

Despite the spate of building that occurred on the reservation in the 1880s, the schools opened during that decade never approached the numbers required by the Medicine Lodge agreement. Between 1869 and 1884 the number of school-age children enrolled rarely exceeded 30 percent of the eligible population. In 1880, for example, the agent estimated the eligible school-age population at 800, but reported that only 250 could be accommodated. Average attendance for the year was 183 students. Three years later the estimated number of eligible children was set at 600, with school facilities for only 160. And in 1897 the agency's annual report announced it would double the size of Rainy Mountain's enrollment from 50 to 100 not by adding additional buildings or staff, but by "the intention to crowd the school." Even with the addition of Rainy Mountain and the new Comanche school by the early 1890s, levels of attendance rarely approached 50 percent. As late as 1892, Agent George Day wrote that education, specifically more and better schools, constituted the agency's most pressing concern.[58]

The Indian Service so completely neglected its duties that fulfilling Article 7 alone of the Medicine Lodge Treaty would require expenditures far beyond the scope of government resources. Hagan, for example, has reported the commissioner's admission in 1878 that "if the United States simply lived up to its treaty obligations to the Comanches, Kiowas, and Kiowa-Apaches, it would consume all the education funds allotted to the entire population of the Indian Territory exclusive of the Five Civilized tribes." Four years later, Commissioner Hiram Price estimated that the government had fallen behind a total of nearly $2 million in meeting its educational commitments. And in his annual report for 1885, Superintendent of Indian Education John H. Oberly admitted "that Congress annually fails to give effect . . . to most of the still vital provisions." The secretary of the interior's report for 1884, he added, revealed that $4,033,700 was necessary to fulfill education obligations throughout the country.[59]

A report from the superintendent of Indian education in 1883 revealed the extent of the negligence. Beginning in 1869, the government's master plan at the Kiowa-Comanche Agency called for the construction of thirty-two schools at a cost of $1,000 each, plus an additional $700 per school for teachers, materials, and supplies. Yet by 1884 the agency had only three government schools with an estimated total enrollment of 120 children out of an eligible pool of more than 600. Moreover, budget appropriations were in arrears by huge sums. On the Kiowa-Comanche-Apache Reservation alone the government owed $249,206, or 22 percent of the entire education budget of $1.1 million for 1885. Figures for other agencies indicated similar failures. The Indian Office owed the nearby Cheyenne-Arapaho Agency $254,100. For the Crow Agency the sum totaled $235,200 and for the Utes, $255,500, and on the Sioux Reservation it was an astonishing $1.2 million.[60] What had happened at the Kiowa-Comanche-Apache Reservation was occurring all over the country. The problem, of course, was that for the year 1885 the total education budget of the Indian Service was only $1.1 million.

Yet year after year the Indian Office announced that, with the exception of annuities, no other government program received as much money. There was truth in that statement, but not the whole truth. Indeed, the annual education appropriation grew from a paltry $20,000 in 1877 $2.9 million by 1900. The number of schools more than doubled during the period, and the number of students went up sevenfold. But what the numbers actually represented was illusory, for nowhere in the country did the government meet its obligations. Most agencies suffered the same kinds of shortages as the Kiowa-Comanche Agency and had only a fraction of their children in school. In 1880 the commissioner's office admitted that at fifty-one of sixty-six agencies fewer than 50 percent of the eligible students had classrooms and teachers, and that on at least seventeen agencies there were no treaty school funds whatever. By comparison, the Kiowa-Comanche Agency enjoyed real advantages; although only an estimated 13 percent of its children were in school in 1879, at least it had schools.[61]

From the very beginning the agency faced serious problems that crippled the government's civilizing programs. Most important, federal policy makers failed to make commitments to the Indian school system and its ancillary civilizing programs, but remained satisfied with what amounted to token attempts. Ironically, although the government considered the Kiowa-Comanche Agency one of the nation's most important, it did surprisingly little to create a stable, orderly environment. The Medicine Lodge agreement promised significant government assistance; its aftermath revealed a stingy, misdirected policy.[62] Far from being the remedy for the so-called barbarism of Indian life, the school system on the Kiowa-Comanche-Apache Reservation was symptomatic of a policy that was ambivalent at best, dishonest and wilfully neglectful at worst. And it was into this maelstrom that Rainy Mountain appeared.

"There Are So Many Things Needed"
A Difficult Beginning

As the 1880s came to a close, the Kiowa-Comanche-Apache Reservation still lacked school facilities for the over-whelming majority of its children. With no indication from Washington that significant improvements would come in the near future, the reservation seemed destined to continue operating with only a handful of schools scattered across its expanse. Agent Charles Adams reported in 1890 that the agency's three schools (Fort Sill, Riverside, and the Kiowa School), had a combined capacity of 190, but added that by his count the reservation had 1,045 school-age children, of whom more than 400 came under the jurisdiction of the Kiowa-Comanche Agency. Even with the new school at Fort Sill and several missionary schools opening in the near future, Adams observed that "there will still be a lack of proper school facilities. I am convinced that the importance of work in reservation schools is much underrated."[1]

The Kiowas, however, were not shy about pressing the issue. Repeatedly disappointed in their demands for more schools, and unhappy at the prospect of sending their children to Fort Sill or Riverside, the tribe campaigned for a school of their own. After all, the Medicine Lodge Treaty had promised a school and teacher for every thirty children, and the Kiowas had proved willing to enroll every child for whom there was room. In the opinion of Kiowas living in the reservation's outlying areas, a school located in a spot convenient to them was the least the government could do.[2]

The situation showed signs of improvement by the summer of 1891. Directed by the Indian Office to survey suitable sites for a Kiowa boarding school, regional Indian schools supervisor John Richardson recommended a site about thirty miles west of Anadarko, at the base of a well-known landmark known to the Kiowas as Tseityaedlta, or Rainy Mountain. In August, Richardson sent a detailed report to Commissioner of Indian Affairs Thomas Jefferson Morgan that, among other things, confirmed widespread support among the local Kiowas for the school. Owing to what he described as a "restlessness in this settlement of Kiowas, for whose benefit the school is to be established," Richardson encouraged the Indian Office to get the school into operation as soon as possible.[3]

From all appearances the site was more than adequate. Located "in the midst of the most beautiful scenery," Richardson reported ample supplies of water and grass. Quantities of timber and native stone for building purposes were nearby. He declared the site "most happily located for health. . . . No dull lake, marshy swamps or stagnant pools lurk within miles of it; nothing that breeds the dread malaria is found here. . . . Fanned by the sweetest of mountain air," the site, exclaimed Richardson, was "a veritable 'health resort.' "[4]

One week after receiving Richardson's letter Morgan authorized Kiowa-Comanche Agent George Day to hire George Moss, a thirty-seven-year-old teacher at the nearby Cheyenne Boarding School, as the new school's superintendent. By the fall of 1891 building plans had been prepared and reviewed, Moss was on his way to the Kiowa-Comanche Agency, and the Indian Office had allocated funds for construction. Finally, the Kiowas would have a place for their children.[5]

As events turned out, however, establishing the school was an omen of things to come. Slow, mixed up, and poorly directed, the building of Rainy Mountain lurched ahead unevenly for the next two years. Although a local construction firm accepted a contract in mid-April 1892, nothing happened at the proposed site for the rest of the spring. In early May, for example, Moss

wrote Day to arrange a discussion about various matters concerning the school. The builder, reported Moss, was still waiting
for the Indian Office to approve construction. "You are aware,
of course," he wrote, "that there is liable to be a considerable
delay in regard to receiving it, so I thought it would be a good
plan for me to come down and go with you . . . to select a site
for the building." Moss especially wanted to begin fencing the
school's pastures and fields so that Rainy Mountain's farm
could be started.[6]

In June Commissioner Morgan inquired about the school's
preparations. Had a site been officially determined? Was it advisable for the superintendent to begin full-time duties? What
progress had been made on the construction of a building or
the breaking of farmland? In late fall 1892, Morgan again made
anxious inquiries about Rainy Mountain's status. He admon-
ished Day to direct every effort toward the completion of the
main building and, although Rainy Mountain as yet had no
teachers, completed buildings, or staff, announced "the earnest
wish of this Office that the school may be filled with pupils at
the earliest practical opportunity."[7]

There was not a single finished building at the site when
Morgan wrote in June, but the commissioner nevertheless directed Moss to report full-time to Rainy Mountain on July 1,
1892. In mid-July W. D. Lancaster, a former missionary from
Kentucky and experienced schoolteacher on the reservation,
joined Moss as the school's industrial teacher and farmer. Agent
Day also hired John Wolf, a local Kiowa, as the school's helper.
In September 1892, Moss finally informed the Indian Office
that "the building is going up nicely now" and that other proj-
ects were also progressing. Several months later the Indian
Office informed Day that a matron was being selected from
Civil Service lists and that other staff members would soon
begin reporting for duty.[8] More than a year had passed since
Richardson's first report, but the school was finally taking
shape.

Morgan's eagerness to get the school into service as quickly as possible ran headlong into the galling realities of reservation life. No students enrolled that fall, and none entered the following spring. Indeed, in mid-November 1892, nearly a year and a half after the government had approved the school, John Richardson reported that Rainy Mountain still lacked many of its basic necessities. There were no facilities for dining, storage, or laundry, and the school needed a barn to shelter its animals and to provide industrial and agricultural training for the boys. And, contrary to earlier assurances, Richardson wrote that "the manner of the water supply should be looked after at once, so that there will be plenty of water when the school is opened."[9]

Despite these and other distractions, the school's small work force pressed ahead. All seemed well until February 1893, when Richardson lodged a series of allegations against the Rainy Mountain staff that were so serious that they threatened to derail the entire operation. "The Superintendent and the Industrial Teacher of the Rainy Mountain School are total failures; indolent and shiftless," wrote Richardson. He described the two as unfit to hold their positions and declared them incompetent and dangerous. In response, Morgan ordered Moss and Lancaster fired on the spot. "It is . . . utterly useless to consider the matter of Mr. Moss remaining in the service in any capacity," wrote Morgan. "You will notify him that his relief is absolute." Surviving records do not explain completely why Morgan ordered the two drummed out of the Indian Service. Day's reports contain no discussion of the episode beyond the fact of the firing, but whispered rumors about moral improprieties swirled around the agency for weeks afterward.[10] The incident threw a shadow over the school and threatened to plunge the project into chaos.

In an effort to sort out the mess as quickly as possible, the Indian Office appointed W. H. Cox as Rainy Mountain's new superintendent. Cox was at that time the assistant superintendent at the Albuquerque Indian School and previously had been a teacher at the Sac and Fox Agency near Stroud. Arriving from New Mexico on March 17, Cox and his wife, Lucy, plunged into the work. Indeed, Cox handled matters efficiently and carefully, and by late April he informed Washington that Rainy Mountain would be ready for occupancy as early as May. Owing to the nearness of the traditional summer vacation, however, Cox delayed the formal opening until the fall.[11]

In the meantime he oversaw the completion of the school's main building and stockpiled supplies, clothes, and other items. An inventory from the summer of 1893 contained an astonishing list of goods from disk harrows to shoe blacking. Included were hand bells, brooms, butter knives, mirrors, thimbles, gingham dresses, shoes, washtubs, and assorted goods and tools that would force the transition from Kiowa culture to Anglo-American culture. Cox also left an interesting record of the school's administrative supplies. His list included the usual foolscap stationery, inkstands, envelopes, and, alas, "one spool—red tape."[12]

Cox also inaugurated the school's agricultural operations. He made provisions to fence part of Rainy Mountain's four sections of land, and in late March he put fifty acres under immediate cultivation and used them as the beginnings of a modest farm operation that would serve as a laboratory and field school for the boys. He also ordered huge quantities of shade trees and decorative plants to beautify Rainy Mountain's rather nondescript campus.[13] His successor, Cora Dunn, was an indefatigable tree planter as well (she was fond of catalpa trees and planted them by the dozen), but their combined efforts to create a tree-lined campus failed in the long run. Today the school's grounds show no evidence that trees of any kind ever existed.

Finally, Cox directed the hiring and training of his staff. Between the time of his arrival, when the number of full-time employees hovered between four and six, and the school's opening in September 1893, Cox assembled a staff of nearly two dozen. A notable exception to the otherwise smooth build-up, however, was the absence of a qualified teacher. Cox's wife, Lucy, reluctantly agreed to serve as a temporary substitute.

Luckily, the agency hired a full-time teacher shortly before the opening. All seemed ready.[14]

On August 14, Kiowa-Comanche Agent Hugh Brown informed Commissioner of Indian Affairs D. M. Browning that Rainy Mountain would open on or about September 1, 1893. Browning authorized an opening date of September 1 but stipulated that because of the lack of a certified teacher, Cox could accept no more than forty pupils. Unfortunately, the woman hired as the school's teacher had resigned before Rainy Mountain even opened. Until a qualified replacement could be found, Browning directed Cox to employ "some competent person as a temporary teacher." To Mrs. Cox's dismay, she was the one.[15]

Rainy Mountain School opened officially on September 5, 1893, with a total of 5 scholars, as the government called them. Two weeks later there were 13; by March 1 it had edged up to 32. At the end of the first year enrollment stood at more than 50, and within two years approached nearly 100 students. After a decade it reached 130. The Kiowas at last had their school, and a great experiment had begun.

We know relatively little of that first year. Cox's letters and reports are sparse, and administrative records reveal little about the day-to-day activities of the school. Moreover, Cox left Rainy Mountain at the end of its first year, transferred to the Fort Sill School, and ultimately ended up in Rosebud, South Dakota, in 1898 as the superintendent of the agency boarding school.[16] His replacement was Cora Dunn, a redoubtable woman of enormous energy and enthusiasm who stayed on for the next sixteen years. Her husband, Alfred, joined her as industrial teacher, farmer, and ombudsman. The Dunns were experienced hands, having worked at both the Kiowa-Comanche Agency and the nearby Cheyenne-Arapaho Agency. She had taught in the Cheyenne-Arapaho school near Concho; he had spent the previous four years at a variety of agency jobs in Anadarko including farmer, flour inspector, and forwarding agent.

Cora Dunn directed the school through its formative years

and was often single-handedly responsible for keeping Rainy Mountain on a firm footing. Forced to endure a fumbling and indecisive Indian Office, saddled with a school that was never properly staffed or supplied, and faced with the rigors of living in a remote area, she nonetheless brought vigor and devotion to the job. With her at the helm, Rainy Mountain confronted an assortment of problems and setbacks that would have disheartened all but the most iron-willed administrators. "A cast-iron constitution, Scotch determination, Irish nonsense, the divine call and the power of the Holy Spirit," wrote her colleague, the pioneering Baptist missionary Isabel Crawford, "are the elements that made for success. Had any of them been lacking the results could not have been the same."[17]

When Cora Dunn arrived in the summer of 1894, she had her hands full just keeping the place afloat and operating. The most urgent problem confronting the school, and the one that best illustrates the chronic emergencies that plagued Rainy Mountain, was the condition of the school's facilities. The new buildings immediately proved to be both inadequate and poorly constructed. Moreover, the indifference of the Indian Office left the school crippled by unhealthy living conditions, obsolete and insufficient equipment and teaching materials, and ineffective staff members. The fact that Cora Dunn sometimes feared for the very roof over her head can be taken as a symbol, literally and figuratively, of what life at Rainy Mountain was like. In an early letter to the Indian Office, Dunn was moved to note, "Should it occur to you that we are asking for a good many things, please remember that we *need everything*."[18]

Rainy Mountain's physical plant was not very large or complicated. The campus, a neat quadrangle at the base of Rainy Mountain's east side, was dominated by a two-story stone dormitory-classroom building. It was the largest and oldest structure on the campus and originally housed the girls, some of the boys, and most of the staff. A similarly sized second dormitory went up in 1899, as did a superintendent's cottage. A laundry, barn, commissary building, mess hall, bandstand,

and various service buildings went up over the next fifteen years. The last major structure was a classroom building added in 1915. In addition to the central campus, 2,560 acres of adjoining land were reserved for the school's exclusive use as a farm. Much of that land was used as pasture or put under cultivation; on rare occasions it was leased.

Building the school had required a significant investment, yet the government showed a curious ambivalence about maintenance, upkeep, and improvements once Rainy Mountain was in service. The school's records are rife with complaints and reports that reveal the disregard of the Indian Office for any but the most urgent needs. And even then, school officials often had to beg for help. Having invested at least $37,825 on the campus during its first six years, the Indian Office, it seems reasonable to think, would have shown considerable interest in protecting and improving its investment.[19] Curiously, this was not the case. In fact, having spent the money, the Indian Office usually appeared reluctant to appropriate more funds, even when conditions at the school were dangerously unsafe.

Several examples illustrate the case. At the end of his only year as superintendent, W.H. Cox issued an annual report in which he concluded that Rainy Mountain was "in need of an additional building for schoolrooms and quarters for either the boys or the girls; that the school also requires a range, and that some porches should be constructed on the present building." Overall, he concluded that the school was already operating beyond capacity and that it lacked critically important facilities. In response, the Indian Office doubted the need for some of Cox's improvements and asked Agent Maury Nichols to look into the matter.[20]

Cox's requests proved both necessary and justifiable. After only one year the school had already outgrown its single main building, built to hold approximately fifty pupils. Attendance increased from an average of thirty-one in May 1894 to more than seventy by December 1894. In the fall of 1895 it was at seventy, and by early 1897 stood at nearly ninety, far more than the school could adequately or safely hold.[21] The absence of employee housing made the situation even worse, forcing staff members to live in the dorms and thus reducing the space available for students. Because it served as dormitory, assembly hall, classroom, staff living quarters, and chapel, the main building quickly suffered from overuse.

Cox left without persuading officials of the school's needs. When Cora Dunn arrived, she addressed the same concerns. Shortly after her arrival in November 1894 she informed the commissioner's office that the school needed an array of general repairs and improvements. "The plastering of the [main] building was originally of very indifferent quality," she wrote, "and is now badly broken." She requested funds to repair the plaster as well as the authority to build three water closets in the main building. In a separate letter she requested $550.00 for a barn and tool building. Noting that the school's livestock and implements were unsheltered, she also pointedly reminded the commissioner that this was the third time in her brief tenure that she had written of the matter. Already aware that the Indian Office did not take her seriously, she prefaced one letter by stating that she was writing at the advice of "Special Agent Able, who appreciates our pressing need."[22]

Eager to limit expenses, the Indian Office suggested that instead of building a large dormitory-style edifice, less expensive smaller cottages would suffice. Unwilling to endure the cost of another major building (the original main building had cost twelve thousand dollars), the Indian Office and Kiowa-Comanche Agent Frank Baldwin agreed that the plan seemed economical and practical. Cora Dunn agreed but had some reservations. Her letter to Baldwin in December 1894 stated that the plan "commends itself to me as the best and most functional method of fostering a love of homelife among these homeless children. Such an arrangement would turn out more permanent work than all the non-reservation schools with their vast machinery." The cottages could also solve other problems. The dining area in the main building could be converted into a chapel, and the kitchen into a classroom. (The pupils would cook in their cottages.) Dunn worried, however, that the school would need a matron for each cottage "to insure the prosecution of the work and sufficient protection for the girls," and that such a need would be a burden on the school's already limited finances. At the same time, she continued, the expense of additional matrons might be offset by eliminating the positions of cook, baker, and laundress.[23]

Nothing ever came of the plan, however, and three years later Dunn again complained to the agent about conditions at the school. "The standing need of this school, as has been stated in all previous reports, is another large building of the same size and general construction of the one now occupied." So desperate was its need, she continued, that it not only would have to serve as a dormitory, but also must contain a kitchen and dining room, for those facilities were pressed well beyond capacity. In addition, she also requested a cottage for the superintendent, a carpenter's shop, and a milking shed. Without these and other improvements, Dunn wrote, the school simply could not be expected to provide the children with adequate instruction.[24]

As if these were not enough, Dunn also requested funds to make extensive repairs across the campus. Flues in the main building were "nearly ready to fall," she reported in 1897. After further inspection she hastened to add that the flues were "in worse condition than we supposed, and it is extremely fortunate that it was discovered in time to save the building from destruction by fire." Shortly thereafter, Alfred Dunn requested permission to build flues in the dining room and playroom. "The children are having chills," he wrote, "and ought to have fires early in the morning." The Indian Office denied the request with the explanation that funds for such purposes were not available.[25]

It seemed to be one thing after another, especially during the early years. Plumbing, plaster, walkways, fire hoses, wells, new buildings, and basic supplies all found their way into Cora

Dunn's correspondence on a regular basis. Her constant pleas for ordinary items and normal repairs were most troubling. Typical shortage lists invariably included shoes, clothing, and food. On other occasions kerosene, lime for the latrines, or coloring paper for the kindergarten topped the list. And as her tenure lengthened, Dunn discovered that she could usually expect little sympathy, and less help, from the Indian Office when it came to keeping her school in good condition. In 1897, for example, she raised the issue of getting a decent water system for the campus; six years later she was still asking for one. In the meantime, the school muddled through by relying on the decrepit original system from 1893. Dunn's immediate successor was reduced to writing angry letters as late as 1915 to an Indian Office unmoved by Rainy Mountain's shockingly tawdry conditions.[26]

By February 1904 the condition of the school's major buildings (including a new dormitory, built in 1899) had deteriorated so badly that Dunn needed more than six thousand pounds of plaster for repairs. Blaming the condition of the buildings on the haphazard and inferior craftsmanship of the original contractors, she described several buildings as "positively dangerous." In the spring of 1905, driven to exasperation by the bureaucratic wrangling that crippled even the simplest requests, Dunn tersely informed the agent that she needed, and had ordered, boiler grates and a range for her cottage. "In order to obviate the extensive correspondence and tedious waiting involved in ordering through the Indian Office," she continued, "I had . . . a hardware merchant in Gotebo order them."[27]

She knew from experience that the Indian Office did not appreciate such maneuvers, but she also knew that the alternative was to suffer the interminable paper shuffling that too often left her with little more than official rejection notices, or with solutions that failed to correct the problem. In the fall of 1897, for example, after receiving repeated requests from Dunn for fire equipment, the Indian Office declined to authorize $220.00 on the grounds that the requests "seem to be about

100% above market price." In the end it allocated $78.05 for the purchase of one hydrant and 250 feet of hose.[28] Such equipment was quite inadequate to protect a campus the size of Rainy Mountain, but Dunn was helpless in the face of official foot-dragging. Adding insult to injury, the Indian Office also refused to upgrade the school's water system, leaving the fire equipment marginally useful under the best of conditions and completely worthless when normal conditions prevailed.

Despite the necessity of extensive repairs, significant improvements did not come until the turn of the century. The school did get a tool building and barn, both built in 1895, but no additional quarters or classrooms were approved. And it was not until late 1899, a full five years after Cox first raised the issue, that an additional dormitory was built. In the meantime, a stable went up in 1895, a playroom and lavatory in 1896, and a slaughterhouse sometime between 1894 and 1900. Certainly the school had need for these facilities, yet the Indian Office did not address the most urgent problem of all, that of better living quarters and expanded classroom space.

The situation became increasingly urgent after 1900, when average enrollment rose to more than 130. The school's facilities, originally built to accommodate 50 students, had not been significantly enlarged, and overcrowding remained a problem. Cora Dunn informed Agent John Blackmon in 1906 that "the need of an additional building for school purposes has so frequently been represented that it is unnecessary to further enlarge upon it." To dispel recent charges of unhealthy conditions, Dunn assured Blackmon that "the only time the pupils really lacked for sufficient air is when all are assembled in the schoolroom used as a chapel." Attendance was 129 at the time of her letter.[29] Relief finally came in 1915, when a third building went up. It marked the last major construction at the campus. By then enrollment averaged more than 160 students.

In addition to continual concern about the physical state of the school's buildings, Cora Dunn inherited an especially critical problem in the form of an unreliable and decrepit water system. John Richardson's original report stating that a spring only one-half mile away would "amply supply water for all purposes" was an exaggeration if not an outright fabrication.[30] The lack of a reliable water source and the unwillingness of the Indian Office to provide anything but the most meager appropriations led to dangerously unsanitary conditions. This was increasingly true for the years after 1900, when the school's inability to provide even minimal levels of sanitation for its students produced increasingly dangerous compromises year after year. Indeed, after 1913, when more than 160 students crowded into the school on an annual basis, poor bathing, laundry, and sanitary conditions produced the highest reported levels of trachoma in the Indian schools.

Dunn and her successor, James H. McGregor, repeatedly brought the health and water issues to the attention of the Indian Office. Indeed, they run like threads through the official correspondence over the entire history of the school. In December 1892, nearly two years before the school even opened, John Richardson advised "that the manner of the water supply be looked after at once, so that there will be plenty of water when the school is opened." Yet when Rainy Mountain opened, the water question remained unresolved. The solution was to haul water daily from a spring located nearly three miles south of the campus. Complaints that it took one employee nearly half the day to haul the necessary amount prompted Superintendent Cox in August 1894 to ask Agent Maury Nichols for permission to hire a man to dig a well at the campus. Because Rainy Mountain Creek was nearby, Cox observed that a well dug some fifteen to twenty feet deep "would likely furnish a supply of water."[31] Nichols apparently did not share Cox's concern and did not approve the request.

Cora Dunn took the matter up in the summer of 1895 when she submitted an estimate for a well to Commissioner of Indian Affairs Daniel Browning. She reported that a small one had recently been dug for the Indians who gathered at the school for rations and annuities and that an enlarged one at the same place "would furnish an inexhaustible supply of pure water . . . at a moderate cost." There was some urgency about the issue, she continued, for the small well was the school's only reliable source of water short of continuing to haul it from the spring three miles distant.[32]

Browning's reply is revealing. To the request for funds to build a water system (estimated by Agent Baldwin at $1,799.24) Browning replied that Baldwin needed first to establish which of the reservation's schools could be expanded to accommodate a larger than anticipated pool of eligible children. Until the Indian Office received such recommendations it would not review the water question at Rainy Mountain School. Obviously there was not enough money to satisfy every school's needs, but because it was unlikely that Rainy Mountain would be significantly enlarged, it was equally unlikely that its water problems would receive much attention. By tying improvements to matters that had nothing to do with the actual problem, the Indian Office virtually assured that pressing needs would go unattended. The merits of its case, clear and convincing though they were, did nothing to help the school. In the end, Cora Dunn's last-ditch plea for $40.00 to purchase a wagon-mounted water barrel elicited a curt response authorizing "no more than $30.00 for one wagon water tank."[33]

By early 1896, however, the Indian Office had a change of heart and approved $1,381.94 for a well, water tower, pump, and pipe. Hopes ran high on the campus, and Cora Dunn anticipated the end of a troubling dilemma. That summer a local contractor plumbed most of the school's main buildings. Another dug a well, and a third erected a windmill with motor, pump, and pipe. Interestingly, the total cost came to $637.71, less than half the allocated funds.[34]

No sooner was the water problem solved, however, than a series of disasters occurred. In December 1896, most of the pipes laid that summer burst. In a letter to the contractor who had directed the original installation, Alfred Dunn implied shoddy workmanship was to blame. (Perhaps a low-budget contract explains the lower-than-estimated cost.) "There are several things that will be a continual source of trouble," warned Dunn, "and they had better be fixed now."[35]

Shortly after this episode, a train of events occurred that defy explanation. On March 21, 1897, Alfred Dunn notified Baldwin that a spring storm the previous evening had wrecked the school's windmill. The apparatus was "torn all to pieces," explained Dunn, and the school had less than a week's supply of water on hand. By early April a new well was ready, and Dunn anxiously inquired when the school could expect a new windmill; without it there was not sufficient water short of hauling it, an onerous task that he wished to avoid at all costs. In addition, Dunn feared he would be forced to tear down the water closets, thus leaving the school with only drop-pit latrines. By May, with no relief in sight, he informed Baldwin that matters were serious. "If we do not get relief soon," he wrote, "we will be compelled to let some of the children go home. We are running our water wagon all the time and our cisterns have given out, so that we are dependent on the water wagon to furnish drinking, cooking, and laundry water, besides water for the closets."[36]

One week after Dunn's plea, but six weeks after the windmill had been destroyed, the Indian Office authorized $225.00 to set matters right. It would be almost another month before the second mill went up. And then disaster struck again. In early June, as the mill was being raised into place, a rope parted and the structure crashed to the ground. "It is in nearly as bad shape as the other mill," reported Alfred Dunn. But, Dunn hastened to explain, Agent Baldwin could take some solace from the knowledge that the broken rope belonged to the man hired to erect the mill, "so no blame can possibly rest on us." Baldwin no doubt found comfort in that fact. After repairing and raising the mill again several days later, however, Dunn reported that it was so badly bent that it could not function. Worse, it was in danger of falling down in even a moderate wind. In early June the Indian Office authorized funds for repairs but did not allocate very much money. Despite Dunn's warning that without a good mill the school would "of course be out of water the rest of the year," he was limited to $28.94, most of which apparently went into makeshift repairs of the previously wrecked mill.[37]

Events then verged on the ridiculous. The third mill went up in late June, but not for long. On June 25, Alfred Dunn wrote again to Baldwin to inform him that "the 'expected' has happened to the windmill." The Indian Office, probably flinching every time it heard from the school, agreed to spend $179.04 for a fourth windmill that went up in mid-August 1897 and miraculously stayed up.[38]

Alas, this did not solve the problem. In early September, Alfred Dunn wrote again to Baldwin. "I am sorry to say it," he began, "but the mill will not put the water in the tank. . . . I am satisfied the tower will have to be raised in order to give wind steady and strong enough to do the work." Until then, he would haul water for the kitchen and laundry as well as for the school's livestock. By October, Dunn reported that the school had water in limited quantity only, and that the water closets had been moved away from the campus. The fire hazard related to the lack of water across the campus worried him greatly. Thankfully, Baldwin approved a steam engine to pump water from the well or nearby creek to the main buildings. Yet even this measure did not end the crisis, for as the winter deepened, so did Rainy Mountain's water troubles. In early January 1898, Dunn told the agency that the school was "out of water and [has] been for three weeks."[39]

Matters continued in this vein for the next several years until a seemingly permanent solution appeared in 1900, when Alfred Dunn oversaw the construction of a reservoir near the top of Rainy Mountain. In October 1900, Cora Dunn requested $535.25 for the "proposed reservoir at the top of Rainy Mountain," and in March 1901 she included as part of a general estimate for campus repairs a request for cement "to be used in repairing the water reservoir and rendering it insect and vermin proof. Its present condition," she added, "is a standing menace to the school and must be remedied."[40] By using a steam engine to pump water up from the well or creek, the system could then rely on gravity to send water at sufficient pressure to the campus below.

It was a good idea. The only problem was that it did not work very well. No matter, for in early February 1900, an event occurred that elevated the school's misfortunes to epic proportions. The fourth windmill was blown "completely to pieces" in a storm that also ruined the limited improvements to the school's still primitive sewer and waterworks. Later that year Cora Dunn informed Agent James Randlett that the "automatic flushing apparatus of the water closet in the girls' building refused to work" and that the plumbing in most of the other buildings was failing. The only water the school was getting was water that it did not particularly need, for all of the main buildings leaked like sieves. In 1903 she continued lecturing Randlett about the "immediate necessity of repairs . . . to the plumbing and water system at this school." The grates at the steam boiler in the laundry had given way, the girls' dorm needed a complete plumbing overhaul, and the water closets would not flush anywhere on the campus. "All the plumbing at the school was originally of the most inferior quality and workmanship," she wrote, "and no repairs have ever been made except such as could be effected by school employees. The health of the employees [to saying nothing of the children] . . . is greatly endangered." Randlett finally authorized the money after an eight-week delay.[41]

The windmill episodes might seem humorous had they not so dramatically impaired the school's operation. The danger from fire aside, the situation compromised the health of the children in ways that contributed to lingering and episodic outbreak of illness, especially trachoma. Employees suffered as well, although they were rarely affected as adversely as the children. Inoculated against disease, and able to take advantage of medical facilities at Fort Sill or in surrounding towns, employees were uncomfortable but rarely threatened. Alfred Dunn, for example, could easily find ways to keep himself and his wife supplied with fresh water and other goods. After all, no one would question the superintendent's need to maintain a certain level of cleanliness and hygiene.

Students, on the other hand, endured primitive conditions. Drop-pit latrines located at a distance from dorms, water so limited in quantity as to allow bathing only once every other week—and only then in tubs shared by two to three children— no regular physician, and susceptibility to a variety of illnesses and diseases meant that boarding school life could be exceedingly uncomfortable. Reluctant to spend enough money to remedy the situation, the Indian Office instead allowed the school to suffer through prolonged periods of neglect that bordered on abuse. Doing so meant that the ability of pupils to learn was compromised in fundamental ways, for schools that would not provide clean drinking water could not possibly create an atmosphere in which learning was nurtured and supported.[42]

The school's physical woes were symptomatic of other problems. Cora Dunn regularly battled the Indian Office about shortages of supplies and necessities. Indeed, much of the school's official correspondence during its first decade reveals a deeply felt sense of isolation. Relatively distant from the agency office in Anadarko, the place was inconveniently located for visits or inspections. Out of sight, and just as often out of mind, Rainy Mountain seemed very much like a remote outpost.

The Indian Office often shrugged off Cora Dunn's endless requests for more help, better staff, improved instructional materials, or else it provided only the bare minimum. Several examples illustrate this point. The Indian Office required that all students wear "citizen clothing," which usually meant some sort of uniform. On most occasions Dunn saw that the children dressed in accordance with such regulations. But Rainy Mountain often had to rely on the charity and goodwill of missionaries, or had to make do with salvaged goods and cast-offs from other schools. In August 1903, for example, Dunn implored agent Randlett to find her enough shoes so that she could open school on schedule. "There are no shoes on hand for the opening," she wrote, "and as yet none received. If you would call the attention of the Indian Office to this also, it would help me out of an embarrassing situation." In September, Dunn raised the matter again. "Where are my shoes?" she queried the agent. "We have none at all for the children. . . . The Indians are greatly dissatisfied over it." Thankfully, the agency received 427 pairs of day shoes and Sunday shoes in time to rescue Dunn from her dilemma.[43]

In the fall of 1905, Dunn was pressed again for shoes and clothing for older students, especially the boys. Three months later she informed the agent that although she had shoes on hand, they were "so coarse and stiff as to occasion the children great discomfort in wearing them. Lighter shoes, I think, would effect . . . the relief that would be afforded the unhappy wearers of those now in use." One year later Dunn was in the same predicament. "I am sorry to mention the subject of shoes again," she wrote, "but a number of our children are barefooted and are really suffering these cold mornings." She noted that their parents either would not or could not buy their children shoes. "Many of the children have colds and I am trembling in fear of some of the barefooted ones having pneumonia." Worse, angry parents confronted her on the matter. "The Indians are greatly incensed over the matter and I cannot blame them." Turning their ire to her use, Dunn reminded the agent that the Kiowas did not know "how perfectly helpless I am as far as providing for their children is concerned," but hinted that she could easily make the tribe aware of the problems. At the end of the month, having received no help, she submitted bills for the emergency purchase of shoes for children who, she angrily noted, "were barefooted."[44]

More than a decade later, one of Dunn's successors faced the same problem. In September 1917, R. W. Bishoff informed the agency that "a number of the parents . . . have ask[ed] me to write you for some money for them to buy shoes and clothes" for their children. Meanwhile, Kiowa parents went away perplexed and angry at a government that confiscated and burned native clothing and shoes, but then proved unable to provide suitable replacements.

Food and supplies posed equally serious concerns. In the spring of 1906, for example, the school was so low on staple foods that Dunn threatened an early closing. "We are now out of bacon, lard, rolled oats, potatoes, hominy, and rice," she wrote. Her supplies of beef, soap, and sugar would last only another three weeks. Dunn suggested slaughtering part of the school's dairy herd but ultimately decided against it because the school lacked ice and proper storage facilities for dressed beef.[45]

A lack of equipment and instructional aids created additional problems. In November 1895, Cora Dunn advised the agency that a sewing machine intended for Rainy Mountain had been sent instead to the Fort Sill School. The foul-up rankled her enough that she dropped her normally respectful demeanor. "Whatever the need for a machine may be there, it can't be as great as at our school, for we have only two machines, one of which is practically worthless, while [I] understand that Fort Sill has five already." Three weeks later she raised the matter again. Not wanting to seem importunate, Dunn wrote, she was nevertheless driven to remind the agent that her personal sewing machine had been pressed into service the preceding year. "I think each of the other schools have as many as five, and I don't quite understand why we are not allowed those that have come for us." She never got her sewing machine from Fort Sill and was forced to divide her two usable machines among forty-nine female students.[46]

The kindergarten was an especially important component of Rainy Mountain's curriculum, for in it incoming pupils received their first taste of formal schooling. Like most of the school's other programs, however, it suffered from a chronic lack of supplies and support. In an 1894 letter requesting materials for the kindergarten, Dunn pleaded for consideration on the grounds that "the material asked for is mainly colored paper and really costs very little." In 1899 she made a similar plea. "Miss Mattoon [the kindergarten teacher] complains that she has not the proper material to successfully prosecute her work," wrote Dunn. "If the present estimate could be filled this year it would aid her greatly. We have received no kindergarten supplies for two years." And in 1905 she simply demanded authority to purchase her own materials. "No supplies of this character have been furnished this school for three years," she wrote, "and there are none on hand now."[47]

Chronic employee turnover represented another source of trouble, especially during the first decade of operation. Between 1895 and 1902 the school had no fewer than fifteen teachers, of whom only one stayed longer than one year. The rest drifted in and out at an average of one every six months. And only once during that span, from September to December 1899, did the school have as many as four teachers. By December the number had dropped to three; one year later the school had only one teacher for the entire spring term, when the enrollment was 110. It average two per year for the years 1895 to 1902.[48]

Other positions revealed similar turnover rates. Between 1895 and 1902 the school employed at least six matrons, three seamstresses, four cooks, five laundresses, and three kindergarten teachers. And on some occasions Dunn did not know who was coming or going. In 1902, Dunn made inquiries about the school's newly appointed teacher—who had not yet arrived and from whom no word had been received—and asked the agent if "another temporary nomination" was in order. In early 1903 an irate new employee "arrived in rather a disturbed state over my failure to send a team to meet her at the station," wrote Dunn. "But I had never even heard of her appointment. . . . The same thing happened when Mrs. Young, the laundress, came out." Alarmed by the high turnover, Dunn plaintively reported in 1895, "I feel extremely anxious to have a full corps of employees at the beginning of school as we suffered such inconveniences last year from late appointments." Rainy Mountain's predicament was not unique; by 1927 personnel turnover in the Indian school system reached 48 percent annually.[49]

Some prospective employees never even managed to find the place. Several appointments to the school appear to have gone unfilled when employees could not locate Rainy Mountain, or having found it, reconsidered their decision after seeing first-hand what awaited them. Perhaps no other statement captures the school's isolation so well as that made by Mary Fleeman to Agent James Randlett in 1905 before Fleeman's arrival at the school. "As Gotebo cannot be located by any railroad agent nearby," she wrote, "I will go to Anadarko. . . . Hope will have no trouble finding the Rainy Mountain School after reaching that place." In 1896, Mr. George Williams wrote to the agency on behalf of his young daughter, who was about to depart from Youngstown, Ohio, to Rainy Mountain. Unable to locate the nearest railhead to the school, Williams asked the agent if he might render a favor by sending "some directions as to how she can reach Anadarko, it is a long distance and a strange land."[50]

Worried that prospective employees could not quite appreci-ate the school's predicament, Dunn often tried to break the news to them as kindly as possible. Virginian Alice B. Mon-cure's inquiries about the size of Anadarko, the region's climate ("is it dry and healthy?"), the number of white inhabitants in the area, and the availability of a physician and "a minister of the gospel" worried Dunn so much that she sought advice from the agent. In a note to John Blackmon, Dunn expressed the fear that "the lady is laboring under some illusions that ought to be dispelled at once before she comes nearly two thousand miles. I have one employee now who wants the earth," she continued, "and I doubt my ability to divide it satisfactorily between the two." On the other hand, she needed a kindergarten teacher and was willing to do whatever was necessary to get one. She enclosed a copy of her reply to Moncure with a note to Blackmon saying that if the letter was "unduly discouraging

. . . I will gloss things over a little more." Whether Dunn eventually had to gloss things over a little is not clear, but agency records show that Moncure accepted the job in November 1907 and was gone by December of the same year.[51]

And those who accepted positions often proved to be of questionable caliber. As discussed in chapter 2, agency personnel were not always of the highest standing. In 1907, Dunn complained to Agent Blackmon that her current kindergarten teacher "has done very much less work than any kindergartner I have ever had and has done that little very poorly." In the same year she reported it necessary to rid the school "root and branch" of a married couple whom she feared would wreck the school. Among other transgressions, Dunn had observed the husband (an assistant farmer) teaching the boys how to roll their own cigarettes ("encouraging them to do so even to the extent of furnishing them tobacco!" she fumed); the wife (a cook) had announced she would not stay without her husband, even though "she came here to get rid of him." Dunn favored an immediate firing with no notice on the grounds that "it would be a bad plan to have him hanging around the school after being discharged as I am convinced he is none too good to do some serious harm such as setting fire to a building."[52]

But willing and manageable souls did appear. In 1901, for example, Dunn happily but wryly reported that a recently hired laborer was working out nicely. "I find he is a trained machinist, a competent musician, and, as he did not during the night develop aspirations to the position of superintendent, I think he will do."[53]

Dunn also supervised a support staff comprised of local Indians and older students, most of whom she regarded as unreliable and incompetent. Required to hire as many Indians as possible for certain subordinate positions, Dunn and her successors dutifully complied but were not usually very happy or enthusiastic about it. It is true that some Indians rose through the ranks and enjoyed status comparable to that of their white counterparts. In October 1898, for example, a Pawnee woman with the unlikely name of Jane Eyre accepted an appointment at Rainy Mountain as a teacher, a position normally reserved for white women.[54]

But Eyre was the exception who proved the rule, and most Rainy Mountain administrators took a dim view of native work habits and dependability. Although some Indian employees earned sincere praise and respect, on balance the Rainy Mountain Indian workers seem to have been rather poorly treated. In 1899, for example, Dunn wearily reported difficulties finding an Indian to hire as the school's baker. She asked for permission to hire a non-Indian based on "a series of unsuccessful experiments with Indian bakers." The previous year's appointment, she continued, "brought about results so disastrous to the health and comfort of the school that I am exceedingly anxious to avoid a similar experience in the future."[55]

In early 1903 she informed Agent James Randlett that the school's Indian assistant (a term used to describe a variety of positions, but generally applied to laborers and workers) had to be replaced at once, even if on a temporary basis. Fortunately the boy she had in mind was a perfect candidate; she needed help for about a month, and "a month's service usually exhausts Moses's usefulness anyway." Three months later she reported the unapproved absence of several Indian employees who were rumored to be off "looking for gold. If it takes them as long to find it as previous prospectors," she noted, "their immediate return is not to be expected." And in late 1906 she informed the agent that despite the fact that "I have used all means in my power to find a suitable Indian" for disciplinarian, "so far I have only obtained the promise of one to come the first of January."[56]

During its early years Rainy Mountain suffered from a list of chronic problems that marked it as an isolated, neglected school. The physical plant was poorly built and maintained, and the campus made do without essentials. And although some of the staff were dedicated and enthusiastic, too many of them proved to be unequal to the task. Hobbled from the beginning, the place worked against great odds. But it survived, often only because of the perseverance of Cora Dunn and sometimes because of good luck and timely aid. She more than any other person or administrator stamped the school with a sense of mission and dogged determination. A more easily satisfied superintendent would likely have seen the place fall to pieces. Cora Dunn remained undeterred in her work, even in the midst of repeated shortages and disasters.

And she even kept a sense of humor, although it was tinged with understandable bitterness. In a letter to Randlett in 1903 decrying the latest in a series of setbacks, she wryly observed that Rainy Mountain's somewhat diminished facilities "could not fail to gratify the practical statesmen who framed the Indian appropriation bill." Five years later she reminded one of Randlett's successors that "there are so many things needed for the school" that she was running out of ideas.[57] But she never ran out of energy or devotion, and this meant the difference between abject misery and heartfelt concern for hundreds of Kiowa children.

Rainy Mountain near our farm.

View of Rainy Mountain from the north, December 1910. The campus is located at the extreme left of the mountain's base, just out of this frame. Courtesy of Archives and Manuscripts Division of the Oklahoma Historical Society.

Main campus ca. 1915, looking northwest. Probably taken from the top floor of the 1915 classroom building, this photo captures the tree-lined campus that Cora Dunn labored to create. Structures left to right are the dining hall, which included the kitchen and bakery (1899); girls' dormitory (1899); and bandstand (1906). Courtesy of Archives and Manuscripts Division of the Oklahoma Historical Society.

Interior of the campus, pre-1915, looking northwest. Photo is taken from what would become the site of the large 1915 classroom building. Structures left to right include the dining hall (1899), bandstand (1906), girls' dormitory (1899), and principal's residence (1899). Courtesy of Archives and Manuscripts Division of the Oklahoma Historical Society.

Interior of the campus, pre-1915, looking southwest. Taken from about the same vantage point as photo number 3, this image shows the school's agricultural and mechanical plants. Structures left to right are the commissary building, which was also the 4–6 grade classroom building after 1910 (1907); employees' dining hall (1907); stable (1895); and boys' dormitory (1892). At the extreme right of the frame, behind the boys' dormitory are living quarters for staff and Indian police. Courtesy of Archives and Manuscripts Division of the Oklahoma Historical Society.

Back of the girls' dormitory looking east, ca. 1910–1918. This photo was taken from near one of the school's main gates, located at the east base of Rainy Mountain. Courtesy of Archives and Manuscripts Division of the Oklahoma Historical Society.

Interior of the campus looking northwest, December 1910. This is the south porch of the boys' dorm, with the laundry and sewing room (1894) in the background. Courtesy of Archives and Manuscripts Division of the Oklahoma Historical Society.

Interior of the campus looking north, 1910. Front porch of the boys' dormitory in the foreground, dining hall and girls' dormitory in the background. Courtesy of Archives and Manuscripts Division of the Oklahoma Historical Society.

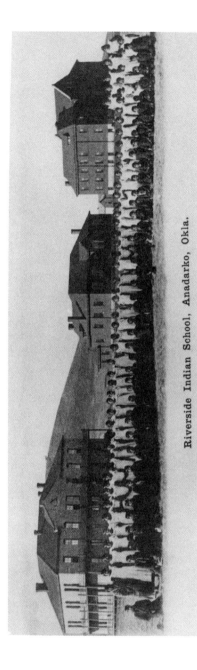

Riverside Indian School, Anadarko, Okla.

School body, pre-1906 (note the absence of the bandstand). Mislabeled as Riverside School. Courtesy of Archives and Manuscripts Division of the Oklahoma Historical Society.

I was head teacher at the govt Indian school almost a year. (Kiowa girls)

Group of Kiowa girls, December 1910, gathered near the school's main gate (visible in the distance, left of center) on the north side of the campus. Structure in the background is not the bandstand, but a gazebo located near the front of the girls' dormitory. Courtesy of Archives and Manuscripts Division of the Oklahoma Historical Society.

Kiowa girls, 1918. Note the uniforms and boots that one student likened to "prison uniforms." Courtesy of Archives and Manuscripts Division of the Oklahoma Historical Society.

Kiowa girls, left to right, Hattie Geimausaddle, Belle Kicking-
bird, Emile Botone, Helen Gooinkeen, and Lizzie Asa were
all schoolmates between 1901 and 1902. Photo is taken on
the front porch of the girls' dormitory. Courtesy of Archives
and Manuscripts Division of the Oklahoma Historical Society.

Marbles game outside of the boys' dormitory, ca. 1902. Courtesy of Archives
and Manuscripts Division of the Oklahoma Historical Society.

Three Rainy Mountain teachers, ca. 1910. Courtesy of Archives and Manuscripts Division of the Oklahoma Historical Society.

Rainy Mountain Bakers' Class, 1917. Parker McKenzie's sister, Nellie, is at lower right. Courtesy of Archives and Manuscripts Division of the Oklahoma Historical Society.

Rainy Mountain track team, ca. 1910. James McGregor is on the left. Courtesy of Archives and Manuscripts Division of the Oklahoma Historical Society.

Rainy Mountain baseball team, 1914. Parker McKenzie's brother Daniel is at lower right. Courtesy of Archives and Manuscripts Division of the Oklahoma Historical Society.

Rainy Mountain School agriculture exhibit, Oklahoma State Fair, 1913. Courtesy of Archives and Manuscripts Division of the Oklahoma Historical Society.

Rainy Mountain campus, 1990. Principal's cottage at center, boys' dormitory at right. Author's photo.

Rainy Mountain campus, 1990, looking northwest across the site of the dining hall and girls' dormitory. Excavation for the water tank is visible at left side of mountain, halfway up. Author's photo.

Ruins of boys' dormitory, 1990, looking northwest. Author's photo.

Parker McKenzie at the Rainy Mountain flagpole, August 1990. Author's photo.

4

"We Had a Lot of Fun, but . . .
That Wasn't the School Part"
School Days

UNTIL FAIRLY RECENTLY, MOST SCHOLARLY ACCOUNTS OF INDIAN education have focused on policy. And although some works examine the boarding school experience from the perspective of students, for the most part these accounts are not from Indians as much as they are *about* Indians. The difference is crucial, for it entails the critical component of perspective. Understanding Rainy Mountain through the eyes of its students presents a rich portrait of life in a reservation boarding school. It offers a revealing look at how and what students learned, and at how schooling affected their lives.[1]

In and around Kiowa communities in southwestern Oklahoma there are many former students who recall life at Rainy Mountain or one of the agency's other boarding schools during the early twentieth century. Except for the Doris Duke Oral History Collection undertaken in the late 1960s, and a handful of scholarly studies, however, few of these people have ever been asked to comment at length on their experiences. Thankfully, many of them have been willing to discuss their school years and in doing so to add an important perspective to our understanding of reservation life. Much of what follows rests on interviews with elderly Kiowas and Comanches who attended Rainy Mountain or another boarding school on the reservation.[2]

As with all sources, some caveats are in order. Because much of what follows rests on memories that reach back as far as the first decade of the twentieth century, the question of reliability is legitimately raised. Despite the caution with which these sources must be used, it is nevertheless true that they have a potency and resonance absent in the school's official records. Moreover, these sources are both historically powerful and historically credible. Michael Coleman's work on Indian schools reminds us that oral accounts make important contributions to our understanding which cannot be ignored:

> The school obviously was such a radically new experience that it imprinted itself deeply upon the minds of the narrators—they recalled the arrival with special vividness. Further, most of them began life in oral cultures, where accurate recall and the faultless performance of ritual and other duties were seen as vital to survival. This is not to claim that memory is infallible in such cultures, merely that the deeply ingrained need to remember accurately did not dissolve the moment the narrators entered the school gates.[3]

Tsianina Lomawaima makes the same argument in her work on Chilocco. The sixty-one former students who spoke to her expressed different opinions and memories, but collectively they created a mosaic that captured the rhythms of boarding school life more completely than any official source ever could. "Marked inalterably by the communion of shared experience," she writes, former students knew that "the memories one has been entrusted with cannot be laid aside or relegated to the attic of the soul or the mind."[4] The same is true for Kiowas who went through Rainy Mountain, Fort Sill, or Riverside.

To begin a discussion of reservation schools, one must start with the most elemental task agents faced: enrolling eligible children. Determined to round up as many students as they could, agency officials took seriously the task of locating and enrolling eligible youngsters. As Rainy Mountain's first term approached in the fall of 1893, Commissioner of Indian Affairs Thomas Jefferson Morgan ordered Kiowa-Comanche Agent George Day "to meet with parents of children and make a thorough canvass among the children of school age [six to sixteen] and suitable health who are tributary to the Rainy Mountain School . . . [and to reach a] thorough understanding with the parents and effect such arrangements that you may get the children into the school without delay as soon as you are ready to receive them."[5]

As discussed earlier, Kiowas and Comanches were generally willing to enroll their children; the problem confronting that reservation was not reluctant parents but too few schools to accommodate the school-age population. Once Rainy Mountain opened, it rarely had trouble filling its quota. And when Kiowa parents resisted, the agent had forces at his disposal normally sufficient to compel parents to relinquish their children. Because a reservation census was taken annually, for example, the number and location of families were matters of record. The agency kept track of where families with school-age children lived and monitored their movements through ration and annuity issues. The annual agency census included statistics on school-age children between the ages of six and sixteen, the number of schools operating and their location, the average attendance at such schools, and the distance that each student lived from both government and public school-houses.[6] Moreover, with the coercive force of the army at his disposal, and with the authority to restrict rations, annuities, and supplies, the agent had clear advantages in the campaign to enroll Indian children.

The reasons for putting children in school varied. Some families believed that education and training meant a more secure future. Others knew that the schools supplied food, clothing, and shelter to every pupil. Some children went to be with relatives or because they had no other choice.[7] Rainy Mountain's students often attended for one or more of these reasons. Myrtle Ware enrolled at Rainy Mountain in 1898 because her family was poor. Living at the time with an aunt and uncle in a tipi near Anadarko, Ware recalled being told "that I can't be taken care of down this way. . . . [My aunt] took me up there to Rainy Mountain. She asked my dad, 'I wanta put her up to school there, where I'll go and see her,' and I went up that way." Annie Bigman, born in 1900, arrived at Rainy Mountain between 1904 and 1905 for similar reasons. "Daddy started me

to school when I was about four years old," she stated. "He
was sick then" she added. "He don't want to take care of a
little one so he pushed me to school."[8]
Missionaries also influenced the decision. Guy Quoetone,
born in 1885, attended John Jasper Methvin's Methodist Institute south of Anadarko before switching to Rainy Mountain.
He would have gone to one of the agency schools in Anadarko,
he said, "if my father hadn't already have joined the Methodist
church . . . [But] the campaign was on in every camp, and when
we started to school he wanted me to go to that school [Methvin]
and dedicated me and sent me." When asked the reason for his
transfer to Rainy Mountain, he replied, "Well . . . we lived
closer to Rainy Mountain." He also recalled that he told his
father "maybe they might give me better grades, but they
didn't."[9]

Lewis Toyebo got to Rainy Mountain because a family friend
prevented missionaries from carrying him away to another
school. In 1897, at the age of five or six, Toyebo and a friend
were on horseback headed for a mission school when a relative
"chased us down and made us get off." Pondering the incident
nearly ninety years later, Toyebo mused, "We might have been
preachers." He recalled that "Daddy and Mother told me they
were to take me to Rainy Mountain School." He spent the next
decade there, eventually becoming an assistant disciplinarian.
Interestingly, Toyebo's father, Edward, attended school with
his son after Cora Dunn granted him permission to stay on the
school grounds and attend classes: "While his progress has been
slow, as might be expected at his age, during his three years
. . . at school he has learned to read and write and can speak
English with sufficient ease to make a very acceptable inter-
preter for the missionary. Deprived of educational advantages
in his boyhood, Toyebo, late in life determined to educate himself. For several years he struggled along with no other help
than his little boy during vacations."[10]

Sarah Long Horn, born in 1902, entered Rainy Mountain in
1910 with a cousin:

We mostly was raised together, and I always want to be with her.
. . . I went down there to see that girl. They say she's going to school,
so I went to visit her and she begged for me to stay. So I thought
to myself, I'll stay for a few days and then I'll go back. Then when
the time came, well I was already in school. So I just stayed there
and never did go back home. . . . That's how I got to school. I went
to school myself. By going visiting, she asked me to stay, so I just
stayed with her.[11]

Fred Bigman, born in 1900, began his education at the Cache
Creek Mission west of Apache, Oklahoma. "Boy," recounted
Bigman, "they is like real missionaries. Sort of like Baptists."
(In fact they were Presbyterian.) From there he went to public
schools near Fort Cobb and then to Saint Patrick's Catholic
Mission west of Anadarko. In September 1915 his parents took
him to Rainy Mountain. "Wanted me to switch schools," he
remembered. "They just took me here and there." The peripa-
tetic Bigman, who attended at least four schools by the time
he was fifteen (most of his cohorts were lucky to attend two
during their entire lives), noted that he was not particularly
happy at Rainy Mountain. "I didn't like that school right there
close" to home. He stayed only for half a year and then returned
to public schools.[12]

James Haumpy entered Rainy Mountain in the fall of 1913
at about the age of thirteen. His parents sent him to school, he
said, to be with "those other boys they was schooling out there."
Haumpy found little solace in that fact: "I was a little boy. I
don't know how to talk English. They put me in school. Well,
I ain't used to it. And I cried and cried, I wanna go home." So,
like other young Kiowas, Haumpy went because his parents
wanted him to and because other Kiowa children were there
as well. Haumpy also remembered that when he got over his
initial displeasure he discovered that Rainy Mountain was not
entirely unpleasant. "I'd take my horses down there," he said,
because "I seen pretty girls at that school."[13]

Parker McKenzie said that by the time his parents enrolled
him and his brother Daniel in 1904, "most of the Kiowas already
were impressed of the benefits of education and took advantage

of schooling." Rainy Mountain School was well known to the Kiowas, he added, and "no one had to inform them about the schools, they were on hand and saw them." As far as McKenzie's family was concerned, "the Indian was already out of us by the time we went to school. . . . Missionaries had already been doing this. . . . After joining the church we began to change."[14]

The willingness of the Kiowas and Comanches to enroll their children compels us to reconsider the history of Indian schools. Conventional wisdom holds that tribes jealously resisted the schools and used any means available to keep their children out of the hands of government teachers. Although resistance did occur on the Kiowa-Comanche-Apache Reservation, Indian parents also indicated a willingness to enroll their children. The seriousness with which Kiowas and Comanches addressed their agents about the distressing lack of schools raises an interesting set of issues: Forced onto the reservation, unwilling to commit to the wholesale cultural change demanded by the government, Kiowas and Comanches nevertheless showed a genuine interest in gaining the best possible advantage when it came to the schools promised to them.

Explaining this requires a reexamination of how the tribes interpreted the role of the schools. In 1896 the agency's annual report noted that instead of forcing children into the schools, "we find no one who has a child of school-age that is not presenting it for attendance in school." Three years later a delegation of Kiowas informed the commissioner of Indian affairs that "we have placed our children in schools provided by the government. . . . We point to these facts as evidence that we are striving in the right way to fit our people for the day when we realize we must" come to the end of the reservation. Individual students echoed this sentiment. Eugenia Mausape entered the schools because her parents "think it's good way." [sic] Cecil Hunting Horse attended both the Methvin Institute and Rainy Mountain to learn what his father called "the right way of living."[15]

Bruce David Forbes has suggested that such actions need not

be seen "merely as capitulations to a foreign culture but might be described more positively as attempts to find a new organizing center for lives which had suffered disruption." And, continues Forbes, other historians such as Angie Debo have argued persuasively that for some tribes the schools and the church became "a steadying influence to compensate them for the disruption of their ancient ways." Howard Harrod continues this line of thinking and writes that "participation in missionary institutions [and, by extension, boarding schools] may provide a needed center of social order and identity for Indians undergoing rapid social change—a conservative, stabilizing function."[16] Schools like Rainy Mountain clearly served such functions.

Important support for the school also came from well-placed authorities inside the tribe. Some appreciated the importance of education; others used it to gain favor with agents. In 1891, Agent George Day informed his superiors that "no branch of agency work has been more encouraging during the past year than . . . the schools. . . . The Indians seem to have a growing confidence in the management of the schools and even the ghost dancers failed to break into a good attendance." The agency's annual report for 1897 noted that the Kiowas were so anxious to get enough schools built that they had agreed to donate twenty-five thousand dollars from their grazing fees to build an industrial school at Mount Scott that could train graduates from the reservation's other schools. And in August 1905, Big Tree, an influential Kiowa and former opponent of reservation life (he eventually became a Baptist), dictated a letter to Agent James Randlett after the agent had solicited the chief's help in getting the school filled. Big Tree replied, "I will tell the people to put these children in school. . . . We are going to the Ghost Dance Friday and I will let the people know about the school and tell them to put these children in school." In closing, the chief reminded Randlett that annuities were due shortly and wanted to know "when the payment will be." It was a friendly reminder that support had a price. Jim Whitewolf remembered that Henry Brownbear, a Kiowa-Apache chief, told the agent that all of the tribe's school-age children ought to be enrolled and that any parent who resisted should not receive rations.[17]

Not every Kiowa parent was anxious to surrender a child, however, and some doggedly refused to comply. Resistance took several forms, the most common of which was simply to hide one's children. In September 1900, for example, allotment negotiations influenced embittered parents to keep their children at home in an attempt to force concessions. Cora Dunn reported only two dozen students on campus at the end of the opening week; in past years opening week had brought in an average of seventy-five children. "The Kiowas are in an ugly frame of mind over the terms of the allotment treaty," she added, "and are determined to be as annoying as possible." This included using their children as a bargaining point. "If the children do not come in by the first of the coming week," she concluded, "some coercive measures will have to be used to fill the school." A group of Kiowa parents remedied the situation when they collected enough children to open the school. On another occasion Dunn reported to the agent that disputes over annuity payments had led Kiowas to hold their children out of school. Quanah Parker, Big Tree, and local bankers interested in "stirring up the Indians," wrote Dunn, had convinced Kiowa parents to "keep their children out of school altogether." Unable to convince parents to comply with regulations ("Persuasion is worse than useless in the present state of mind," she wrote), Dunn concluded that "all I can do is to wait until the pending questions are adjusted" and hoped that some of the "right-minded Indians" would enroll their children.[18]

Administrators also used the school's policeman to round up students. In early 1899, Cora Dunn informed Agent James Randlett that a local Kiowa "came to the school to tell me that he had recently been appointed policeman and wished to collect children for this school," a task she set him to immediately.

In 1913, James McGregor reported that he was going to use Rainy Mountain's policeman to "forcibly bring in" several children but worried that he might need the assistance of the agent to get two other truants, whose father was "such a notorious kicker I am of the opinion that it will take more than an Indian police to bring them to school."[19]

More often than not, however, parents discovered that they could not challenge the system for very long, especially with rations or annuity payments in the balance. In March 1905, Cora Dunn advised Agent James Randlett that one such case had been resolved after a father agreed to enroll his daughter and that the man's grazing money should not be held up. Moreover, she added, the case ought not to be pressed too vigorously "as he promises he will voluntarily place the child in school next year." Another parent "placed in school his daughter . . . on account of whom his per capita payment was withheld." Cora Dunn believed it was absolutely necessary to take a firm stand. "I know from experience," she wrote, "that nothing is to be gained by temporizing with a Kiowa." Not even widows could escape Dunn's reach. In 1906 she reported that "Doyebo's widow has put her children in school and there is now nothing in the way of payment of her money."[20]

If withholding payments failed, agents might cut off rations to parents who refused to comply with regulations. In 1898, for example, Commissioner William A. Jones informed Kiowa-Comanche Agent William Walker that failure to enroll children in the schools specified by the government would result in the suspension of rations. "And if that does not suffice," he continued, "I will send their children anyway. Make it peremptory, and let them understand that I do not care and will not have any obstacles in the way of these children going." Citing an 1896 circular, the commissioner called for "more vigorous measures" and ordered the arrest and "suitable punishment" of children who deliberately avoided school. Parents and guardians who resisted were to be punished as well. "The wisdom of this course," he imperiously observed, "is fully evidenced in the largely increased enrollment and average attendance for these schools."[21]

On rare occasions, however, officials refused to enroll children or would even expel them for various reasons. Such was the case in 1906 when Cora Dunn expressed the desire to send two young boys home. In her opinion, one was more trouble that he was worth, and the other was stricken with some undisclosed malady. "The Whitefox boy is a most flagrant case of insubordination," she wrote. "The father and grandfather . . . put him in school and drew his money, then stole him away and now defy the police to come after him." Weary of the time and effort required to lay her hands on the boy, Dunn was willing to write the episode off as a loss. In the case of the second boy, she wrote that "I would rather not have the Pauquodle boy, unless you feel it necessary that he shall come as a matter of discipline. He is horribly diseased and I had to send him home last year." In 1895 she happily expelled a boy on the grounds that "his moral influence was bad," and in 1913, James McGregor dismissed several girls with the explanation that they "have no contagious disease, but were naturally weak and as I did not have room for as many girls as applied for admission, I allowed those to go home that appeared to be on the decline." Another girl met the same fate in 1918 because of "weak lungs and she needs money each month for clothing and food."[22] These cases, however, were the exceptions that proved the rule.

Once enrolled, Kiowa youngsters entered a new world. For forty weeks a year they lived according to a regimen grounded on diligence, individualism, and discipline. It was to be a wholly transforming experience in which no detail was too small to be spared, no lesson too limited to be ignored. "A close examination of the institutional life of Indian schools," writes David Adams, "reveals that they were waging an all-out assault on the child's 'otherness.' For the war against savagery to be successful, reformers decided, it must be waged uncompromisingly on every aspect of the child's being." What Indian children learned, and how they learned it, observes Bruce David Forbes, had enormous implications: "More than simply offering an education in certain subjects, the boarding school lifted young people out of native contexts and immersed them in white, American culture. The intention was to raise godly, civilized, educated children, with all the implications that those words carried. The goals were difficult to achieve if the child remained in touch with old ways and life-styles; the separation of the boarding school made children more educable in new patterns."[23]

The change began immediately upon arrival. Because physical appearance was an important measure of a civilized life, the children went through a process designed to take the Indian out of them. For some the transition was not so difficult. Parker McKenzie, born in a tipi on the reservation, grew up in a home where he learned much about white culture. "I am sure I was not surprised that knives, forks, and spoons were on the cloth covered tables" at school, he recalled. A visiting missionary once described the home of McKenzie's maternal grandparents as "neat and clean, two beds well made, chairs, a table, a polished cook stove, a cupboard well arranged, pictures on the wall."[24]

Other students, however, came to the place with considerably less exposure to white culture. Guy Quoetone recalled that he was "still in my Kiowa costume" the first time his parents left him at the Methvin Institute. Staff members assured his parents "We'll take care of him. You don't have to worry. Just don't come back for about a month or two. . . . He'll be alright," and ushered Quoetone into a room where two men and a woman waited for him:

> They shut the door and about that time I get excited and they got a chair. This man set me there and they commence to hold me. He set me down in that chair and that lady talked to me and tried to get my attention. While I was talking at her . . . this barber . . . he come from behind and cut one side of my braid off. . . . About that time I jumped up and they grabbed me and hold me down. And I turned tiger! I commenced to fight and scratch and bite and jump up in the air! They had a time, all of them, holding me down. Cut

the other side. Two men had me down there and that white lady tried to hold my head and then that barber cutting all the time. It was almost an hour before he finished cutting my hair. And you ought to see how I looked. I sure hate a haircut!

Following his encounter with the barber, Quoetone received uniforms and shoes ("Big heavy shoes. . . . That's why my feet's so large—wearing oversized shoes!"), and was sent on his way to the boys' dormitory.[25]

Every student received a set of uniforms. Like haircuts and baths, this marked the deliberate subordination of Kiowa culture and helped to enforce discipline, order, and dependence. "Everything that was needed was furnished by the school," said Lewis Toyebo. "The Indians didn't have to buy nothing." Styles varied from year to year, but the school always attempted to provide some standard dress for boys and girls. At Methvin, Guy Quoetone remembered getting "a suit—jeans—kind of grey." During Annie Bigman's Rainy Mountain years the girls wore grey uniforms that resembled sleeveless jumpers. A white blouse, black shoes, and stockings completed the ensemble. Boys wore "little brown suits. Boys' knee pants. Brown caps." Sarah Long Horn's uniforms had a distinctly military look. She commented that girls wore ribbons in their hair identifying them as members of company A, B, or C in military style. Lewis Toyebo also remembered a martial look to his clothes. "Our school uniforms were grey with red stripes and our play clothing were plain jeans. We were a sight on earth." Juanita Yeahquo described her Riverside uniforms as "awful clothes. . . . I guess we got prison uniforms and didn't know it." She especially disliked the fact that girls wore heavy boots.[26]

For some the transformation included receiving a new name. Because tribal names often seemed a babble of indecipherable syllables, schools and agents translated them whenever possible, or used what John Wesley Powell described as "suitable or euphonic" replacements. Botone, for example, became Beavertail, and Setainte (or, as more commonly rendered, Satanta) became White Bear. When asked if his son had a Christian,

English name, Lewis Toyebo's father said that he did not. "Okay, we'll call him Lewis," replied a Rainy Mountain administrator. James Haumpy received his name in similar fashion. Guy Quoetone was named after the principal at the Methvin Institute, and Eugenia Mausape was named after Mrs. Methvin's sister. Sometimes the transition was not very smooth, and more than one student remembered being disconcerted by the fuss over new names. Ethel Howry, who attended the Methvin Institute, remembered being confused when summoned by a name she neither recognized nor understood.[27]

Each student also received a permanent number. Lewis Toyebo was number forty-one from the day he entered Rainy Mountain in 1898 until he left in 1909. Myrtle Ware was number nineteen, "which I kept for so many years until I was dismissed from the school." Parker McKenzie said that "like prison convicts we were mostly identified by our assigned numbers rather than by name, except in classrooms where we were 'respected' by our given English names." At the school's first-ever reunion in June 1963 the schedule noted with some poignancy that "an appropriate program is being rounded out for the afternoon and will start with roll calls of 'boys' and 'girls' by numbers, as was the practice at Rainy Mountain."[28]

Along with a bewildering array of new cultural looks and practices, schools strictly separated students by age and sex in all aspects of life in order to establish control, which was the hallmark of the school experience. Matrons hovered over their wards, and were unstinting in their punishment of any who tried to cross the line. Hagan reports that barbed wire was often strung across transoms, and he notes the Victorian moral codes that influenced the schools. Former students corroborate this. "Keeping the sexes apart was routinely strict," said Parker McKenzie. "We were under strict discipline, we were never free." Boys and girls not only maintained separate living quarters, but also ate at separate tables, occupied different portions of the same classrooms, and were kept apart at chapel services. School officials allowed them to mix only at the school's carefully

chaperoned social functions. And even then it was not quite
an open field. Students "all marched to and from in military
order—and separately, too." Despite what McKenzie called
"some unavoidable togetherness," for the most part staff members tried to keep boys and girls as far apart as possible.[29]

Although students flirted, they also recognized the imaginary
line that separated boys and girls, and "most feared to cross
it," Mckenzie recalled. But Sarah Long Horn remembered that
boys often tried to find ways around the wall of separation.
Boys attempted an occasional daring foray into the girl's dorm,
but the odds of success were long and punishment was swift
and sure. There were more auspicious moments. When students
made the trek to Boake's Trading Post about a mile from the
campus, for example, an opportunity to test the rules often
presented itself. But staff members guarded against such lapses
and often foiled the best laid plans. "They watch us real close,"
Sarah Long Horn said. "There's got to be one teacher up in
front and there's got to be somebody else in the back that will
watch the boys and the girls." Fred Bigman grumpily recalled
that "we never did get to talk to any girls."[30]

Despite the concerted efforts of teachers and matrons, students sometimes managed to get around the carefully constructed rules and regulations. During free time in the evenings
boys and girls slipped away to socialize and visit. Some students
recalled sneaking around campus buildings to arrange clandestine meetings. The summit of Rainy Mountain afforded a safe
haven for love-struck youngsters and became a sort of student
hangout over the years. Occasionally, tactics assumed a level
of sophistication unanticipated by the school staff. Parker Mc-
Kenzie wooed his future wife Nettie by passing her messages in
phonetically written Kiowa, a practice that prevented teachers
from confiscating the notes and reading them out loud. (The
practice led eventually to the first written syllabary of the Kiowa language.) Others carried on what amounted to whispered
courtships that escaped the attention of matrons.[31]

Like all boarding schools, Rainy Mountain ran according to

military-style regimens. Administrators organized students into companies or squads and designated older pupils as cadet sergeants. A former Riverside student said that boarding school "was really a military regime. . . . Every year an official from Fort Sill would come down and review our companies and our drilling maneuvers. We marched everywhere, to the dining hall, to classes; everything we did was in military fashion. We were taught to make our beds in military fashion, you know, with square corners and sheets and blankets tucked in a special way. . . . On Sundays we had an inspection . . . just like the military."[32]

McKenzie wrote, "I distinctly remember . . . how odd it was to line up like I imagined soldiers lined up." Students queued up for every occasion, he said, and marched to meals, classes, and chapel services. Boys drilled every day before breakfast, except on Sundays. "It was not unusual for the little ones' skins to appear blue from the cold," wrote McKenzie. "It was very sad to see 6, 7, and 8 year-olds being compelled to learn the rudiments of soldiery as early as 6:00 am."[33]

Those who stepped outside the bounds received quick lessons. "Everything you do, you get punished," recalled a former Riverside student. "You'd get tired and get punished." Another Riverside student remembered that school officials openly distrusted students, "treated you like a criminal," and allowed the older girls to "slap them (young girls) around." Disciplinary responses ran the gamut from stern lectures to draconian whippings, with the most severe punishments meted out for the most serious offenses. Yet even minor transgressions brought stern responses. By far the most common sin was speaking Kiowa, and getting caught meant enduring a variety of punishments from which there was virtually no escape. Typical disciplinary measures included soapy teeth brushings, extra drill duty, carrying stepladders on the shoulders for several hours, or restriction from the school's social events. One former Rainy Mountain student remembered being forced to hold quinine tablets in her mouth for speaking Kiowa.[34]

Sometimes punishment humiliated rather than hurt physically. Sarah Long Horn said that boys caught speaking Kiowa had to wear sandwich boards reading "I like girls." At other schools administrators forced boys to wear dresses. Rainy Mountain girls stood face-first in room corners until they spoke English. Myrtle Ware said that getting caught speaking Kiowa brought demerits that restricted trips and outings. "There's one of the matrons, you know, she goes around and listens . . . [and] when one of them gets six marks, they don't let them go to the store." Jim Whitewolf reported that he was ordered to spend an entire Saturday alone in the school chapel and that on another occasion he was required to work two days in the laundry with the girls while wearing an apron and washing socks.[35]

For all of the attention given to eradicating the Kiowa language, however, the campaign rarely succeeded. Children carried on conversations in Kiowa "when the matron ain't listening," said Myrtle Ware. Despite the punishments they had to endure, McKenzie said that Kiowa "nevertheless remained the dominant language away from the campus, particularly with the younger boys." One Comanche who attended Fort Sill in the 1930s remembered holding conversations with visiting relatives that were literally whispered. Kiowa remained the language used in the majority of Indian homes where children went for holiday visits or during the three-month summer vacation when they spoke it daily. Many if not most students became bilingual and never relinquished their native tongue. The failure to eradicate the Kiowa language was costly in view of the school's mission. The survival of the Kiowa language meant that an important barrier to assimilation remained in place. The full meaning of this became clear in the decades that followed. The generations of young people who went through the school proved to be a galvanizing force in the continuation of Kiowa culture in the middle and late twentieth century. They played the central role in transmitting crucial knowledge and traditions in this century.[36]

By far the most serious offense short of violence or sexual

misconduct was running away or, as school forms reported it, going AWOL (absent without leave). According to its official records, Rainy Mountain suffered only about two dozen runaways during its twenty-seven-year history. It is not likely that this is an accurate count. Reluctant to admit that runaways even occurred, school officials tended to consider only repeat offenders as true runaways. Moreover, if children returned within a reasonable amount of time (usually several days), an appropriate punishment was given but the offense was not recorded as a runaway. In March 1918, for example, Rainy Mountain superintendent R. W. Bishoff nonchalantly reported to the agent that one of his students "deserted from our school about a week ago and I have heard that he is with his mother at Anadarko. If not too much trouble will you have your police find out if he is around there and let us know."[37] On the other hand, runaways could not be tolerated, and those who turned out to be incorrigible often discovered the punishment was severe.

For those who doubted the harshness of a reservation boarding school, runaways provided a painful reminder of the price paid for resistance. On balance, boys seem to have been treated more harshly than girls, but both sexes were subjected to humiliating and painful punishments. In typical cases offenders suffered whippings or were forced to wear a ball and chain. Commonly administered punishments for running away also included paddlings, standing on tip-toe with arms outstretched, whippings across the palm of the hands, and kneeling on two-by-four boards for extended periods. Some schools locked children in darkened closets, forced boys to shave their heads, or made them wear dresses. One former student recalled runaways being forced to eat their own vomit after being subjected to a meal of spoiled food. Occasionally, however, students made the best of a bad situation and defused their punishments. Several boys locked in a darkened closet at one school, for example, joined together in a rousing hymn they had learned in church: "Light in the darkness, sailor, pull for the shore."[38]

Once the school located runaways, it dispatched the police or disciplinarian to bring in the offenders. Annie Bigman said that the school's male employees would administer the punishment, usually a whipping. Students genuinely feared such occasions, because they sometimes got out of control. "The men . . . do it," Annie Bigman recalled. "When they whip 'em some would half kill them." Fred Bigman said that "some boys get away, but they got 'em back. Whey they get 'em back they punish them. . . . They whipped them."[39]

In extreme cases administrators arrested students and subjected them to the vile conditions of the Fort Sill stockade. In May 1895, Cora Dunn informed Agent Hugh Baldwin about "a case of most willful disobedience" involving a young Kiowa boy who had requested permission to leave the school. When Dunn refused, the boy left anyway. "I think the punishment he really needs is about thirty days in the guard house at the Agency," she wrote. "In the Cheyenne and Arapaho schools that seemed to have the most salient effect possible in such cases." She left the final decision to the agent, but closed by observing that the young man in question came from a family "that needs a good lesson."[40]

In February 1900, Dunn sent two students to the agency under armed guard and ordered them "punished by imprisonment in the guard house for at least one month." The two boys had "given trouble in every way," she wrote, and normal disciplinary measures had proved "wholly unavailing." Frustrated by her inability to prevent them from making more trouble (which included fighting and running away), Dunn said, "I feel they both deserve more severe punishment than I am prepared to inflict on them, hence I send them to you." There were no mitigating circumstances, she assured the agent, and any defense offered by the boys "will be a product of their imaginations."[41] Cases like this were extreme, however; most disciplinary problems were less serious, and school officials normally handled them.

Still, boys and girls alike tried to leave. Some were lonely, others were scared, and a few simply did not intend to stay in school. A Wichita girl who attended Riverside in the late 1910s said, "I don't exactly know why, but I was all the time running away. There were two older girls who at the end of the week would say, 'let's go home.' And since I was the little kid, I'd always say, 'Okay.' Whenever we'd run home, my folks would just bring us back the next day. I don't ever remember getting punished for that."[42]

James Haumpy gained a reputation at Rainy Mountain for running away and was probably typical of the boys who would not stay put. He usually ran away because the older boys tried to pick fights with him. "I don't fight," he said. "You know how it is." But he also discovered that the girls did not particularly like him either, and that was more than he could take. "Young and got to go to school," he said, "and some girls they don't like you. That's why I wanna' go home."[43]

Many students stopped short of running away but tried to convince their parents to rescue them from the schools, or at least to arrange a transfer to a school closer to home. In early 1916, for example, Nora Cailis wrote from Colony, Oklahoma, imploring her father to "please come after me" and to enroll her at Fort Sill or at one of the mission schools in and around Fort Sill. "I don't want to stay here," went her plaintive letter, "but be sure and come after me please. I don't want to stay here." Her postscript continued the plea: "Come after me please, papa, I am so lonesome for home."[44]

Despite the effort to enforce strict order, serious breaches of the rules occasionally occurred. One such incident at Rainy Mountain came in the spring of 1909 amid accusations of sexual misconduct involving two white female employees, a white male employee, and some of the school's older Indian boys. Cora Dunn carefully hushed up the situation and transferred or forced out of the Indian Service any employees who admitted complicity. Interestingly, the school's official records housed at the Oklahoma Historical Society do not contain a single letter, memo, or reference to the 1909 incident. The agency's files at the National Archives, however, contained full reports on the investigation.

The case centered on rumors attached to Arthie Edworthy, the assistant matron; Theresa Connor, the assistant seamstress; and Arthur Curtis, the school's disciplinarian. The government's investigator ultimately came to the conclusion that "there has been an undertone of gossip at the school for sometime. . . . Only in Miss Connor's case does it appear there are any grounds for the gossip being true." Nonetheless, it was Edworthy who seems to have come in for most of the criticism. According to S. W. McMichael (a local citizen), Curtis had carried on an affair that had left Edworthy pregnant. "He thought he had Miss Edworthy in a fix," reported McMichael's affidavit. "They were unable to knock it and he wanted money to get away." When the rumors reached Cora Dunn, she ordered an investigation that produced fifty-one sworn letters, affidavits, and statements that ran to more than 120 pages of testimony.[45]

The investigation produced disturbing evidence of student involvement. In addition to the rumors about the affair between employees, witnesses testified that Edworthy and Connor often kept the company of male students at night. All those implicated, including the two women, admitted that this was true but insisted that nothing improper ever occurred. But Sydney Holmes, a clerk at Boake's Trading Post, testified that he often observed older school boys "go down to the blacksmith shop near the store and wait for Misses Edworthy and Connor to come by, when the boys would join them. I seen this happen four or five times after nightfall." Corwin Boake, owner of the trading post, testified that he found Edworthy's actions "indiscrete. . . . I based my opinion on having seen her at times leaving the store after nightfall to be met by Arthur Curtis." He also testified that a number of "the bigger school boys wait for her to come out of the store and join her on her way back to the school." The real bombshell came when an eighteen-year-old former student reported that he and a handful of other students visited the women in their rooms regularly. He admitted having sex with Connor, but not with Edworthy, whom he said never approached him."[46]

In his statement Curtis said that he often bragged to students about sleeping with Edworthy but maintained this was actually a lie. "I was fooling," he said. "We were joshing around." His roommate, Lewis Toyebo, testified that he did not believe Curtis slept with either of the women. Edworthy admitted to having male visitors but said that they were always gone by the 9:00 P.M. curfew. She denied all the accusations and threatened Cora Dunn with a lawsuit for libel. Alarmed by rumors of sexual impropriety, Dunn quietly arranged a visit by the agency physician on February 12, ostensibly to examine her father, who was at the school on a visit. Once the doctor arrived, however, Dunn sent him to Edworthy's quarters to administer a pregnancy test, which proved negative. A month later the affair resolved itself when Edworthy took an unpaid leave of absence and subsequently resigned. Curtis and Connor soon followed.[47]

Order and discipline lay at the core of the boarding school experience, but the true test of the civilizing program came in the classroom, for it was the laboratory of change. Under the watchful eyes of their teachers, Kiowa children would be molded into citizens freed from the temptations of a wild life on the plains. The great emancipation would liberate them for lives as civilized citizens. At least that was the plan.

Students at Rainy Mountain were expected to matriculate through the sixth grade. The education given them rested mainly on the acquisition of industrial (later vocational) skills in the form of farming and industrial arts for the boys and domestic training for the girls. To these were added lessons in the rudiments of history, grammar, arithmetic, civics, the English language, and the truths of the Christian religion. The curriculum focused on giving students practical skills and training. In 1895, Commissioner Daniel M. Browning observed that the majority of the schools were equipped for "thorough industrial work, and great stress is laid on this portion of the educational curriculum. While literary branches are by no means neglected . . . the necessity of giving Indian youth an all-round training, which shall equip them for their own living, is kept constantly in view. To teach the Indian boy and girl to work intelligently, effectively, and hence remuneratively, is the first consideration."[48]

The 1902 annual report for the superintendent of Indian schools summarized the government's goals. Drawing on a series of papers delivered at a summer seminar for Indian schoolteachers, the report highlighted the work of schools like Rainy Mountain. In "Essentials of Indian Education," the Most Reverend John Ireland argued that above all "the Indian needs a practical education. It is well for him to know that he must live as a white man, and consequently he must learn to work." Because "work is the basis of all civilization," continued Ireland, Indians must be exposed to strict lessons of industry and discipline in the classroom:

> Teach the boys a trade of some kind, and teach them farming, which is, of course, the most important of all. Teach the girls the ordinary industries for which they are fitted . . . and I believe it will do much more for the elevation of the race than teaching boys. Let the spirit of the home be what it should be, and the father and son will be all right. Teach the girls to take care of their homes and make them attractive. Teach them cooking, teach them neatness, teach them responsibility. Teach the girls to milk and take care of poultry; and teach them how to serve a nice appetizing meal for the family; do this and I tell you you have solved the whole question of Indian civilization.[49]

From the beginning, the Indian school curriculum placed more importance on practical training than on academic development. To that end, students spent only one-half of each day in class. The other half was used learning job-related skills. All that was necessary, opined policy makers, was enough general knowledge to instill respect for Anglo-American values. Anything more was a waste of time and effort. The result was a curriculum of limited expectations and goals that, according to Sally McBeth, "were not intended to meet any specific Indian problems or needs."[50]

How well did all of this work at a typical reservation school? A 1914 report from Rainy Mountain provides some answers. (The regimen it detailed had not changed significantly since the school's opening. The most notable additions were evening classes and activities; otherwise, it was much like the curriculum that Cora Dunn had perfected.) The day began at 6:00 A.M. with drilling and cleaning. Morning roll call came at 6:45. Breakfast followed from 7:00 to 7:30, after which students returned to their rooms to do routine chores. Classes began at 8:00 and ran until 11:45. Lunch came at noon. Instruction resumed at 1:00 and continued until 5:00. Supper was served at 6:10. Evenings were filled with more classes, vocational training, reading circles, recreation and free time, lectures, and various programs.[51]

The calendar also indicated numerous evening socials (designated for "small, middle, or large-sized" boys and girls) as well as lectures on topics ranging from the humane treatment of animals to patriotism. Evening roll call came at 7:15 for young pupils and at 8:00 for the older ones. At 9:00 it was lights out. Weekends brought some respite from the routine. Saturday mornings usually found students engaged in chores or work from 8:00 to 11:00, but afternoons were considered free time. On alternate Saturday afternoons groups made the trip to nearby Gotebo or to Boake's Trading Post to buy treats and see the sights.

It was a long and arduous schedule, and many children went to their beds exhausted from the frantic pace. One former Rainy Mountain student recalled how much she looked forward to going to sleep:

> I think that in remembering I treasure most the last half hour of each busy day. Scrubbed and in their pajamas each girl sat up in the middle of her cot hugging her knees and with bowed head chanted: "Now I lay me down to sleep. I pray the Lord my soul to keep. If I should die before I wake, I pray the Lord my soul to take." Each

word was spoken in unison, sharply and without expression, then
the last three words of each phrase were run together as one word
in a lower tone. One loud Amen and then Plop! they fell back upon
their pillows. There was a long sigh and rustle of sheets and all was
still.[52]

Sunday meant worship services from 10:00 A.M. to noon,
recreation and free time for much of the afternoon, and church
service from 5:00 to 6:15. Because officials believed that lessons
learned from the scriptures ought to be joined with those
learned in the classroom, religious training was a standard component in the boarding schools. The Indian Office reminded
administrators that "the Sabbath must be properly observed.
There shall be a Sabbath School or some other suitable service
every Sunday, which all pupils shall be required to attend."
Interestingly, employees were encouraged to attend, but could
be excused on personal or doctrinal grounds. As for students,
however, "you went to church; there was no *not* going." Juanita
Yeahquo remembered that "we had to go. Some girls would
hide under the beds to get out of going. But you would get
punished if you weren't there. They took a count."[53]

Religious training contained heavy doses of cultural learning
designed to sever the ties to native rites and beliefs. At Rainy
Mountain this meant a strict Baptist regimen that relied on
regular Sunday worship and on as many evening meetings as
could be reasonably arranged. Mary Clouse, an agency field
matron and wife of the Baptist minister who preached at the
school for nearly two decades, reported in 1915 that she and
her husband regarded religious training as the most critical
element in the transformation of Indian children. "Mr. Clouse
preaches very plainly to the children," she wrote, "and when
in the face of this they break the commandments we are very
much grieved." Yet the fact that students sinned and broke the
rules was merely evidence of how badly they needed the gospel,
said Clouse, and so she and her husband continued on with
their work.[54]

Thus the school's typical schedule kept students busy at a

variety of occupations and chores designed to maintain order, enforce discipline, and accomplish a transformation. The school's academic programs complemented this approach. For most of Rainy Mountain's history, students were organized in two divisions: kindergarten through third grade, and fourth through sixth grade. After 1910 the school formed three sections: kindergarten through second grade, third and fourth grades, and fifth and sixth grades. Students in kindergarten through the third grade typically concentrated on primary-level learning skills, especially English language training. They also received simple lessons in hygiene, manners, music, and exercise, among other things. By the fourth grade students added history, classics, agriculture, and civics. At this stage vocational training began. Fifth and sixth graders intensified their vocational training as well as their language training.

In 1916 a redesigned curriculum designated schools as either prevocational or vocational. Reservation boarding schools usually concentrated on the former, and off-reservation boarding schools the latter. As a prevocational school Rainy Mountain would in theory offer a wide variety of training classes suitable for the age and experience of its students. First, second, and third graders concentrated on lessons in music, manners, health, arithmetic, and some limited vocational skills described by the Indian Office as "industrial work." Instruction in reading, grammar, and spelling rounded out the academic day. Beginning with the fourth grade, academic skills were scaled back in favor of more intense vocational instruction. Academic training in the fourth grade, for example, consisted of 145 minutes a day of instruction in reading, history, geography, and other topics; vocational work, however, took up 240 minutes of the day.

According to this regimen Rainy Mountain would train students for what the commissioner described as "useful lives under the conditions which they must meet after leaving school." For the small number who moved on to off-reservation schools such as Carlisle or Phoenix, the reservation school training provided a foundation for more specialized training. For the vast majority, however, the rudimentary skills learned in the barns and kitchens of the boarding schools would be the extent of their school experience.[55]

It all sounded fine in theory. In reality most schools never had a chance of putting such plans to work, at least not consistently. Limited facilities and too few teachers meant that Rainy Mountain usually provided its students with parts of the program but rarely all of it. A 1911 inspection, for example, revealed a distressing lack of critical facilities, including a dairy barn, carpenter shop, and industrial cottage. Worse, because of the lack of teachers, classes were enormously overcrowded. In December 1912, Rainy Mountain's attendance stood at 146, but the school employed only two academic teachers plus an industrial teacher. Rosters showed that 47 percent of the student body (67 pupils) were in the first grade and 28 percent (41 pupils) were second and third graders. Thus, 110 of 146 students attended grades one through three with one full-time teacher. In September 1913 the situation remained unchanged. With 108 students on campus (soon to top off at 166), 85 pupils were assigned to the first grade with one full-time teacher. In a masterful show of understatement several months earlier, the agent described the situation to the commissioner's office as "somewhat difficult."[56]

Over the next two years huge numbers of students crowded into the lower grades, where they languished and suffered from glacially slow progress. Parker McKenzie remembered many boys well into their teens who were in only the second or third grade despite five or six years of instruction. And a 1915 inspection report revealed that 10 percent of the school's first and second graders had been at Rainy Mountain for as long as seven years.[57]

Alarmed by such statistics, field matron Mary Clouse recommended in 1916 that the agency add "another teacher and two more grades to our boarding schools" in order to prepare the children more fully for what lay ahead. Concerned that the schools were not adequately training the children, and alarmed that former students often fell into disreputable habits after school days were over, Clouse concluded that the schools could combat such conditions with more thorough instruction. Agent Stinchecum's reply was a masterpiece of government rhetoric. Clouse's suggestion was "impracticable," wrote the agent, "for the reason that . . . schools are conducted in accordance with well defined plans laid down by the Commissioner of Indian Affairs. The reservation schools are only expected to take the boys and girls through the first six grades."[58]

The language barrier represented one of the chief causes of poor advancement rates. Strictly forbidden to speak Kiowa, the children encountered serious difficulties from the first day in class. The transition was especially grueling for very young pupils, many of whom were so frightened that, according to McKenzie, they "just clammed up." McKenzie recalled an experience that helps to illustrate the difficulties involved. Resolute in her determination to teach the children English, his teacher plunged into an intensive program to provide them with the essentials. To demonstrate the use of articles, for example, she placed a boy's hat on a stool and said that it could be "a" hat, or "the" hat. The lesson, however, left most of the children confused. "Some of us were puzzled," said McKenzie, "because she was seeing two hats where we only saw one. . . . How she managed to get it across to us still mystifies me."[59]

Fred Bigman said that learning English was the most difficult task he faced. "Boy, I had a hard time," he said. "When they start talking English I don't know what they are talking about." Once, when called to the board for spelling and grammar exercises, he panicked: "I didn't know what to write. I didn't know what she said. So I ask a guy . . . what'd she say. . . . She said for you to run out. Boy I jumped up and grabbed my cap and away I went. I went plumb back to our boy's building." Bigman eventually improved "to where I got to learn to talk English pretty good. Wasn't extra good." Indeed, he admitted, his limited language skills meant he never did "get to that Bible" study

required of more advanced students. As a result he went only
as far as the third grade. Looking back on the experience he
commented, "I had a hard time. I think about it sometimes
myself. Oh, it was painful."[60]

Ethel Howry had similar experiences at the Methvin Institute. Years later she recalled the mysteries of boarding school
life and a language that she did not yet understand:

> So she [the teacher] says, "Come here Ethel." Here I went. Oh, she
> was so glad and she says "Good, Good," she says. I didn't even
> know what she wanted. So she picked us all up and took us back
> to the school. To our building. Just then I didn't know what she
> done but that was where she cleaned us up and we had the clothes
> on and she named us. And we went and oh we just cried and our
> brothers would come over and put us to bed, and we'd go to sleep,
> and they'd have to go back to their quarters. First thing in the
> morning they'd come [back to help the girls]. We didn't know
> nothing."[61]

Myrtle Ware said that she spoke no English before her enrollment at Rainy Mountain. "We had to learn," she said. "They
write it on the blackboard when I first started to school." Every
pupil went to the board, something that frightened many of
the young children. "Our names are called, we go there and
she tell us, write, give us a word, and then we have to write it
down. Spelling so that she'll know that we know how." Ware
adjusted fairly easily and even began to enjoy trips to the board
to spell her favorite word, Mississippi.[62]

Students occasionally received unexpected lessons, as was
the case with one young boy whose introduction to English at
Rainy Mountain came from the school's farmer. As the man
tried to harness several uncooperative horses, the youngster
heard him growl "stand still" at the animals, a command punc-
tuated immediately with several obscenities. Asked to share
his beginning knowledge of English in class later that day, the
boy stood up and enthusiastically said, "Stand still, you son-
of-a-bitch!" By all accounts the teacher was not amused.

Because many students took several years to attain even minimal English fluency, academic training remained remedial. Vocational training overshadowed academic skills almost without exception. Former students often said relatively little about their academic experiences (except for language lessons) but had quite a bit to say about vocational training. Most believed that they learned valuable skills but often regret that they were forced to learn in an environment where, said Juanita Yeahquo, "they worked us like dogs." When asked if she remembered any of the classes she took in school, Sarah Long Horn said she did not, but commented at length on her vocational training. She remembered that girls were assigned to the school's bakery, laundry, and ironing room and that kitchen work was standard for all girls. "That's where I got all my work, my neatness and my sewing, most of my cooking, things like that, because we stay there and do all that work."[63]

Myrtle Ware's memory of the classroom was that her teacher taught them "how to write and sing and read and spell." Beyond that she offered no specific information on academic training except to say, "I like to go to school in the morning 'cause I feel a little fresh to learn something. . . . At a certain time you go to school, you know, so many hours, and then you're out to work so many hours, too." She spent much of her time working in the laundry, where she was so proficient that after several years as a student she took a job as an assistant matron.[64]

William Lone Wolf, who enrolled at Rainy Mountain in 1905, remembered that "mostly they teach us how to work; it was a nice school, I learn some—I learn to work there." Students from the reservation's other schools made similar comments. "We were taught practical things such as sewing and cooking, laundry and how to care for a family," said a former Riverside student. "All the things we learned were things we needed to know for our immediate living." Some students regretted not getting more academic training. "It didn't take me long to realize how far behind I was," noted a former Fort Sill student. "I had a little math and science . . . compared to those who attended public school." One Riverside student lamented the

lack of academic instruction, and a Fort Sill student said "I
don't think it was good because it was really academically
inferior to the public school." Parker McKenzie put it a bit
more bluntly and characterized one man's teaching qualities
as "mostly bossing." Jim Whitewolf said that he "didn't like
the jobs they gave me, but I knew that if I did them all right
they wouldn't bother me. But if I didn't they might whip me."[65]

The discipline expected in the classroom and at work extended into other areas of school life as well. Relations between
staff and students tended to be formal and reflected the school's
ordered regimen. "There was very little personal contact between white employees and students," said Parker McKenzie.
The school "seemed to have that segregation business going
real strong." But this did not mean an adversarial relationship.
When teacher Lillie McCoy transferred from Rainy Mountain
in 1896, for example, she regretted leaving "my sweet little
Kiowa children." A former Riverside student said that "the
employees have empathy for the students. . . . The teachers
influenced us a lot and we liked them a lot." Lucy Gage, a
Riverside teacher in the early twentieth century, observed that
"teachers . . . were for the most part refined and well-prepared"
and cared deeply for their work. Sally Cowgill, who worked
at the Fort Sill School in 1875, believed that Indian children
deserved compassion and loving attention. "I consider it a noble
missionary work," she wrote to the commissioner's office, "and
should it be the will of Providence, I would be glad to go back
to the work, and labour for the good of their precious immortal
souls."[66]

Rainy Mountain students held mixed opinions about their
teachers. Fred Bigman, who matriculated under teachers in public schools and reservation schools, saw no real distinction
between the two. "I don't see any difference," he said. "Teachers always teachers. . . . I do what they tell me. I mind them."
Guy Quoetone schooled under missionary teachers before enrolling at Rainy Mountain. He preferred missionaries because
"I think that they were really more interested that we learn."[67]

Students also genuinely liked some teachers. Flora A. DeLay, for example, was still alive in 1963 when former Rainy Mountain students held their first-ever reunion. They invited Delay, said Parker McKenzie, because she was a "dedicated teacher and well liked." At the time of her death two years later, McKenzie sent his condolences to Delay's niece: "The hearts of many Kiowa men and women . . . were made very sad when they learned of her passing. . . . We Kiowas are indebted much to our former teachers and counsellors. They were most assuredly dedicated individuals, as demonstrated by the very 'raw' material they molded into the stream of American life."[68]

Thankfully, there was more to school life than the training that dominated students' lives. A wide variety of extracurricular activities offered welcome diversions. On the campus students could participate in reading circles, evening meetings, lectures, club meetings, and other group activities. Dances and socials were especially popular and often featured prizes for the best performances. Juanita Yeahquo remembered many such dances at Riverside School, but also recalled that some students found such occasions awkward. "It's like we've got our feet in two paths," she observed, one Indian and one white. Because they were forced to "dance all those white man's dances— like the boogie-woogie," Yeahquo said, socials were not always enjoyable affairs.[69]

The schools celebrated important holidays, especially Christmas, when a week's vacation sometimes allowed children to go home for virtually the only time during the school year. The vacation was not automatic, and in some years Cora Dunn queried the agent about whether the children could be released. In 1905, for example, she noted that parents "are very anxious to have a Christmas vacation . . . though in my judgement it is not advisable." Rainy Mountain sponsored an annual Christmas dinner, complete with turkey (or pork in years when the budget was tight) and small gifts. Students observed Halloween, New Year's Day, and Easter ("which was the only time I ever saw eggs," said Parker McKenzie). Indeed, to encourage "the inculcation of patriotism," the Indian Office regularly issued guidelines reminding the schools to observe appropriate holidays. In 1891, for example, Commissioner Morgan called attention to all of the usual holidays plus Washington's Birthday, Arbor Day, and Franchise Day.[70]

These occasions included the school's annual closing ceremonies. In many years the number of graduates was small, so the event served as part celebration and part academic ceremony. Cora Dunn usually referred to it as "our closing entertainment." Local citizens anxiously anticipated it, and administrators often went to extravagant lengths. The staff usually constructed an elaborate platform surrounded by bleachers in the center of the campus, and officials from surrounding towns, Fort Sill, and the agency office addressed the assembled multitudes. In some years the event stretched to two days and was filled with games, student presentations, and picnics. In 1905, Cora Dunn admitted to a shortage of supplies (and graduates) but commented that "the Indians I think would be quite as well pleased to have a big dinner and band concert instead of the entertainment" and usual speakers. J. H. Crickenberger declared the 1915 closing ceremonies a rousing success after more than two hundred local citizens paid admission to the campus to enjoy the concert and other events. "We had two nights, a full house each time," wrote Crickenberger. "This is an annual affair to which the people of Gotebo look forward," he continued, "and they pronounced it the best they had attended. To say the least the whole affair was a success."[71]

A number of other pursuits kept students occupied. Playing in the band was one of the school's most popular diversions. Cora Dunn started the band sometime in the late 1890s, and it became an institution unto itself. A bandstand was built in the center of the campus in 1906, and Dunn personally directed rehearsals and performances. Music played an integral role in the introduction of Anglo-American culture at Indian schools throughout the country, and in Dunn's opinion no other aspect of Rainy Mountain's curriculum was as effective in that process. In 1895 she requested funds for a piano, justifying the purchase in part on the grounds that it would greatly improve the school's ability to cultivate the students' sense of advancement. "I attend personally to the instruction of the music pupils," she wrote, "and find them more enthusiastic and responsive in this than in any other branch of study." She was counting on the Indian Office's support "to make the musical features of this school a power in the intellectual and moral elevation of the pupils." The government agreed and in late November 1896 approved funds for a piano.[72]

Applicants for positions at the school were queried about their musical training, and Dunn went out of her way to find and hire employees qualified to teach music. In 1897, for example, Dunn requested authority to hire a disciplinarian for the school who could not only drill the boys but also teach music. On another occasion she wanted an assistant matron who could also play the clarinet or cornet. The actual duties for the job "are those of farm laborer including milking," she noted, but as long as she was hiring she wanted an employee with musical ability.[73]

The band proved to be a huge success. "The proficiency of the Rainy Mountain band is a matter of pride and no school influence has contributed more to the advancement of the pupils," she wrote in 1907. Indeed, students eagerly participated and showed impressive talent. Parker McKenzie said that Dunn produced "wonderful school bands from fourteen to twenty-year-olds who learned to play the masterpieces even before some mastered the fourth grade." On a visit to the campus in the summer of 1990, he stood by the remains of the principal's cottage, motioned in the direction of the bandstand, and said that he could still see Cora Dunn striding purposefully toward her waiting students, baton in one hand, sheet music in the other.[74]

Off-campus trips provided an especially welcomed (and rare) respite from school routines. With the exception of the Christmas holiday, students did not leave the campus during the year except in cases of illness or emergency. The outing system, popularized at schools like Carlisle, where advanced students were sent to live and work in surrounding homes and businesses, was not used at Rainy Mountain. In response to an inquiry in 1910 concerning the absence of the system at Rainy Mountain, Agent Ernest Stecker replied that the number of pupils old enough to participate was not large. "All of those who are of proper age are needed at the schools to successfully conduct the school farms, gardens, laundries, etc.," he wrote, and he feared that Kiowa parents would not only hamper the program and unduly influence the students, but would also likely regard the outing system as "enforced labor."[75]

Athletic teams were among the school's most popular extracurricular activities. Rainy Mountain sponsored a variety of teams for both sexes. Like the band, these were a source of school pride and offered the chance to get away from campus. Policy makers also regarded sports as another way to inculcate the children with American values and ideas. The hard work of sports, for example, and the stress laid on individuality, could tear down traditional cultural identity. Cora Dunn endorsed sports at the school (though not as enthusiastically as she supported the band) and always included athletic equipment in her annual request for supplies. Baseball games against neighboring reservation schools and local teams began around 1902. "The boys are taking great interest in playing ball," Dunn reported that year, "and have arranged match games with the ball clubs of the surrounding towns." Lewis Toyebo, who played shortstop for the team, remembered that "about the only other team we played was Gotebo, then we just played among ourselves, just to have some exercise," and he recalled years later that his dream was for the New York Yankees to discover him. Girls were especially fond of basketball and started their own teams about 1910.[76]

The failure to destroy the Kiowa language occasionally paid dividends at athletic events. One Kiowa who attended boarding school in the early 1930s recalled a revealing episode from his days as a member of the football team. As a Kiowa at the predominantly Comanche Fort Sill School, his assignment during games against Riverside (largely Kiowa in those days) was to linger around the line of scrimmage and eavesdrop on the plays being called in Kiowa by the Riverside players. He would then quietly translate the plays from Kiowa into English for his Comanche teammates and they would then plan their defensive strategy accordingly. Sixty years he still chuckles at the memory and smiles ruefully at the thought that "for once, it was okay to talk Kiowa!"

After James McGregor's arrival as superintendent at Rainy Mountain in 1910, the school's athletic programs grew rapidly. "Principal McGregor," recalled Parker McKenzie, "knew such extra-curricular activity was not only of physical benefit to the students, but also provided a sane outlet for their excess energy." By 1912, McGregor had arranged an athletic meet of Rainy Mountain, Fort Sill, Riverside, and Saint Patrick's schools that included baseball, high jumping, running, and pole vaulting. To this was joined an academic meet with contests in writing, reading, spelling, and arithmetic. The event proved to be so popular that in 1913, 1914, and 1915 it was expanded to three days and moved to Anadarko, where the city's opera house was used for oratorical contests and nightly entertainment provided by students. (McGregor's enthusiasm also got him elected president of a newly formed athletic association among the reservation schools. The letter informing him of this development noted dryly that the vote had come during a meeting "at which you were unable to be present.")[77] In addition to baseball, which seems to have been the most popular sport at the school, students eagerly participated in volleyball, tennis, and track. At the age of ninety-two Parker McKenzie once playfully jogged in place during a visit to the campus and attributed his good health to his once having been a member of the Rainy Mountain track team.

The athletic program rallied the students, gave them a sense of identity, and fostered real pride in their school and teams.

School songs and yells, popularized during McGregor's tenure, exalted Rainy Mountain's teams. One favorite made fun of the archrival Fort Sill School:

> A big long train comes 'round the bend, good-bye Fort Sill, good-bye;
> It's loaded down with Kiowa men, good-bye Fort Sill, good-bye;
> We got your goose, so what's the use, good-bye Fort Sill, good-bye;
> We got your scalp, that makes us yell, good-bye Fort Sill, good-bye.

Another song extolled Rainy Mountain's character:

> You may talk about your baseball team of Riverside and Fort Sill; the Anadarko Boarding School, you mention if you will.
> The Rainy Mountain Kiowa Kids are going to do all this;
> We're from the place of knowledge, honor and grace;
> For we are jolly students of this Indian land;
> We've got to send our colors o'er the white and blue;
> We make cheers and yells of our dear old school;
> We're the kind who play the game.

Yet another song declared Rainy Mountain "the place most dear to me, / It's where we all get in the game—where the Kiowas eat gravy."[78] It worked a bit too hard for the rhyme, but the meaning was clear just the same.

Finally, a rich and often closely guarded private world kept students busy when not in class or otherwise occupied. Although school administrators tried to control the lives of students, the children inevitably found ways to create space between themselves and their superiors. James Silverhorn said that after the school day was over "the boys used to all go up on the hill—up on Rainy Mountain and stay up there until supper time. Just to take a walk."[79] Likewise, clandestine conversations in Kiowa preserved an important measure of identity.

Other activities combined mischievousness with a determination to make do for themselves. Parker McKenzie recalled late-night raids on the kitchen after "gravy day," when the boys would break into the dining hall, fill their hats with gravy and biscuits, and then sneak back to their rooms for a feast. Jim Whitewolf did the same during his years at the Kiowa School in Anadarko. He and his friends often stole food when they worked in the kitchen and would slip away on Saturday afternoons and cook it. "We wanted to cook it in our own way," he recalled. There were other diversions as well. On mornings when a heavy frost or rare snowfall came to Rainy Mountain, the older boys sometimes borrowed the fire escape ladders and dashed to the top of the mountain for a ride down that was as exciting as it was dangerous.[80] Such activities relieved the monotony of school life and enabled students to maintain some sense of autonomy.

McKenzie reported that students also engaged in a wide variety of games and self-made amusements. In addition to the usual pursuits of baseball, tag, or marbles (the impending showdown of self-designated world champions caused eager anticipation. "We regarded it almost as much as the World's Series now is regarded," he noted), students maintained a circus behind Rainy Mountain. Cast-off furniture and other junked odds and ends were scavenged and put to use as props. A band provided accompaniment on imaginary instruments made from wooden sticks, and drums fabricated from discarded tubs. Aerialists, tumblers, and acrobats wearing long-handle underwear for tights performed on mattresses, while cowboy rope artists and clowns entertained the crowd. A menagerie of rabbits, possums, "a rat or two," squirrels, and snakes was a popular attraction. One boy won acclaim for his gorilla act, featuring a fur suit crafted from a worn-out mohair mattress and wooden teeth, during which he growled and hung from a chain. Two others created a buffalo complete with cow's skull and horns. Admission was a uniform button, preferably brass.[81]

School administrators probably knew about the circus, but there is no indication that they ever tried to close it down or restrict it. But there were moments when Dunn and her staff must have wondered what their students were up to in their spare time. Matrons and disciplinarians fumed over the mysterious wholesale loss of the uniform buttons required for admission and waged a never-ending battle to keep students properly clothed. School supply invoices from May 1909 and April 1910, for example, showed orders for a total of six gross of coat and vest buttons. A note in Cora Dunn's hand on one such invoice asks plaintively why so many uniform buttons were constantly missing.[82]

Once school days were over, most students disappeared back into the local Kiowa communities. Agency records show that small numbers went on to Chilocco, Phoenix, or Carlisle, but the total never amounted to more than a handful of those who went through the reservation's schools. Trained only in agricultural, mechanical, or domestic skills, students faced limited prospects, so returning to their old homes and towns was about all that most could look forward to. Military careers took some away, and others, such as Parker McKenzie, successfully parlayed their education into professional careers. For the most part, however, Rainy Mountain sent its students back to their communities.

Agents attempted to track the movements of former students and sent detailed questionnaires to field matrons in an effort to ascertain the whereabouts and occupations of former students. In 1914, for example, the Indian Office notified James McGregor of its wish "to know something of the success you have achieved in following up the careers of Indian boys and girls who have attended only reservation schools." The letter noted the importance of securing meaningful work for former students "so that they may have opportunity to practice the training they have received at school and become self-supporting." The office was especially interested in McGregor's "ideas and plans for placing these youths at work, also of their responsiveness in availing themselves of the opportunities presented for their benefit."[83]

A series of field matrons' reports from 1915 offers some evidence on life after school days. Asked to survey her district's "returned students," Mary Given wrote, "Most of our young people are married soon after coming out of school. We have a cooking club for girls. Good books and magazines [are] lent to boys and girls." Mary Clouse added that "we assist them, invite them to our Sunday School, encourage them to be workers, are planning a Summer School of ten days, and a camp meeting." Anna Heersma "attempted to interest boys and girls in the work of their homes, suggesting good reading matter," and Mary Wilkin reported that "some have done well with their crops and caring for their homes. Have given out good reading and had little social times for them." Above all, field matrons and missionaries tried to keep former students on the straight and narrow path and energetically opposed the introduction of peyote or other practices that might lead students away from the lessons and values championed in the schools.[84]

From the perspective of former students, Rainy Mountain represented a collection of contradictions. When measured against the government's expectations, the school did not succeed in erasing the cultural identity of Kiowa students; at the same time, however, despite its numerous limitations it did provide a level of education that proved useful for most of the children after their school days were over. Some students learned well and left the school with advantages they otherwise would have missed. "If it hadn't been for Rainy Mountain School, I probably would not be typing this account," wrote Parker McKenzie in 1987. "Despite the hardships we encountered there, they were well worth the time. . . . It provided us the opportunity for an education, though rudimentary for most of us."[85] Yet McKenzie, who spent nearly forty years of his adult life as a Bureau of Indian Affairs employee, never gave up his Kiowa identity. He originated and perfected a written system for the Kiowa language and assumed prominence as a tribal historian.

Other former students also carried fond memories away from

the school, despite its often unpleasant circumstances. "But I really did, I really did like that school," said Sarah Long Horn. "I'm always thankful that I went to that school because that's [sic] lots of things that I had . . . learned from that place." On the occasion of his ninetieth birthday Lewis Toyebo told his descendants that he had "fond memories [of Rainy Mountain]. . . . I now see the Kiowa people have made rapid progress from the tipi to the halls of higher education. . . . That was the wish and prayer of our ancestors who have gone on."[86]

For most of these students the school did not succeed in destroying their cultural identity, which it was meant to do. It sought transformation but could not force its students to abandon their lives as Kiowas. Rainy Mountain forced an accommodation, but no more. Although some students surely left the schools ashamed of their Indianness, many others survived with their sense of identity intact. Try as it might, Rainy Mountain School could not take from them the fact of who they were.

"Education Does Not Eliminate These Differences"
The Shifting Priorities of the Progressive Era

DURING THE EARLY TWENTIETH CENTURY NEW POLITICAL, SCIEN-tific, and social attitudes created a climate of opinion that shattered the previously widespread faith in the schoolroom's ability to solve the Indian Problem. By the end of World War I, critics largely discarded Thomas Jefferson Morgan's vision of a school system that would assimilate and integrate Indian youth into the American mainstream and replaced it with a new, severely limited plan. Specifically, critics questioned the suitability of educating Indians if such schooling were inconsistent with the more narrowly defined roles that social scientists and policy experts assigned to Indians. As a result of these shifts, the usefulness and practicality of boarding schools lay open to a searching reevaluation. Even more important, Indian schooling, traditionally based on the common school system attended by whites, now assumed distinctly new and different goals.

Because experts rejected integration into the mainstream as education's ultimate task, Indian schools no longer aimed at transformation. Instead, their function, said policy makers, should reflect more realistic and limited plans for Indians. The timing of this transition was imporant, for Rainy Mountain opened just as these currents began to gather strength, and it matured in an environment dominated by them. The Jeffersonian position asserting progress as a natural condition gave way to profoundly pessimistic opinions. New interpretations labeled Indians as racially backward, culturally deficient, and intellectually feeble. As a result, notes Robert Trennert, Americans quickly lost interest in the campaign to turn Indians into imitations of white men.[1]

By 1920, Commissioner of Indian Affairs Cato Sells spoke for a generation that had retreated almost completely from the vision embraced by Richard Pratt and Thomas Jefferson Morgan. Reflecting a much more limited view of assimilation, Sells believed that policy makers had "no other choice than to regard the Indian as a fixed component of the white man's civilization." By "fixed," he meant an unchangeable group assigned to a permanently subordinate position on the periphery of American society and not, as Morgan imagined, meaningfully participating in it. Previously used interchangeably, education and assimilation soon came to represent different things, especially when Indians, immigrants, and other non-Anglo-American groups were concerned. Indians, it seemed, could not be remolded after all.[2]

As long as popular opinion, scientific observation, and policy assumptions shared the belief that the classroom could remold Indian children, schooling remained a vital and efficacious process. Shifts in that core belief, however, endangered the Indian schools, for the loss of any part imperiled the system. And that is what began to occur in the late nineteenth and early twentieth centuries. A new generation of social scientists came on the scene, surveyed the issues, and arrived at radically different conclusions from those of an earlier generation. Often casting aside the idea that progress was a natural condition, these new experts perceived a much greater distance between the races than had been previously assumed. Professionals and experts replaced Morgan's optimism with a kind of skepticism that described Indians as alien, backward, barbarian, "zoo-mimic," subhuman, or unable to rise very far above their natural state. Instead of seeing Indians as merely culturally underdeveloped, observers increasingly regarded them as static and blighted, imprisoned by their race in a world from which few could escape. Indeed, Francis Leupp described the difference between Indians and whites as resembling the distinction between substance and shadow.

A preoccupation with race marked an especially dangerous precedent. By popularizing interpretations of culture based on the authority of science, leading figures such as Madison Grant and Daniel Brinton opened the way to a redefinition of culture that resisted the possibility of change. Craniology, for example, offered new clues and apparently irrefutable proof of the vast gaps between the civilized and savage races. Moreover, defining culture on the basis of racial characteristics instead of environmental ones changed the course of debate significantly. Environment is malleable and changeable; race, of course, is less so. Thus, racial determinists accepted certain racial and cultural characteristics as evidence of inferiority and assailed assimilation as an unrealistic hope for Indians who, among others, were to be assigned to a permanently inferior position in society. Embracing what Robert F. Berkhofer labels "virulent racism given the patina of science," policy makers rationalized their changing assumptions by giving them the imprimatur of science.[3]

Popular ideas and cultural icons joined this new intellectual climate and contributed to the impression that assimilation was wrong-headed. Literature and photography, for example, presented an increasingly romanticized, nostalgic view of Indians. Pulp westerns, dime novels, and arcade movie reels all highlighted Indians as a vanishing race. Wild West shows promised scintillating re-creations of Indian life and the Old West that locked Indians into the frontier that, by the 1890s, was declared closed, if not dead. When Hollywood joined the fray the metamorphosis was complete.

Photographers such as Edward Curtis rushed to capture the last fleeting moments of a disappearing race and had an especially powerful effect. Careful to retouch any evidence of the modern world that tainted his meticulously planned scenes, Curtis convinced audience and patrons alike (Theodore Roosevelt was one) that a once glorious way of life was on the way to extinction. Considering the enduring power of his work, it can be argued that Curtis succeeded in creating the aura of a vanishing race that survives to this day. His work, and that of other contemporary image makers, had nothing to do with civilizing Indians and everything to do with immortalizing them before they were gone.[4]

Some of the clearest expressions of the conquered Indian doomed to extinction came from artists and sculptors. Like Curtis, the so-called cowboy artists Charles Russell and Frederic Remington, among others, captured and popularized a mythical image of Indians that quickly became part of the cultural baggage of early twentieth-century America. This image supported the perception of Indians as a race that flourished only in the old, now vanquished West. Why worry about their assimilation (or their schooling) if they were soon to be gone? Robert Berkhofer has correctly observed that Remington's self-styled "cowboy philosophy" (to use Remington's phrase) "regarded Native Americans as an inferior race deserving of extinction. His archetypical Indian scowled and skulked as he passed off the stage of history."[5]

As long as the frontier represented a wild and open place, the Indian was critical to its history. Now that it was closed, according to Frederick Jackson Turner, the U.S. Census Bureau, and the makers of popular opinion, what place remained for Native Americans? In a country rushing pell-mell toward an industrial revolution and the age of the machine, they said, why be concerned about Indians who were, after all, ill suited to modernity and unable to change? Once the frontier was closed, went the new reasoning, so was the Indian Problem. As the Goetzmanns have observed, all that remained for the sculptors, painters, and photographers was to sanitize the legend of the frontier so that the scenes portrayed merely chivalric idols. The "glory paintings" of Remington and Schreyvogel extolled an Indian West that "could have been army recruiting posters."[6] Add to this the West of Zane Grey, or the pathetic Indians of Rodman Wannamaker or Joseph K. Dixon, and the public's understanding of the Indian Question understandably shifted from present tense to the glorious shadows of the past tense.

Obviously, changing the goals and assumptions of assimilation brought the entire civilizing program under scrutiny. For the Indian Office this meant a critique of allotment, citizenship, and education—the centerpieces of the old approach. Critics leveled severe blows against these institutions, but nowhere was the attack more keenly felt than in the Indian schools. Clear evidence of the shift came from sources such as the Board of Indian Commissioners, which announced in 1905 that far from attempting to transform Indians according to the vision of Pratt and Morgan, "the effort should never be made to 'make a white man out of an Indian.' "[7] Even Paul Prucha, who does not believe that Progressive Era policies marked a significant retreat in goals or quality, concedes that the preeminence of old-line reformers and philanthropists was "severely shaken, if not indeed shattered" during the first decade of the twentieth century. Prucha is correct, for even before the century was over prominent voices raised a hail of protest against the Indian schools.[8]

To their dismay, many Peace Policy reformers discovered that they no longer controlled policy making and did not particularly influence those who did. Faced with politically powerful adversaries like Theodore Roosevelt, who scorned friends of the Indian as "foolish sentimentalists," reformers confronted western politicians whose influence and patronage now directed policy decisions. Even Roosevelt admitted ruefully that when it came to the Indian Office he could not "get a man confirmed unless the senators from that state approve him."[9] Patronage battles over the appointment of agents were bad enough, but now the process tainted the highest levels of the Indian Office. Of course, this had always been the case, but it was surely a different situation to have men like Frederic Remington influencing policy rather than Albert K. Smiley, Lewis Henry Morgan, or even Richard Pratt. Groups such as the Indian Rights Association and the Lake Mohonk Conference now saw their prestige and influence slip away. Once gone from the scene, reformers like Morgan would not be replaced by like-minded individuals.

In their stead came a generation of administrators who carried the banners of Progressive Era reform and scientific management. Often lacking the philosophical and personal passion that characterized the earlier generation, new policy makers tended to be less patient, more concerned with achieving goals, and generally suspicious of passion when it came to Indian rights. For them, the ultimate goal was to dismantle the Indian Office, something policy makers had desired for decades. But this would occur not because Indians had been brought into the mainstream via Pratt's cultural baptism, but because they had been cast aside. Rather than continuing to struggle with the difficult problems posed by assimilation, new policy makers thought in terms of finding solutions quickly and efficiently. It was an old goal; achieving it, however, necessitated speeding up the process and redefining the goals of assimilation. As John Berens has observed, the commissioners who held office after 1900 "discovered that it was difficult if not impossible to follow these principles [that is, Morgan's line of thought] in practice. Forced to choose between abstract theory and concrete actuality, the Commissioners chose the latter."[10]

In the minds of most policy makers, not much changed as far as overall goals were concerned. For example, the Board of Indian Commissioners thundered in its 1901 annual report, just as it had in previous years, that the object of the Indian Office was to "make all Indians self-supporting, self-respecting, and useful citizens of the United States. The Indian Bureau should always aim at its own speedy discontinuance!" Success was measured not by self-perpetuation of the Indian Office but by "self-destruction."[11] The rhetoric of the Peace Policy had been no less strident. But what was a self-supporting, self-respecting, and useful citizen? In the new era how was such progress to be realistically and practically defined? Would the lofty goals of the Lake Mohonk Conference dominate the process, or would they fall before a determined assault?

Rather than continuing to endure the frustrations of an earlier era, Progressives advocated new agendas. Accelerate the pace of allotment, they said, and make it easier to obtain clear title. Limit the time students could stay in school, roll back curricular expectations, and make Indians subject to citizenship and state and federal laws more quickly. Some otherwise respectable voices even advocated throwing Indians to the wolves; Cato Sells, for example, was only too happy to speed up the competency process that allowed Indians to claim title to their individual allotment. If doing so exposed them to temptations and situations with which they were not prepared to deal, well, the government could no longer coddle its wards. Sells argued they must either sink or swim; for his part he was willing to let large numbers sink. This was a new attitude.

Sells and his colleagues reminded their critics that it was a greater disservice to keep Indians in a state of near thralldom than it was to release them to find their own way. In 1907, for example, Commissioner of Indian Affairs Francis Leupp observed that the Indian Office was engaged in a multitude of works for which it really had no legitimate responsibility—irrigation, forestry, and reclamation, for example—and which only reinforced the dependence of Indians on the government dole. "All my work," he wrote, "is guided by my general aim of preparing the whole Indian establishment for going out of business at no very distant date." Of course, this had been the goal of Pratt and Morgan as well, but they envisioned a fundamentally different way of achieving it.[12]

By the turn of the century the general understanding among policy makers concerning the Indian schools began to crumble. Never crystal clear, it now became clouded by increasingly loud complaints about what the government could reasonably expect from a backward race. South Dakota Senator James H. Kyle (chairman of the Senate Committee on Education and

Labor) observed in 1894 that although the government had certain obligations toward its wards, its obligations ought to be guided by rational decision making. "I would not approve giving them superior educational advantages," the senator noted somberly.[13] In his assessment of the relationship between literacy and industrial training, Carlisle Assistant Superintendent A. J. Standing wrote in 1900 that in "the battle of life," the Indian student must receive "such industrial education as will place him clearly beyond the ranks of the incapable. . . . To do this, rational industrial training is a necessity." But most Indian schools, continued Standing, too often misunderstood their mission and gave far too much attention to literary studies, textbooks, and methods of writing and thus pretended to spin silk from a sow's ear.

Standing aimed at "the proportion of ninety-nine manual workers to one lawyer or doctor." Do this, he assured his audience, "and Uncle Sam will be proud of his red children." After all, added one of Standing's colleagues, "the diverting of an Indian from his natural bent is not to be done without serious consideration and especially good reasons." Livelihood came not from carpentry, blacksmithing, or skilled labor but from "reading and writing, welding and planing, cooking and sewing." Others also took the hard line when it came to the Indian schools. James Mooney, a man often accused of *protecting* Indian rights, wrote to Albert Smiley in 1903 to tell him that the government should "throw out the fancy eastern education. . . . Shape the whole Indian policy to make it impossible for an Indian . . . to get a dollar except by earning it. . . . I doubt if more than a small percentage can meet this test, but that is the percentage worth saving."[14]

This line of thinking represented much narrower opinions about the ability of Indians to transform themselves. Challenging the "natural bent" had once been at the very center of the campaign for forced assimilation. Now educators began to give greater attention to a less comprehensive scheme. Miss Alice Robertson, school supervisor for the Creek Nation, Indian Territory, for example, observed in 1902 that "we should not try to make the Indian too much of a white man," but ought to focus instead on "training the pupils to be better Indians." In 1905 Superintendent of Indian Education Estelle Reel, already gaining acclaim as one of the new voices, applauded an Indian Office that recognized the new order of things. It was a mistake, she said, to "attempt to make the Indian over and transform him into a white man, with the idea that this is necessary in order to bring him into harmony with the established order." The superintendent of Hampton's academic department agreed. Rather than providing the common school education advocated by Morgan and Pratt, with its implied promises of equality and citizenship, George P. Phenix announced in 1907 that "if the children learn to speak and write the English language, acquire thru [sic] pictures and books some knowledge of other places . . . and get a little knowledge of numbers, it is quite enough."[15] These ideas became the harbingers of a new order.

Such thinking had a decisive effect on policy makers, especially the commissioners of Indian affairs. Beginning with William Jones, who took office in May 1897, and continuing down through Charles Burke, who served during Calvin Coolidge's administration, the men who held the commissioner's post accepted an increasingly narrow definition of assimilation and married it to a similarly narrow view of what Indian schools ought to achieve. After 1900 such ideas prompted what Prucha admits were "explicitly more modest" goals. Another scholar is less charitable, saying that the "period was distinguished by the extreme oppression of Government policies, and by desperation arising from a slower than expected movement toward civilization."[16]

Commissioner Jones heralded these more modest hopes himself in his annual report for 1900: "The Indian school system aims to provide a training which will prepare the Indian boy or girl for the everyday life of the average American citizen. It does not contemplate . . . an elaborate preparation for a collegiate course through an extended high-school curriculum. . . .

It is not considered the province of the Government to provide either its wards or citizens with what is known as 'higher education.'"[17]

Like the experts on whom he relied ("the soul of the Indian is different from that of the Caucasian," they told him), Jones believed that practical knowledge and training should lie at the heart of the Indian schools. Rudimentary math, science, history, geography, hygiene, and music were necessary but should not be considered major components of the curriculum. The greatest amount of time should go to more practical areas: agricultural training, domestic skills, cooking, dairying, tailoring, upholstering, baking, and the like. This so-called industrial training, of course, had formed the core of the Indian school curriculum since the days of Carlisle, but it had also been tied to a specific set of goals. Now, lowered goals meant lowered curricular standards. Thus simple vocational training that recognized implicit limits became the rule. Having convinced themselves that Indians were perpetually backward people, policy makers could safely construct policies that ensured their backwardness. Lake Mohonk conferees would have blanched at such thinking.[18]

Estelle Reel, the outspoken champion of such thinking, wrote in 1901 that the Indians' future lay in vocational training and not in more formal strides. Referring to lessons for plowing, for example, she argued that "upon this work more than any other depends the advancement of . . . the Indian." Emphasizing domestic skills for girls, Reel believed that every girl should learn to bake bread and "be taught how to cut bread into dainty, thin slices and place [them] on plates in a neat, attractive manner." Of history and civics, she observed that students should know only enough "to be good, patriotic citizens." Recognize the "natural impulses" of the Indian child, she said, and do not attempt anything more than is consistent with those impulses." In Hoxie's opinion, this represented a fundamental change. Industrial education "was consistent with the holistic

approach of nineteenth-century educators. . . . Vocational training . . . merely prepared students for jobs."[19]

Jones also campaigned to reduce the number of Indian schools
and to pare the government's commitment to off-reservation
boarding schools. Convinced that off-reservation schools were
poor investments, Jones closely reviewed Carlisle's program
and concluded that Pratt was not working any miracles. "Analysis of the data obtained by this office," Jones wrote in 1901,
"indicates that the methods of education which have been pursued for the past generation have not produced the results anticipated."[20]

Leading experts concurred. At the 1901 annual meeting of the
National Educational Association, Pine Ridge School teacher
C. C. Covey argued that nonreservation schools failed to prepare students in a practical fashion. "The non-reservation
school will send home polished and perhaps refined students,"
wrote Covey, but "we who have come in contact . . . know that
nine-tenths of them are idle because the education . . . given
them . . . cannot be applied to anything they find to do on the
reservation. They were to wash by steam at school, but they
find no steam washers or steam wringers at home."[21]

Covey's charge became a standard canard by the end of the
decade. Schooling was a good idea only if such education reflected the limited abilities and limited futures faced by all
Indian children. "The school must be within the circle of Indian
sympathies," wrote Calvin W. Woodward in 1901. "The training must be of such a simple and practical character, as to win
the approval of the Indian people." Rejecting Thomas Morgan's
optimism, Woodward added that "the course of study, textbooks, and manual features of the schools in Boston or Detroit
are out of place in an Indian community." And, in an important
blow to the assimilationist agenda of the schools, he advocated
actually allowing Indian children to learn about their own history and cultural heroes.[22]

When he left office at the end of 1904, however, Jones had

not succeeded in closing any of the government's more than two dozen off-reservation schools. On the other hand, he did begin a shift in where the majority of students were schooled; not surprisingly, reservation boarding schools showed the highest growth rates. It would be only a matter of time before more significant changes became apparent.[23]

Francis Leupp followed Jones into the commissioner's office. A journalist, one-time member of the Board of Indian Commissioners, and agent of the Indian Rights Association, Leupp advocated even bolder changes. With Leupp's appointment, notes Hoxie, "the Indian office embarked on a comprehensive reorganization of its educational programs." These changes mirrored Leupp's opinion that Indians were intellectually feeble, culturally moribund, and best suited to menial jobs. Speaking to the National Educational Association in 1907, the commissioner observed that "the Indian is an adult child . . . [combining] the physical attributes of the adult with the mentality of about our fourteen-year-old boy." Moreover, much about the present school system was wasted on a people who could not use and did not desire the training given them. "The present practice of feeding and clothing and lodging an Indian free in order . . . to force upon him a degree of learning which he does not wish, and in which cases he can and will make no use of," said Leupp, "is folly." Unpersuaded by the old Jeffersonian notions of change and transformation, Leupp believed Indians incapable of rising beyond a very modest level of civilization. It was therefore unwise and foolish to ignore their limited capabilities. "Improvement, Not Transformation" was his creed.[24]

Agreeing with those who thought Indians racially defective, Leupp advocated lowered standards and decreased government involvement. After all, there were limits, he said, to what might realistically be accomplished. "The Indian," he wrote, would "always remain an Indian." It was a mistake to "push him too rapidly into a new social order." For those who hoped the commissioner might eventually form a more enlightened opinion of the Indian, his first annual report suggested that such optimism was unwarranted. "Nothing is gained," he said, "by trying to undo nature's work and do it over."[25] Thomas J. Morgan's optimism was in total eclipse.

Like Jones, Leupp focused his attack on boarding schools. Calling for "a marked change in the Indian educational establishment, always in the direction of greater simplicity and a more logical fitness to the end for which it was designed," he endorsed enlarging the day school system and opposed any increase in boarding schools. Such a move had numerous advantages, the most important of which was that it would save significant money. Like Jones, Leupp considered the cost of educating students at off-reservation schools to be exorbitant. "We spend on these now nearly $2,000,000 a year, which is taken bodily out of the United States Treasury and is, in my judgement . . . a mere robbery of the taxladen Peter to pay the non-taxladen Paul and train him in false, undemocratic, and demoralizing ideas. The same money . . . would have accomplished a hundredfold more good, unaccompanied by any of the harmful effects upon the character of the race." On average, he continued, the government spent between $167 and $250 per student in the boarding schools. At the day schools, by contrast, the sum was between $36 and $67 per student. Accepting an average of $50, Leupp argued that day schools could accomplish the same work as boarding schools at one-fourth or one-fifth the cost.[26]

Leupp had other concerns about the Indian schools. First was the fear that schools did not engage in practical work. Calling them "simply educational almshouses" and a "well-meant folly," the commissioner argued in 1907 that the schools were unrealistic: "The pupil grows up amid surroundings which he will never see duplicated in his own house. Steam heating, electric lighting, mechanical devices for doing everything— these cultivate in him a contempt for the homely things which must make up his environment as a poor settler in a frontier country. His ideas of the relations of things are distorted; for his mind is not developed enough to sift . . . between the comforts which are within his reach and the luxuries which are beyond his legitimate aspirations." The schools indulged Indian children so badly that in the end they fell prey to "an ignoble willingness to accept unearned privileges" on the basis of "false, undemocratic, and demoralizing ideas." The contrast between Leupp and Morgan is stark. Morgan had insisted that a "paltry reservation" was not a proper home; Leupp saw Indians as "a poor settler in a frontier country" for whom a reservation was a natural environment.[27]

Hailing Leupp as a hard-headed realist, *The American Monthly Review of Reviews* applauded his ideas in a 1906 editorial. Commenting on Leupp's recently published essay "The Failure of the Educated American Indian," the magazine took sharp aim at "certain well-meaning philanthropists" who failed to understand the situation. "In striking contrast with the sane and sensible policy of negro education . . . [at] Hampton and Tuskegee," went the piece, "is the mistaken attempt . . . to give the American Indian an education of which he can make no possible use in actual life." Blaming Leupp's "unbalanced white friends who have deceived him as to the real meaning and benefits of education," the essay ridiculed the eastern-style schooling forced on rustic, simple Indians and called for an approach based on "what there is for the young man to do after he has finished his schooling, and then adapt what you teach him to that."[28]

On a second matter, Leupp worried that maintaining separate schools for Indians was not a justifiable policy. "Where else does the United States Government maintain special race lines in education?" he asked. Certainly the government undertook no similar programs for the millions of immigrants pouring into the country, and did not do so even for the millions of freedmen in the post–Civil War South. Thus, why should the government insist on a separate school system for Indians when public schools could adequately meet their needs? The alternative, of course, was to force Indian children into public schools. "The more Indian children we can get into them," he announced in 1907, "the better it will suit me. I should like to have every one of them in a public school instead of a Government school."[29]

Others agreed, but built their cases on the racial determinism and social Darwinism already infecting American society. Some of the critics were influential. Herbert Welsh, for example, supported Carlisle and Hampton but attacked Thomas Jefferson Morgan directly in 1902 when he wrote that the Indian race was "distinctly feebler, more juvenile than ours."[30] Another expert was even harsher. Charles Dyke observed in 1909 that the issue confronting Indian education was one of educating the "child races." Moreover, such education "to be sane . . . must rest upon scientific knowledge." Convinced that racial characteristics, especially blood quantum, determined intellectual ability, Dyke delivered a tortured account of how "passive . . . ancestors" had doomed certain childlike races (Polynesians, Filipinos, and, of course, American Indians). Because of their racial heritage, he went on, "it is absurd to theorize about the propriety of a college education for the mass of negroes, or Indians, or Filipinos, or Hawaiians," because "they lack the intelligence to acquire it." And to those who might argue that education could lift a race out of its degraded position, Dyke calmly insisted that "education does not eliminate these differences."[31]

In his attempts to close off-reservation and reservation boarding schools and to limit educational opportunities, Leupp revealed not only a new attitude toward Indian education, but also a similarly disturbing opinion on where nonwhite peoples belonged in American society. Any man who could argue that Booker T. Washington had been successful because "the black man [was] to him a black man, and not merely a white man colored black," could hardly be counted on to endorse a school system founded on the premise that education could successfully change Indians into models of white America.[32]

In mid-June 1909, Leupp left the commissioner's office to his hand-picked successor, Robert G. Valentine. For the next four years the trends set in motion by Jones and Leupp continued apace. Described by Prucha as "a solid Progressive, committed to economy and efficiency," Valentine enthusiastically embraced Leupp's plans and pushed for further reductions in education. For him, public schools and day schools represented the most attractive solutions.[33] In his annual report for 1910, Valentine concluded that with the exception of the Apaches and Navajos, who lacked even the most basic schools, "there will probably be no further need of new boarding schools." Moreover, he continued, those still in operation could ultimately be closed when public schools enrolled sufficient numbers of Indian children. Calling the public schools "a definite means of prompting the assimilation of the Indians into American life," the commissioner said they were the "final step" in getting Indian youth into schools and the government out of the education business. Indeed, the record suggests significant success in the matter. By 1912 the commissioner's report showed 17,011 Indians in public schools; two years later the number stood at 25,180, a 50 percent increase. Similar changes lay in store for day schools. Aware that public school facilities remained inadequate in most Indian communities, Valentine increased the number of day schools from 138 in 1905 to 167 by 1908.[34] The movement begun by Jones and continued by Leupp finally reached full speed under Valentine.

Like his predecessors, Valentine accepted a pessimistic view of Indians and believed that their education ought to reflect more modest goals. He revealed this opinion in 1910 when he wrote that students at nonreservation schools should receive the "kind of training that will best fit [them] for the conditions prevailing at home."[35] Far from liberating Indians from the reservation and preparing them for entry into the mainstream, schools now prepared them for a return to the communities from whence they had come. "Every Indian, like every white man, is best fitted for some one thing," Valentine wrote in 1912. "We are trying to find that thing." But he had already settled on what that thing was; in 1911 Valentine announced that "the whole policy of the Government concerning the Indian race may be described as an attempt to make it function industrially in the civilization with which it is now surrounded." The "great emancipation" predicted by Hailmann had become a one-way trip back to the reservations.[36]

The last of the Progressive commissioners, Cato Sells, came to the position in 1913 with the Democratic victory of Woodrow Wilson. Like almost all of his recent predecessors he had no previous experience in the Indian Service and was not well versed in the issues. A Texas banker and faithful soldier in the Democratic Party, Sells did not move very far from the policies of previous administrations. He announced in 1913, for example, that he intended to protect the rights of Indians so that they could "ultimately take their rightful place as self-supporting citizens of the Republic." His "fixed purpose," he added, was "to bring about the speedy individualizing of the Indians." This he did by working to remove guardianship restrictions, to lower the barriers to competency certification, and to limit more sharply than ever the role of the Indian schools. "The aim of the Indian schools," he noted in 1915, "is not the perfect farmer or the perfect housewife, but the development of character and sufficient industrial efficiency . . . through instruction in the agricultural, mechanical, and domestic arts."[37]

When Sells modified the Indian school curriculum in 1918 he made the connection between education and race unmistakably clear. "We must . . . take into account the development of those abilities with which he is peculiarly endowed and which have come to him as a racial heritage," Sells wrote, including "religion, art, deftness of hand, and his sensitive, esthetic temperament." Those who understood the reality of the circumstances would appreciate the fact, he continued, that the work of the Indian schools was "essentially practical rather than idealistic."[38] To that end Sells eliminated from the curriculum what he termed "nonessentials." These included geography, arithmetic, history, and physiology. "It is a savings of time and expense to

leave them out," he wrote, and "thus make room for more
practical and useful subjects." On the one hand, Sells eliminated such subjects as powers and roots, ratios, averages, ap-
proximations, divisibility, foreign money, metric system, par-
tial payments, duodecimals, and stocks and bonds from the
course of study in Indian schools. Public schools for white
children, on the other hand, routinely required study in these
areas.

The Indian Office, however, openly rejected the call to dupli-
cate the standard public school curriculum. Sells moved toward
a specialized curriculum that suited the needs both of Indians
and of the society that defined them as second-class citizens.
In unapologetic language, he noted that "the development of
the all-around efficient citizen is the dominating feature." By
eliminating "needless studies" and using "a natural system of
instruction," Indians would conceivably be prepared for their
"rightful place as self-supporting citizens of the Republic."
Three years later Sells's successor, Charles Burke, a South Dakota real estate broker and political hack, echoed that sentiment. What really mattered, Burke opined, was that schools
operate efficiently and orderly. Only then would Indian students get through "the dangerous transition period between
the close of school and the time when they should fill worthy
places in our social order."[39] The metamorphosis of the Indian
schools was complete.

The ideological distance between the administrations of
Thomas Jefferson Morgan and his Progressive Era successors is
dramatic, clear, and troubling. In 1889, Morgan insisted that
schools, especially public ones, were vital to the campaign for
Indian reform because they would do "what they are so successfully doing for all the other races in this country, assimilate
them."[40] By the turn of the century a new set of attitudes
prevailed. Education, thundered Reel, Leupp, and others, ought
to recognize that Indians, hobbled by race, could not be transformed. And that is exactly what occurred. "Federal boarding
schools did not train Indian youth to assimilate into the American melting pot," notes Tsianina Lomawaima. It had never

really done so in the first place. Instead, it "trained them to adopt the work discipline of the Protestant ethic and accept their proper place in society as a marginal class. Indians were not being welcomed into American society."[41] The door to membership, never opened wide to begin with, now began to close.

Although the era produced many significant changes for Indians, none was more notable than the decision to roll back the forced assimilation campaign. No longer devoted to Pratt's injunction to kill the Indian and save the man, schools ironically included room for Indian-related subjects because such topics fit more naturally in the curriculum. In the search for a barometer of change inside the Indian Office, one can hardly find a more persuasive example of changing goals than the government's decision to allow and even to encourage Indians to protect certain parts of their heritage. Previously determined to destroy the very roots of Indian culture, by the 1920s the government retreated completely from such efforts.

The decision to do so is significant for several reasons. Most importantly, we must acknowledge that negative impulses dominated the shift. Influenced by theories of racial impurity and inequality, policy makers accepted and embraced a set of values that played down the abilities of Indians and emphasized their limitations. If assimilation is not a meaningful or practical goal, said policy makers, why waste time and money? Let them have their menial careers, made endurable by superstitions and uncivilized notions that education could not erase. Thus, the rollback amounted in some ways to a capitulation, a recognition that a once grand plan had foundered on the shoals of modern science and experience.

An unsigned 1901 column in *Outlook* gives a clue to the new direction. Lamenting the inability of the schools to elevate the Indian, the essay plaintively admitted failure:

> After one hundred and thirty years of dealing with the American Indian, we may quite frankly admit that, so far from developing what was best in him, the methods hitherto followed have produced in the modern Indian on the reservation a lower type than the

colonists found. . . . Did we try to learn what industries he already possessed? Not at all! Precisely the same sort of book education was given—where offered at all—as was set before white children in the public schools. Later, when trades were taught to the select few, they were invariably the white man's trades, at which he naturally excels . . . and in which fierce competition already exists.[42]

Fortunately, continued the essay, there was a solution to this sorry state of affairs. The Indian Office had recognized the wisdom of letting Indians engage in the arts and crafts that were their cultural hallmarks. Canoe making might return to a highly perfected craft and, incidentally, save Americans the unfortunate inconvenience of having to buy such goods from Canadian Indians. (Those tribes, sniffed the essayist, had never forgotten how to be Indians in the first place.) Weaving, pottery, beadwork, and other simple crafts, not extensive and wasteful schooling, were the answers to the crisis of civilizing Indians. Reviving basketry classes, for example, was a stroke of genius, for it would singlehandedly create the "quickening influence of an appreciated, remunerative industry."[43] This amounted to the worst kind of trivialization.

Other observers voiced the same opinion. G. Stanley Hall took a more serious approach to the issue but agreed with the need to recognize limits. "Why kill the clever Indian art of basketry," he asked, and replace it with skills that have less market value? "Why substitute the life of the barrack-like government schools for that which Sitkla Sa [Gertrude Bonnin] has described? . . . Why not make him a good Indian rather than a cheap imitation of the white man?"[44]

Saint Paul Superintendent of Schools S. L. Heeter struck a similar note when he observed that "if you proceed to impose upon him the trimmings of a white man's civilization, if you destroy his racial comfort, break up his customs . . . there is the danger that you remove the foundation and source of his old life and slaughter his very soul . . . all for a mongrel education aiming at a caricature of a white man." It was necessary, Heeter added, to remember above all that an Indian was not and could not be a white man. "You cannot transform your Indian by the wave of the hand into something other than an Indian. You cannot . . . crop his hair, give him a modern bath, and make him anything more than a little cleaner Indian." Far better to recognize the true talents of the Indian—"his splendid physique; his racial instincts; his fondness of fresh air"—than to attempt something beyond the range of possibility.[45]

As Trennert, Hoxie, and Dippie show, the decision to adopt such a position also paid dividends with the public. At the various world's fairs and expositions held between 1892 and World War I, for example, interest in the government's Indian school exhibits declined with such stunning rapidity that by the 1910s the public clamored to see troupes of dancing Indians trucked in from the reservations but could not have cared less about hearing Indian school children recite scripture. The Indian Office went to extraordinary lengths on several occasions to build and staff model schools at such events, but enthusiasm waned quickly. By the turn of the century, writes Trennert, "public interest in a romanticized vision of the Indian had become so overwhelming that no school exhibit could compete for attention. . . . Morgan had believed the American public would always be more interested in progress. By 1904 he was proven wrong. Americans were not interested in seeing an imitation white man with red skin."[46]

So, the schools began to allow the inculcation of Indian arts and crafts because such skills fit more comfortably with the lowered expectations of Progressive Era policy. If they were content to live with the basic lessons associated with the crude vagaries of tribal life, said policy makers, so be it. Yet the move was significant for other reasons as well. If there was a silver lining in the otherwise dark cloud of the era, it was that schools ironically began to provide an environment in which Indians might continue to be Indians. Of course, many Indians had never given up to begin with, but now they had breathing room. By relinquishing its hold on the lives of Indians, and simultaneously allowing them to protect and use certain elements of their own culture, the Indian Office made it possible for some accommodation to occur. The government undertook this accommodation out of no sympathy for Indian ways but only because the mood of the era was so pessimistic that it seemed more practical simply to admit defeat and get on with matters. Still, such a decision must be reckoned as a turning point in the government's long-term assimilationist agenda.[47]

The repercussions of these decisions resonated deeply at reservation schools. As challenges against the basic assumptions of assimilation began to mount, boarding schools came under withering attacks. Whether challenged on the basis of fiscal necessity, educational priority, or policy direction, schools such as Rainy Mountain rarely survived the onslaught. Even in the relatively hopeful years of the late nineteenth century, Rainy Mountain had never been an especially secure place. When policy makers adopted a more limited view of assimilation, education came in for closer scrutiny. This meant that the school would fall in line with the new wisdom or it would be closed. Either way, the future looked unappealing. And as a result of such thinking, Thomas Jefferson Morgan's vision of a new Indian race transformed by the diligence of learning died aborning at the Rainy Mountain School.

"Is It Not Time That Relief Be Furnished Rainy Mountain School?" Declining Fortunes

As PROGRESSIVE ERA CHANGES WENT INTO PLACE, THEIR EFFECTS began to filter out through the entire Indian school system. Reservation boarding schools were obvious targets. Caught in the bureau's drive to produce a more efficient, streamlined operation, schools such as Rainy Mountain proved easy to close. With public school facilities within short distance of most of Rainy Mountain's students, and with three other boarding schools serving the same agency, the Indian Office could marshal a strong case for reducing the number of schools on the Kiowa-Comanche-Apache Reservation.

Serious problems began to appear as early as 1905 when a series of official reports and inspections revealed dangerous deficiencies in virtually every aspect of the school's operation. As she had done for much of her tenure, Cora Dunn shouldered the burden as well as she could and tried to stem the flood of complaints that tainted the school. By 1909, however, several poor evaluations ended her career and that of her husband. Her forced resignation late in the year marked a turning point in the school's administration. Rainy Mountain would never have another administrator like her, and much of what had made the place a success was lost. Replaced by a series of well-intentioned but ill-prepared successors, the school literally began to fall to pieces.

The warning signs had never been far from the surface, and by the first years of the twentieth century the tide turned against Rainy Mountain. In 1909 indications of what was coming appeared in the wake of two major inspections. The first, in April, reported that the school was functioning as well as could be expected. Special Agent C. L. Ellis wrote that "the several departments . . . seemed to be run in an efficient and orderly manner." With the exception of badly overcrowded sleeping arrangements, the school seemed well run. Ellis took special care to note that despite difficult circumstances, the school had no trouble getting full enrollments. Indeed, unless accommodations were improved, he feared it would be "necessary to reduce attendance. . . . There is no difficulty in keeping up the present attendance from the surrounding scholastic population."[1] Except for the usual problems typical of most reservation boarding schools, Ellis found little out of order. It was a charitable report, but not an entirely accurate one.

Only months later a second inspection produced a decidedly different assessment of the school and of Cora Dunn's fitness to continue as superintendent. In early July 1909, Commissioner Robert Valentine informed Kiowa-Comanche Agent Ernest Stecker that Inspector Robert McConihe's report indicated serious shortcomings at Rainy Mountain. Worse, it contained an evaluation of the Dunns that was so uncomplimentary and derisive that it proved to be their undoing.[2]

Unlike the previous inspection, this one portrayed a school teetering on the edge of disaster. Inspector McConihe concluded that most of what he saw was far below acceptable standards. What little good he found was restricted almost entirely to the girls' dormitory, which he found cramped but otherwise neat. Like Ellis, McConihe described uncomfortably crowded sleeping arrangements that violated regulations. Classrooms were likewise cramped, suffered from poor facilities (blackboards were "miserable affairs, . . . a menace to the eyesight of the pupils"), and were enormously overcrowded. A single teacher was responsible for 110 pupils spread through three grades, all meeting at the same time and in the same room. McConihe judged this "too great a task for one teacher," even by Rainy Mountain standards.[3]

Turning his attention to the boys' dormitory, McConihe reported a litany of problems. "This school is badly overcrowded," he wrote. "Children are being compelled to bear with discomforts entirely unnecessary," including doubling up in single beds. McConihe judged the general appearance of the boys' building to be quite poor. "Dirt and disorder abounded. . . . The linen rooms were in much confusion. . . . Closets [were] strongly impregnated with impurities." The washroom so overwhelmed him that McConihe declared it a menace to health. "I pronounce [it] as filthy," he wrote. "Towels have been up for five days [a well-known source of trachoma] and most were as muddy as though the boys had wiped their shoes with them, others were too soiled to be used on the face." Employees set a poor example, too. McConihe described their living quarters as "keeping with the rest of the building showing an utter lack of cleanliness and tidiness."[4]

McConihe charged that school officials only worsened the situation by ignoring sanitation regulations. Although the health of the students was good at the time, McConihe warned that "it would not take much to start an epidemic here under the present conditions." This was completely unacceptable in a school where "lung trouble" and trachoma often spiraled out of control. The safety of living quarters also came in for criticism. McConihe specifically expressed alarm over the absence of fire drills and the poor quality of the school's fire fighting equipment. Fire drills, he reported, were "virtually unknown," and when he attempted to turn on the water at one fire plug he could not do so, noting with barely hidden disgust that the device "appeared to be rusted."[5]

As he surveyed the rest of the campus, McConihe found more evidence of mismanagement and neglect. The study room was "the most unattractive . . . I have ever seen," with "dust and dirt on all sides." He found the outdoor privies "in a frightful condition" and ordered them hauled off and burned and new ones constructed in their place. The storehouse for the school's oil and other flammable supplies also failed to meet standards.

The commissary building (including the dining hall), which had been pressed into service as a classroom, was overcrowded and poorly organized.[6]

The school's agricultural and industrial areas also came under McConihe's withering scrutiny. He declared them unfit, like so much of the rest of the campus. The horse barn, he said, was "in a filthy condition. . . . The extreme disorder clearly indicated to me that the person in charge of this work was not fitted to instruct boys in industrial work and the example set for them tended to be wasteful and careless." McConihe was even more blunt in his evaluation of Alfred Dunn: "I am thoroughly convinced that Mr. Dunn is not giving as much attention to the affairs of the school as he should and that he has other interests in the neighborhood that are taking up some of his time. I was told that he is interested in hog raising and has a small place near the school where he has some hogs. He told me that one time he took some of the school hogs to his place because there was not sufficient feed for them at the school."[7]

Other things caught McConihe's eye as well. Although he judged meals to be amply prepared and varied, milk and butter were "two things unknown to the children." McConihe reported that the school had only three milk cows, two of which were nearly dry. Further, he discovered that only a portion of the school's meager milk production was allocated to students, and the balance (by which McConihe implied the majority) went to the Dunns for their personal use. Parker McKenzie remembered that "I must have spent nearly nine years at R. M. and never saw a pint of milk or a jar of sugar on the boys' tables in particular. The girls got real milk once in a while." Justifying the practice on the grounds that he and other employees were paying for the feed for the milk cows, Alfred Dunn said that Agent Stecker approved of the practice.[8] McConihe was outraged. Nothing, it seemed, ran according to government standards.

Turning his attention to the school's staff and administration, McConihe was stunned by what he described as utter and widespread incompetence. Having already noted the overcrowded classrooms and the teaching problems associated with them, McConihe wrote that the employees rarely met to discuss matters of curriculum. "I asked the employees when they had their meetings to discuss the affairs of the school and to make suggestions for its betterment. None had been held I was told." Worse, when McConihe inquired about Cora Dunn's attention to administrative details, employees informed him that general inspections "were rarely made" and that Dunn had almost never visited classes. The impression overall was that the staff lacked substantive direction and was generally deficient in many areas. Indeed, wrote McConihe, "there was on every hand the appearance of a lack of system and no head."[9]

In his concluding remarks, McConihe identified what he considered to be the chief source of the school's ills:

> I am constrained to believe that the interests of the Service would be better served by causing a change in both the positions of the Principal Teacher and the Industrial Teacher. I do not believe that the head of this institution should be filled by a woman and have as one of her subordinates her husband. . . . I do not believe that Mrs. Dunn has given such attention to her work and her duties as her position demands. From the conditions existing in the boys' dormitory and building it is very evident that she has been very lax. This plant needs new blood at its head, a man to build it up and put it on a basis where it will go ahead and show something from its resources. It is essentially a man's job, and a man, too, that has had some experience. . . . The other employees are doing the best they know how but they need more supervision and encouragement than I think they are at present receiving. I respectfully recommend the transfer of both Mrs. and Mr. Dunn to other positions elsewhere.[10]

McConihe's report produced immediate effects. Although no knowledgeable person at the Kiowa Agency could have been completely surprised at the report's conclusions, its tone was markedly different from that of previous inspections. The Indian Office seemed to be losing patience with the school, and the commissioner angrily lectured Agent Stecker about improving the situation at Rainy Mountain. Anxious to salvage the situation, Stecker submitted a detailed response to Commissioner Valentine in September. Among other things, Stecker promised that "proper care and attention" would be paid to neatness and health. Privies would be destroyed and a requisition submitted for construction of new ones. Likewise, an estimate was forwarded for consideration with regard to a new oil house. The barn was receiving close attention. The "milk question" was thoroughly understood, and fire drills would be regularly practiced. He also reported that "the Principal's attention was promptly called to the shortcomings of this school and a copy of this letter was furnished Mrs. Dunn with such instructions as were deemed necessary under the circumstances."[11]

Unfortunately, the Dunns found it impossible to deflect McConihe's report, and sullenly accepted the resignations forced on them by the Indian Office. Alfred left the school in August, but Cora agreed to stay on for the coming school year. As events turned out, however, she stayed only through the first half of the school year before retiring. On December 18, 1909, Dunn submitted her resignation to the Indian Office with the request that it take effect February 28, 1910; when James H. McGregor arrived at the school on March 1, 1910, to assume duties as superintendent, Cora Dunn joined her husband in retirement.[12]

A remarkable era thus came to an end. For fifteen years Dunn guided the school through its calamitous, troubled existence. Her letters and official reports reveal a woman devoted to the children and determined to put them on the road to what she believed was a better life. For much of her tenure, however, the place taxed her and, in the end, overwhelmed her. Caught between demands for efficiency and order and the difficult circumstances that characterized Rainy Mountain School, Cora Dunn made the place as liveable as she could. Arriving as a young and energetic thirty-four-year-old schoolteacher in 1894, she left at the age of forty-nine worn out by the experience and finished with her career in the Indian Service. As she departed in the winter of 1910, Dunn left a school that began as, and remained, a beleaguered haven. Nonetheless, Rainy Mountain was a better place because of her presence.

With Cora Dunn's departure the Indian Office hoped for a fresh start at the school. Unfortunately, this was not the case. Despite some important changes and several attempts to strengthen the school's overall operation, the superintendents who followed Dunn inherited a situation that did not improve much over the next decade. Caught between the momentum of the era to scale back Indian education and the desire to economize where possible, officials began seriously to consider closing Rainy Mountain.

In fact, the future was so shaky that an attempt to close the school came in the spring of 1910. On May 4, 1910, Supervisor of Schools H. B. Pears acknowledged a letter on the matter from the commissioner's office. "I am of the opinion that it would be well to act favorably upon the recommendations," wrote Peairs, "provided of course that the Rainy Mountain School can be disposed of in a satisfactory manner." On May 16, Valentine reported that the office could not move on it until Congress enacted legislation. Luckily, J. H. Dortch, chief of the educational division, had already issued a memorandum to the appropriate House and Senate committees for such action. "The office wishes to see Rainy Mountain Boarding School closed," he wrote, and would "apply the proceeds to the enlargement and improvement of the Fort Sill School. . . . A proposed draft of a bill for the sale of the plant is submitted for your consideration."[13] The proposal went before committees in both houses of Congress by late March.

The House draft explained the closing by noting that the Fort Sill School was suitably located to take in Kiowa students and that "in the interest of economy and good administration the future maintenance of the Ft. Sill School in lieu of the two schools as at present conducted is deemed advisable." Similar action occurred in the Senate. On May 25 a bill to authorize the sale of the school was introduced and referred to the Committee on Indian Affairs. It authorized the secretary of the interior to appraise and sell "the lands, buildings, and appurtenances known as Rainy Mountain Boarding School" and to use the proceeds for the construction of new buildings and for repairs and improvements at the Fort Sill School.[14]

News of the action in Washington did not reach Stecker at the Kiowa-Comanche Agency until late August. On August 24 he informed Valentine that Special Agent Edgar A. Allen had told him only that day of the developments. "As this was the first information I have received since I recommended the disposition of said school to Mr. Allen, I respectfully request . . . a copy of the bill . . . in order to keep in touch with all matters pertaining to schools under my supervision." It took Dortch nearly a month to respond to Stecker's request. On September 23 he sent Stecker a copy of the Senate bill and reported that it was still before the Committee on Indian Affairs. Stecker agreed with the arguments being made in Washington, and his annual report for 1910 concluded that "the Rainy Mountain Boarding School should be disposed of. . . . [It] is poorly located and never was properly fitted out to do the work expected of it."[15] Surprisingly, Congress and the Indian Office dropped the matter and the bills died in committee. No effort being made to revive them, Rainy Mountain survived to start the 1910 school year.

Having averted the attempted closing, McGregor and Stecker still faced the considerable task of putting Rainy Mountain in order. McConihe's report of June 1909 and its litany of violations and substandard conditions called for significant changes and improvements. McGregor took over with a determination to reorganize and revitalize the school. He ran a much more organized operation than did Cora Dunn, and there was a fair amount of administrative housecleaning, especially personnel changes. If he lacked the almost parental love that Cora Dunn had shown for the place, McGregor countered with a rigorous improvement program that attacked weaknesses in the school's various departments and programs. Parker McKenzie later remembered that "in no time he injected new life into the school."[16]

McGregor responded to McConihe's complaints by initiating a full review of the school's operation that in turn produced a request for extensive repairs and additions for fiscal year 1911. It is a revealing list in that it amounted to an open admission of the poor conditions at the school. McGregor listed repairs to existing buildings as the top priority. "The buildings are in need of much repair," he wrote. "Both dormitories are defaced vert badly. Sixty-eight window panes in one dormitory and fifty-six in the other were broken when I came." All of the walkways needed repair, and the sewer, water, and lighting systems required extensive improvements. The boys' dormitory, for example, still lacked a modern lighting system of any kind.[17]

Most pressing was the need for a new classroom building and an improved water system, problems as old as the school itself. The two main dormitories had served since the turn of the century as combination dorms, classrooms, employee quarters, lecture halls, and meeting rooms. To Agent McConihe's estimate of needs for the school McGregor added ten thousand dollars for a new classroom building. He also asked for employee quarters, something the school had never had. The custom at Rainy Mountain was for staff to live in the dorms or to take up residence in various buildings throughout the campus. Hoping to provide a more comfortable and professional environment, McGregor requested private quarters for his staff.[18]

McGregor got the walks repaired and the window panes replaced, but he did not get a new building. And the Indian Office refused to allocate funds to repair or renovate the other main buildings to his satisfaction. In October 1910, for example, McGregor informed Stecker that despite repeated requests for repairs to the water system, the situation was once again desperate. A recent drought only made matters worse, prompting McGregor to report that "the water supply at this school is

almost exhausted." Preparations were under way to haul water
from a spring three miles distant.[19]

In the fall of 1910, another official inspection (most schools
received two or three such visits a year) revealed that the school
still failed to meet health and hygiene standards. Referring to
a report filed the previous April, the Indian Office inquired
whether sufficient bedding had been procured to alleviate the
crowded sleeping conditions in the dormitories. The office
could not promise to assist the agency in paying for such goods
but commented that a report was necessary "in order that it
may be determined whether or not it will be possible or advisable to make the expenditure at the present time." The office
also wanted to know if the fire extinguishers it had finally
authorized had in fact arrived.[20]

In reply McGregor wrote that the school needed "60 beds,
60 mattresses and 180 blankets. The estimated cost of this is
$1,000.00. The beds and mattresses now in use are old and
badly worn . . . [and] . . . unsanitary." He promised to maintain
higher standards of cleanliness and noted that new towel racks
had been installed, complete with numbers corresponding to
those put in students' clothing. And fire extinguishers had indeed arrived. He could not get a new building, employee quarters, more staff, or repairs to the water system. But he could
get towel racks with personalized numbers above them. It was
a troubling comment on the level of support rendered by the
government.[21]

Matters did not improve much over the next few years. In
his estimate of needs for fiscal year 1912, McGregor once again
reported numerous urgent repairs and major renovations. Under
repairs he listed five major buildings (both of the dorms, the
dining room and kitchen, the barn, and the laundry) and requested $1,100.00 for work he characterized as "absolutely nec-
essary." He once again requested a new school building (but
lowered the sum from $10,000.00 to $7,000.00) and employee
quarters, saying that the "present building permits care of about
only one-half of scholastic population. . . . School has no em-

ployee quarters. Necessary for employees [to] take rooms in school building." Continuing, McGregor noted that repairs to the water and sewer systems were "urgently needed" and that the "school urgently needs installation of a new [lighting] system." As if those were not enough, he concluded that the telephone line "was urgently in need of repair." All told he listed "urgent needs" at $16,360.00. "Absolute necessities" were less, only $1,960.64. Together the two categories totaled $18,320.64. McGregor knew that he would probably get little if any of what he requested. The previous year, for example, his request for a mere $875.00 was answered with $200.00, less than 25 percent of what he needed.[22]

By now McGregor's correspondence to Stecker and the Indian Office took on an air of increasing frustration and irritation. Criticized by inspectors for failing to meet standards, he replied that appropriations rarely covered the school's barest needs, making it impossible for him to meet those standards. His superiors reduced or ignored those items he considered basic necessities: new water systems, lighting, and improved facilities. Forced to cobble together his own solutions, hobbled by limited funds, and faced with an openly indifferent or, at best, unsympathetic Indian Office, McGregor continued as best he could to make the place work.

In March 1913, McGregor and Stecker once again found themselves answering to Washington for a series of recurring problems. The commissioner's office had refused to approve McGregor's repeated requests for repair funds but had the temerity to inform him that "the water system at the school must be improved. . . . Toilets cannot be used, the children are not properly bathed, and the laundry is hampered by this lack of water." Luckily, the bureau's supervisor of engineering had recently submitted plans for a major renovation of the water and sewer system. McGregor eagerly endorsed it, but the estimated cost of $1,800 seemed beyond reach. The entire repair budget for the school being only $600, the office requested that McGregor postpone his estimate for general repairs "until it is

known what action the Indian Office will take in the matter
of supplying funds for the water system." Even if the funds
available proved to be insufficient, however, another remedy
presented itself. Fifty of the school's ninety-four dairy cattle
might be sold at $30 per head, suggested McGregor, producing
$1,500. Combined with the anticipated $600 from the office,
this would cover the cost of a new water system. Once again,
the commissioner's office refused to authorize the action. "The
cattle are valuable . . . and should not be disposed of," noted
the office.[23] The plan never gained authorization, and three
years later McGregor's successor was still asking for a new
water system.

The matter of a reliable water supply was especially serious,
for it produced disastrous consequences at the school. By far
the most dreadful of those consequences was trachoma, an
infectious disease of the eye that if left untreated often led
to irrevocable blindness. Indians called it "sore eye disease"
because of the pain caused by exposure to light. Usually a
consequence of unsanitary conditions, especially dirty water,
the disease caused acute suffering. In severe cases the eyelids
fused shut from secretions and could be safely reopened only
with surgical procedures. Because of the lack of medical care
at the school, students who came down with trachoma were
often simply confined to darkened rooms or given dark glasses.[24]

By coincidence, McGregor arrived at Rainy Mountain just as
it entered a prolonged trachoma crisis directly and indisputably
linked to poor hygiene and sanitation. For anyone who doubted
the cost of neglecting basic necessities such as modernized
water and sewer systems, the situation at Rainy Mountain was
a sobering reminder. In April 1912, the temporary physician
assigned to the school reported that seventy-nine of 147 students were infected, 10 percent of them so badly that they
required operations.[25] The following December, McGregor advised Stecker that in order to ward off the disease he had installed sanitary drinking fountains and ordered the construction

of new vaults for the outdoor toilets. Lime and carbolic acid in liberal amounts would help to keep the pits from breeding disease. But the continuing battle to secure clean water for bathing and washing remained. "It is hoped," wrote McGregor, "that the Office will take IMMEDIATE action and provide funds for constructing an auxiliary water supply.... Until more water can be procured ... three small boys must be bathed in the same bath water and then only every other week. I am aware that this is a bad thing to do." The appointment of a regular physician "would enable us to fight the trachoma scourge systematically," noted McGregor.[26]

Despite such pleadings, no significant improvement to the water system appeared over the next few years. The health of students declined accordingly. In mid-April 1913, McGregor wrote angrily to Stecker and lectured him about the government's negligence. Having requested a trachoma specialist months earlier, McGregor reminded Stecker that the request had been held in abeyance for reasons never explained. McGregor curtly directed Stecker to inform Washington of the prevalence of trachoma at the school and took the opportunity to speak frankly and harshly about conditions at the school. Of the two specialists sent to Rainy Mountain in the preceding two years, McGregor reported, "one of them stayed six days and rushed away.... Another stayed, by urging, three days." McGregor was especially peeved at the government's seeming disregard of the school's circumstances. "It seems to me that the fact that Rainy Mountain is isolated ... does not lessen the obligations of the Indian Office. I have taken the trouble to note that the specialists and other visiting officials from the Indian Office spend much longer periods at other schools."

McGregor reminded Stecker that he had submitted plans months before for a new water system but had been told, as usual, that funds were not available. "The statement that no more funds are available does not satisfy me when I read of an Agency here and there being furnished an automobile." Anxious to find a remedy, McGregor requested authority to begin work himself on a new water system, and he implored Stecker to appoint a physician to the school.[27]

When Washington informed Stecker several days later that no funds existed for a new water system, McGregor flew into a rage. It was difficult to understand how such a decision could be made, he wrote, in light of all of the information available to the Indian Office. "I must, in duty to a deplorable condition and suffering children," he wrote, "request the Office . . . to reconsider. . . . Surely the Indian Office will not allow [these] conditions to longer exist." Rainy Mountain had the highest trachoma rates in the Indian schools, its students bathed irregularly at best, clothes were not properly washed and rinsed, and the school had no fire protection. "Is it not time," he asked, "that relief be furnished Rainy Mountain School?"[28]

McGregor's wrath had some effect. In December 1913 the Indian Office authorized funds for a physician at the school. In the meantime it directed the school to hold special meetings devoted to eradicating disease. In early December 1913, for example, "Tuberculosis Day" featured a discussion titled "Our Efforts, Handicap, and Results along Hygienic and Sanitary Lines at Rainy Mountain School." After opening comments by McGregor, students from the fourth, fifth, and sixth grades read compositions about health. A series of five-minute talks by staff members followed on topics ranging from work and exercise to "Danger of Dust and How to Avoid It." The agency physician came next with a thirty-minute lecture on the prevention of tuberculosis. William B. Freer delivered a rousing finale on "The Dangerous Fly."[29]

The Riverside and Fort Sill schools faced similar crises and held similar programs. At Riverside the meetings resembled religious convocations supplemented with lessons on the prevention of tuberculosis and other diseases. One such event opened with a doxology and the Lord's Prayer, continued with readings from scripture, and then climaxed with a lecture on "Causes of Tuberculosis and How to Avoid the Disease." A local pastor followed with an address titled "The Bible on Health," and the student body closed out the program by singing "The Fight Is On."[30]

How much good this did is not clear. It surely did not solve the problems, for Rainy Mountain's predicament did not significantly improve. In the same month that "Tuberculosis Day" was held, a visiting inspector recommended that a specialist be sent to Rainy Mountain as soon as possible to begin "a campaign against trachoma. Reportedly 98% pupils affected." McGregor did report in late January 1914, however, that Dr. B. A. Warren had achieved good results in treating cases of trachoma at the school. Many cases were so advanced, however, that the assistance of another doctor or trained specialist (or both) was advised. "I wish to add that this school has the highest per cent of trachoma of any Indian school in the United States," wrote McGregor. Given the situation, he asked, how could the Indian Office fail to provide another specialist?[31] There is no evidence in the surviving records that another physician or trained specialist was ever appointed.

Over the next several years the situation worsened. Medical reports from 1916 and 1917 indicate rates of trachoma that can only be described as epidemic. From a student body of 168 in March 1916, an astonishing 163 were listed as infected with trachoma. By 1917 school medical logs showed 154 children afflicted. To give sick children some measure of comfort, the school purchased fifty pairs of dark glasses in late 1915 and another thirty pairs in late 1917. In the absence of a physician, and without a modernized water and sewer system, it was the best that could be done. Jim Whitewolf, who attended the Kiowa School in Anadarko, recalled treatment at the hands of an Indian woman who removed hardened secretions and cut eyelids open with pieces of broken glass. To discourage such home remedies and the sometimes frightful results they yielded, field matrons entered the fray and gave hygiene lessons to Kiowa women. Weekly field reports contain numerous accounts of such meetings. In May 1919, for example, Susie Peters wrote that she had "treated eyes." One month later Allie Brewer noted that in addition to meeting with the school girls' canning club during the week, she "gave medicine for sore eyes."[32]

The expenditure of less than $2,000 on a new water system would likely have solved the problem. In McGregor's opinion it was little enough to ask. In an Indian Office obsessively concerned with efficiency and economy, however, Rainy Mountain did not receive much attention. McGregor could not even get a new school building; how could he ever expect something as mundane as a new water system?

Comparison with the agency's other boarding schools suggests similar conditions. Like Rainy Mountain, the Fort Sill School also suffered form outbreaks of trachoma. In the late summer and early fall of 1911 the school reported alarming rates of illness. Of 154 students then enrolled, eighty-six were diagnosed with trachoma. Medical reports listed fifteen others with "old trachoma." Thirteen more had conjunctivitis, and nine showed "suspicious" symptoms. Only thirty-one students were uninfected. That meant illness rates only slightly better than Rainy Mountain' s. For example, 56 percent of Fort Sill's students suffered from trachoma as against more than 90 percent at Rainy Mountain. Yet there was not much comfort in that disparity; when old trachoma cases, conjunctivitis, and suspicious symptoms were added, Fort Sill's rates shot up to 80 percent. Interestingly, the agency's response to Fort Sill's epidemic was strikingly different from its response to Rainy Mountain's. In March 1911 the Indian Office authorized three full-time nurses for Fort Sill's "special trachoma work." Rainy Mountain could get neither help nor sympathy.[33]

In addition to poor physical facilities and dangerous conditions, McGregor also endured a staff that was often only marginally talented. Like Cora Dunn, he discovered that turnover was rampant and that those hired as replacements were likely to be the rejects or malcontents from other schools. A December 1912 review of the employee corps produced an exceedingly poor evaluation. Although the report ranked four employees as excellent, it found eleven others "not up to the standard of efficiency to accomplish the work that is required at an Indian school." Reminding McGregor of the obvious, the report noted that "with so many employees of mediocre attainments the principal cannot accomplish the best work." The inspection did not specifically name those judged to be problems, but it did list their positions. Included were laundress, physician, seamstress, industrial teacher, disciplinarian, matron, and academic teacher.[34]

In other words, several of the school's most important staff members were deemed incompetent. Four of the eleven resigned within a month, but McGregor admitted to the Indian Office that "in one or two instances the present employee is no improvement over the one who previously held the position, but in general there has been a marked improvement in the personnel of the school force." McGregor defended his staff in a letter to the agent, noting that if some of them were not the best caliber (he described the seamstress, who shortly resigned, as "a moral degenerate"), the rest were doing the best they could under the circumstances.[35]

Matters showed no significant improvement by the end of the 1913 term. A year-end inspection concluded that advanced and intermediate students seemed to be receiving competent teaching from capable instructors, but the youngest pupils suffered badly by comparison. Although the inspection found the teacher "conscientiously inclined and willing," her class "was almost in a continual state of confusion." Students were listless and disrespectful, the report continued, and showed little progress in language training and other critical areas. Overall, the school was barely satisfactory only because McGregor and a handful of employees "support the school and hold it up to the standard it now maintains. For the most part, the work of the greater part of the other employees is neutralized by their very apparent lack of initiative." The school could not possibly "do efficient work with so many weaklings among employees." Noting that it was only fair to mention the difficulties under which the school operated, the report closed by stating that a new school building, more instructional materials, and replacements for the kindergartner, girls' matron, disciplinarian, and boys' matron would improve the situation.[36]

All of this took a heavy toll on McGregor. As the opening of the 1913–14 term approached he poured out his frustrations in two letters to Stecker. In the first, written at the end of July, McGregor told Stecker that the fall term "brings to mind very vividly the fact that nothing has been done, so far as I know, to provide a suitable school building for this school." Acknowledging that hundreds of other requests from other schools and agencies would soon flood the Indian Office, McGregor wrote "I doubt if there is another school that can present as strong a claim for the need as Rainy Mountain. Without exceptions, the Inspecting Officials readily concede this point. The facts are this School has not received its just dues and its importance has not been appreciated." Again he pressed for a new building and reminded the agent that a long-needed classroom facility had never been built despite the fact that the school served a population desperately in need of education. "I believe they deserve better treatment," wrote McGregor.[37]

In his second letter, sent just after the school opened in September, McGregor was more adamant in his criticisms and expressed great resentment at what he perceived as willful neglect. His comments capture the reality of the school's predicament:

> School is in session again and for the fourth time I am compelled to use unsuitable and unsanitary rooms for the children. I have tried in vain to get a few of the very essential improvements needed at this school and after four years I am discouraged.
>
> Last year we had . . . an excellent school. The attendance was good—more than 150 pupils—and the interest manifested by the pupils better than in previous years. Yet the Indian Office refused to give us any of the new buildings or equipment requested. Here is the condition. An unfinished plant with an attendance greater than Riverside and almost equal to Fort Sill and the two latter schools well equipped, yet Rainy Mountain received $1175 for all improvements for the year and the other two schools received more

than $7000 between them. . . . [Rainy Mountain] children are forced
to use the old fashioned lamps at night, the Comanche child has
an excellent electric light, the Kiowa boy is forced to go 100 yards
through the cold to get to a toilet, the Riverside boy steps across
the porch to a toilet. The Rainy Mountain Employees are forced to
room in the building with the pupils while the Employees at the
other two schools [have] comfortable rooms. . . . The Indian Office
must have some good reason for this neglect. I can see but one
legitimate reason and that is the early abandonment of the school.
I have been in the Indian Office and believe that it would not allow
such an injustice to be dealt to Rainy Mountain if it were the
intention to continue the school.

   It will be remembered that I have in an application for transfer.
. . . I like the work very much and am interested in the Indian
problem . . . but I cannot long remain at Rainy Mountain among
the many handicaps that surround me. Further, I have been here
almost four years and if I have not earned a promotion in that time
I am free to say that I should get out.[38]

Surprisingly, an inspection in December 1913 described
Rainy Mountain as "well managed" despite the "lack of proper
housing and equipment and some rather inefficient employees." McGregor was credited with "excellent work, and is a
strong influence for good among the somewhat difficult Kiowa
Indians." The school's attendance "is regular and the discipline
good. I found here the most enthusiastic body of Indian boys
and girls that I have seen in any reservation school," noted the
inspector. He attributed much of this to McGregor's presence.
"The Principal is indefatigable," went the assessment: "A comparison of the condition and spirit of the Institution as they
exist now and as they were four years ago, when Mr. Mcgregor
took charge, shows not only gratifying but surprising advancement, and the more so when it is remembered that the improvement has been made under conditions the most disheartening
at times, discouragements . . . of such a character that only the
most tenacious, patient and self-sacrificing work could overcome them."

   The report went on to note that "successful work of so persistent a kind should bring practical recognition at an early day"
in the form of a promotion for McGregor. Moreover, it was the

inspector's opinion that such a promotion ought to be given at Rainy Mountain. Calling such a suggestion "a plea for the Kiowas and the Rainy Mountain School, the report asked that McGregor "be given his promotion here. . . . His personal inclination would no doubt be for a transfer; but that course would be likely to interrupt seriously the splendid advancement being made by this institution." Hoping that the Indian Office would induce McGregor to remain at Rainy Mountain, the inspector closed by noting that "permanency, combined with efficiency, brings results that can be secured in no other way."[39]

Despite such acknowledgments, McGregor's resolve weakened by early 1914. Since his arrival at the school no substantial improvements had been made. And as each year passed, McGregor's letters revealed a deepening sense of despair. In March 1914 he once again wearily approached Stecker on the matter of his predicament. "I have passed the fourth year at Rainy Mountain without a change in salary," he wrote, "and without the help from the Indian Office that the school deserved. I am tired of it." The situation was also a strain on his wife, who had agreed to serve as a teacher since arriving at the school. He asked for a salary increase but added that what he really desired was a transfer. He did not like the idea of leaving Rainy Mountain, he wrote, "but I know that it is an injustice to my family to remain much longer." Unless the agent could arrange a transfer, McGregor announced that he would "make other arrangements. It is my intention to leave Rainy Mountain during the next school year." He had not fixed a date but wanted to give Stecker ample time to locate a replacement.[40]

McGregor was not alone in his concerns. In February 1914, Delos K. Lonewolf, a prominent Kiowa, wrote to Commissioner Cato Sells on behalf of the Kiowa Business Committee to express the committee's fears about the condition of the school and about the obvious neglect of the Indian Office. "Having learned of the deplorable conditions at the Rainy Mountain Indian School," went their letter, "we come not only as the business committee, but as fathers, humbly beseeching your good office to immediately take action toward placing our school on an equal basis with the other Indian schools." The letter listed a number of items "needed to our certain knowledge," including a new school building, laundry and sewing rooms, employee cottages, a modern lighting system, and a dairy barn. The estimated cost of such improvements ran to more than $35,000. "We saw with our own eyes that these repairs are needed and needed now," they concluded. "In closing we wish to say that this school has been neglected and our children have not had an equal chance with the other schools, and we appeal to you for justice for the Kiowa school."[41]

In reply, Assistant Commissioner of Indian Affairs E. B. Meritt told them "that the Office has been quite fully informed as to conditions there and the need of extensive repairs. . . . I wish to be as liberal" as possible. "You will understand, of course," he continued, "that there are many other Indian Schools in need of the same assistance. . . . At this time there is almost no money available for constructive purposes or repairs, but I assure you that the Rainy Mountain School will not be overlooked next year." It is worth noting that the Kiowa Agency's entire budget for school support (including repairs) in 1917 was a mere $4,500. The Kiowa business committee's requests totaled more than eight times that amount.[42]

For once, however, the office was true to its word. Shortly after Lonewolf and McGregor voiced their worries, the bureau authorized funds for the construction of a new school building. More than that, the money allocated actually represented sufficient funds to get a sturdy, worthwhile building. Instead of the $7,000 McGregor had requested earlier, the office authorized $10,000. Finally, good fortune had come to Rainy Mountain. The building, completed in early 1916, had classrooms and a large assembly hall with a seating capacity of 210. In March 1916 the office also approved expenditures for an acetylene lighting system on campus.[43]

Some relief from the water problem also appeared in 1915. Parker McKenzie remembered that water closets were added to the boys' dorm as part of an annex built sometime in 1915. A new pipeline running from the side of Rainy Mountain to the school was laid in the same period and was connected to a pumphouse and reservoir that dated from 1913. It was not the kind of system McGregor had requested, but it did alleviate some of the worst problems. Ironically, all of this came at about the same time that McGregor left Rainy Mountain. Unwilling to endure another year under such conditions and anxious to provide a better environment for his wife and family, he left the school in late 1914 to accept a position at the Rosebud Agency in South Dakota. He transferred again to the Pine Ridge Agency and school shortly thereafter.[44]

Between Cora Dunn's forced resignation in 1910 and McGregor's transfer in late 1914, Rainy Mountain made no significant progress. The problems that had troubled it during its first two decades continued. Unfortunately, McGregor could not convince the Indian Office that improving Rainy Mountain's facilities should have high priority. McGregor can be credited with making some improvements and for attempting to rejuvenate the place, but the severity of the situation was more than he could handle. By the time he left, the school was entering its last years of service.

"The Kiowas Need Their School;
They Cannot Very Well Get Along Without It"
The Last Years

McGregor's departure opened the final chapter in Rainy Mountain's history. Ernest Stecker also left as the Kiowa-Comanche agent, replaced in April 1915 by C. V. Stinchecum, the memory of whom prompted Parker McKenzie to remark "Boy, he was all business!"[1] By then the school's future was clearly imperiled. Despite McGregor's vigorous attempts to improve Rainy Mountain's situation, he did little more than muddle through one crisis after another, surviving in the midst of the usual dilemmas. Like Cora Dunn, he discovered that he simply could not overcome the school's numerous weaknesses. By 1915 Rainy Mountain had only a handful of years left.

McGregor's successor was John Crickenberger, who arrived with his wife in January 1915 from Tohatchi, New Mexico. Crickenberger stayed only about one year before giving way to R. W. Bishoff, who ran the school until it closed in the fall of 1920. Crickenberger was little more than a caretaker, and it did not take long for him to run afoul of the Indian Office.[2] In March 1915, Agent Stecker learned that the school had once again received a poor evaluation. "Many of the children are not making good progress in their studies," read the report. "This leads to the conclusion either that the instruction has not been efficient . . . or that teachers have not been alert . . . or else that some of your pupils are mentally backward." In support of its findings, the office referred Stecker to Rainy Mountain's recent quarterly attendance reports, which showed that a number of pupils had been at the school for as long as seven years but languished in the first and second grades. Nearly twenty such cases appeared on the report, almost 10 percent of the student body. Stecker instructed Crickenberger to ascertain the cause of the school's poor performance and warned him that "class room instruction will have very careful attention in future visits to all schools."[3]

Crickenberger replied that his teachers "are all good. . . . Certain pupils have made good progress . . . [and] there are no children here who [are] . . . feeble minded." The cause for the school's lack of progress lay not with its staff or students, he continued, but with its poor facilities. Evening study sessions were impossible, for example, "because we do not have the lights." Crickenberger wrote: "Give us up to date classrooms, good lights for evening work, another teacher, and give the Principal time to supervise closely the work," and the children would made adequate progress. In answer to the Indian Office's query about students who lingered in the first and second grades despite years of effort, Crickenberger suggested that many reasons could explain the situation: irregular attendance or sickness, for example. Yet he was unwilling to give up on such students or to dismiss them. "These, like the poor, are ever with us," he intoned.[4]

In May, Agent Stinchecum reported to Commissioner Cato Sells his opinion that Rainy Mountain "is the worst equipped institution under the jurisdiction of this office," but he also believed that with careful guidance and some physical improvements the school could meet the government's standards. "The possibilities for successful work are splendid," he wrote, "provided proper equipment and an adequate force is provided." Stinchecum noted that he was taking bids for several new buildings on the campus and was going to hire a full-time farmer.[5] For the first time in several years there seemed to be official support for change. But deep problems remained unresolved.

An official inspection in September 1915 produced only lukewarm praise. Noting that industrial education was given "some attention," the inspection observed that because of the "lack of facilities and of sufficient number of employees, little in the way of systematic instruction can be given. There is great need ... of better facilities ... in order that the children of this school may be given opportunities to which they are entitled." The litany of complaints sounded familiar. But all was not lost; the inspector noted with pleasure that "great care" had been taken to prevent students from marking books and destroying property.[6] This was damning with faint praise indeed.

A subsequent inspection five months later revealed some improvements. Crickenberger had implemented a new course of study emphasizing industrial training, including evening study three nights a week. The Indian Office received the news with pleasure and went so far as to recommend hiring a domestic science teacher. With the exception of trachoma, which still plagued the school "to a considerable extent," Rainy Mountain seemed to be in a more satisfactory condition than it had been in for some time. Anxious to find a way around the nettlesome problems, Commissioner Sells reminded Stinchecum and Crickenberger that he wanted "to get this school on a basis of successful industrial operation as rapidly as possible."[7]

Crickenberger did not have the chance to effect such changes, for he left the school at the end of the 1915–16 term. His replacement, R. W. Bishoff, stayed until Rainy Mountain closed in September 1920. Until then, the usual barrage of complaints continued to flow out of the Indian Office, and in December 1916, Bishoff got his first taste of an official inspection when Edgar Allen made a stop of several days at the school. Allen's report was mixed. The course of study was finally being followed, wrote Allen, but only "as [it] is in most schools ... followed in part." There was no music instruction; pupils were judged to be "quite large and old"; and industrial instruction was satisfactory in a few classes, fair in some, and scarcely existent in the rest. The health of the students seemed to be good.[8]

It was not an especially laudatory report, but it did find some bright spots. It is worth noting that in reply to Allen's report,

Stinchecum asked the commissioner to remember that in addition to the school's well-known problems, there had been "no less than twelve changes in teacher's positions . . . since July 1, 1915." He also commented that as Rainy Mountain was patronized almost entirely by Kiowas who "did not take readily to the school" (which was decidedly untrue), the agency faced a continual struggle just to get and keep children long enough to make some meaningful change in them.[9] Stinchecum's comments notwithstanding, the school's usefulness was coming to an end. As negative or barely acceptable evaluations piled up year after year, and as conditions continued to remain only marginally acceptable, it was simply a matter of time before the government decided to close Rainy Mountain and transfer its students.

In fact, the school had little time left; in late 1919 the Indian Office announced plans to close twenty-five reservation boarding schools in Oklahoma, including Rainy Mountain.[10] The office noted that this was consistent with the government's well publicized intention to scale back its education program by placing Indian children in public schools. And with other schools within easy reach of most of Rainy Mountain's students, the commissioner concluded that closing the plant would not cause undue hardship. Not surprisingly the decision to close the school was poorly communicated to the Kiowa-Comanche Agency. Informed by the Indian Office in September that it was decreasing his agency's budget for school and agency buildings by $4,000 for the coming year, Stinchecum requested an explanation. "Absolutely impracticable to keep property in condition with such meager allowance. Request reconsideration." In reply Commissioner Sells wrote that because Stinchecum's annual report for the agency indicated "that practically all children on the Kiowa Reservation live within three miles of a public school," and because of declining enrollments in the agency's boarding schools, one of those schools would have to close. As a result of its poor condition, Rainy Mountain was at the top of the list. Thus Stinchecum would not have to allot any of the agency's funds for that school, which explained the reduction of the agency's funds. Stinchecum replied that although the views of the office about closing Rainy Mountain "correspond exactly with my own," he still needed the $4,000 for repairs at the agency's other schools and buildings. Without it "we cannot make a dollar's worth of repairs during the rest of the year."[11] Sells remained unmoved by the request.

In February 1920 the Indian Office ordered a complete review of the agency's schools. Dr. R. S. Russell's report in March uncovered appalling conditions at Rainy Mountain. With the exception of the principal's cottage and the boys' dormitory, Russell found the rest of the school "in a generally disreputable condition. . . . The plant, taken as a whole is a disgrace to our service." The girls' dormitory, "once the pride of the school, is in such a state of repair that it is a crime to house nice girls in it." Most of the other buildings were judged to be beyond repair or "falling to pieces," and Russell estimated that the school required a minimum of $25,000 in repairs. The work force was small, demoralized, and inefficient, and students showed little evidence of schooling. That most of the girls wore shawls and blankets in the Kiowa style, wrote Russell, was striking evidence of the school's failure. The boys, he conceded, were "a more progressive looking lot." Russell was especially distressed that he heard "no Indian pupil use a word of English, a fact that is, in my judgement, one of the strongest arguments for the discontinuance of this school."[12]

Russell built a compelling case. Riverside and Fort Sill were in excellent condition, produced well-trained students, and were reputable schools. Moreover, the trend toward putting Indian children in public schools was already well established. Between 1916 and 1921, for example, the number of Indian children from the Kiowa-Comanche-Apache Reservation enrolled in public schools in the area increased from 152 to 749; meanwhile, the enrollment in boarding schools declined from 628 to 431. Russell estimated that for 1921 there were only 467 eligible school-age pupils in the area, not enough to fill the agency's four boarding schools unless one was closed. The best interest of the Kiowas, he continued, lay in enrolling their children in public schools at the earliest opportunity. Rainy Mountain should close, reasoned Russell, "if for no other reason than to force the Kiowa children who attend it into contact with the White children in public schools." To those Kiowas who objected, Russell indignantly replied that it was they, in fact, who had first begun the present turn of events by enrolling their children in public schools, "cutting thereby the total number of available children to a number insufficient . . . to allow an enrollment at the four [boarding] schools" run by the agency.[13]

It was an imaginative argument, and one that was not altogether credible, but it satisfied the Indian Office. Far from dooming Rainy Mountain by sending their children to area public schools, however, the Kiowas, statistics indicate, enrolled only modest numbers of their children in local public school districts. A 1913 statistical summary showed a total of 1,147 eligible school-age children from the reservation, 199 of whom were in public schools (and of that figure only 75 Kiowas); 683 others were in government schools, mission schools, or nonreservation schools. In late 1915 field matron Mary Clouse reported only 17 children from the Rainy Mountain district enrolled in the nearby Mountain View Public School; two years later the number had risen to 32. These developments did not significantly weaken Rainy Mountain's enrollments. Indeed, a case could have been made that with a number of the district's students now in public schools, the pressure would abate and Rainy Mountain could more effectively handle its students. The Indian Office was not sympathetic to any of these arguments. It clearly considered Rainy Mountain the least suitable of the agency's schools to save, "an opinion with which," noted Russell, "I have no hesitancy in saying, I am in full accord."[14]

The decision to close the school set off a storm of protest ranging from outraged whites who objected angrily and loudly to the threat of schooling their children with what they considered half-civilized Indians, to the Kiowas themselves, for whom the school seemed both a legitimate debt owed to them and an indispensable component in the tribe's progress toward membership in American society. Word had barely gotten out before the tribe began an extensive campaign to keep Rainy Mountain open. Writing to Congressman Scott Ferris in Washington in November 1919, Sherman Chaddlesone, a Kiowa who had worked as a disciplinarian at Rainy Mountain a decade earlier, spoke passionately against closing the school. He reminded Ferris that if Rainy Mountain closed there would be no school for the Kiowas, but the Comanches, Caddos, Delawares, and Wichitas "will still have their schools." He did not wish to see the tribe "deprived of their good school, they loved Rainy Mountain School."[15]

In Chaddlesone's opinion all the school needed "was a little more backing by the Indian Office and it will do twice as much for the Kiowa children." The school had turned out scores of good students who had gone on to become successful citizens, who, he insisted, owed their chance in life to Rainy Mountain. "If Rainy Mountain School can do these good things for Kiowa children," he asked plaintively, "why should it be abolished?" Chaddlesone implored Ferris to help the tribe: "The Kiowas need their school, they cannot very well get along without it."[16]

Ferris and fellow Oklahoma congressman James McClintic sent separate inquiries to the commissioner's office and requested that it reconsider its decision. In late January 1920, McClintic informed Sells that the "rumor" concerning the school's closing had reached him. "I do not know of any school that is more ideally located than this institution," wrote McClintic. "Inasmuch as the attendance is sufficient to maintain it I cannot see how your Department could consistently entertain an idea looking towards its discontinuance. I trust there is no truth to this report." Ferris and McClintic received curt replies from Assistant Commissioner E. B. Meritt who stated simply that because of the large number of Kiowa children in public schools, and the extraordinary expense involved in repairing the Rainy Mountain campus, the school could not be maintained. The twenty thousand to twenty-five thousand dollars necessary for repairs, wrote Meritt, could hardly be justified for "a school plant which is not actually required for the education of Indian children."[17]

When word of the proposed closing reached Oklahoma a flurry of complaints from Rainy Mountain supporters poured into the Indian Office. Representative Ferris took a particularly active role in the campaign. In a series of telegrams to high-ranking public officials, he insisted that the Indian Office was making a mistake that would cause great harm to the Kiowas. Ferris made his case in separate (but identical) pleas to Secretary of the Interior Franklin Lane, Commissioner Sells, and U.S. Senator Robert Owen of Oklahoma. "The Kiowa Indians feel hurt that an order has been established abolishing the Rainy Mountain School," he wrote. "The Indians are heart broken about it," continued Ferris, and had sent a delegation with a petition to Washington. "Will you not be good enough to see what can be done for them?"[18]

Weary of the browbeating his department was taking, Sells shot back a terse answer to Ferris in February 1920. "It is policy to place Indian children in public schools whenever they are available," wired the commissioner. Large numbers of Kiowa children were already in those schools, he continued. Moreover, the sum required to repair the plant was not the twenty thousand dollars cited earlier, but more than forty thousand dollars. In reply to Senator Owen, Sells hastened to explain that "the closing of the Rainy Mountain School will not deprive any Indian child . . . and I feel it is the proper course to pursue."[19]

Unswayed by the commissioner's tough stance, Representative McClintic personally delivered the Kiowa petition to Sells. Signed by 146 members of the tribe, including many former students, the petition was a plea against taking the school from a tribe that very much wanted and needed it. In a letter to Kiowa spokesman Robert Onco, McClintic promised to present the petition and to continue discussions with Sells about "the unjustness of the order." McClintic went on to say that the suddenness of the decision to close Rainy Mountain had caught him off guard. "I have watched the Indian legislation . . . in order that the appropriations for the maintenance of the Indians in western Oklahoma would not be reduced." When the Committee on Indian Affairs did not take any action indicating a drastic reduction in the number of the state's government boarding schools, McClintic said he felt sure that no significant changes were going to be made. Still, in an effort to ascertain Rainy Mountain's actual conditions (and unimpressed by Sells' suggestion that forty thousand dollars was needed to put the plant in working order), McClintic told Onco that he had commissioned a friend in nearby Gotebo to investigate the facts and report as soon as possible. In the meantime, McClintic would push the issue as hard as he dared. Surprisingly, Sells received word of McClintic's actions and then courteously notified Senator Owen in mid-March that he "had not entirely completed my further consideration of the situation" and would be happy to give it and the tribe's petition "due attention."[20] A window of opportunity seemed to have opened.

The tribe's petition revealed an attachment to the school that was much stronger than the Indian Office realized. Rainy Mountain represented a vital link to the non-Indian world for Kiowa children, and many Kiowa parents believed that it was virtually the only chance their children would have to receive the training and instruction necessary to make successful lives. Although agents and inspectors had complained over the years about the occasional obstinacy of the Kiowas, it was equally true that the school was filled to capacity every year. As Parker McKenzie observed, his parents as well as many others never doubted the school's importance and never tried to keep their children away. Losing it meant having to send their youngsters to public schools, where they were not welcomed, or to the agency's other boarding schools, which were not as conveniently located and which were dominated by other tribes.

"To discontinue the institution would mean the removal of the very backbone of the tribe," began the petition. Rainy

Mountain was where their children got their first knowledge of the outside world. Sending them to white schools was impractical and dangerous. "No white teacher . . . who even has an interest and sympathy for the Indian child will long endure the patience required to remold" that child. The circumstances of Kiowa life would only "breed contempt for the Indian children in public schools." The petition charged that several local school districts had previously gone so far as to refuse to enroll Indian children; another had relegated them to separate rooms. Prejudice and distrust ran deep in the white communities, and Kiowa parents feared the worst if their children were forced to attend public schools. "The best Indian pupil in every respect . . . is the one that has been in attendance at a Government school long enough to learn to speak English, understand the necessity of cleanliness, good health, right living, and the general habits of the whites."[21]

The document closed with a plea for the rights of the Kiowa tribe. "We need more education and better education," it said, "but little progress will be made if the circumstances cited above are permitted." Discontinuing the school might seem wise for financial reasons, "but the welfare of the tribe ought to be paramount." The Kiowas requested that a member of the Board of Indian Commissioners be authorized to investigate the matter thoroughly; it was sure that such an investigation would recommend that the school be continued because, very simply, "We need it."[22]

Shortly after the commissioner received the petition, Agent Stinchecum delivered to the Indian Office evidence that he believed would discredit the tribe's position. The agency's day school inspector, wrote Stinchecum, had "carefully analyzed" the petition and had reached the conclusion that most of its signers had little to do with Rainy Mountain. According to Stinchecum's findings, most of the petition's signers either had no children in the school, did not live in the Rainy Mountain district, had children in public schools or other boarding schools, had withdrawn their children from Rainy Mountain, or refused to send them to school. Fifty-six signers, for example, were listed as either having no children at the school or as being too old or too young to have children.[23]

Stinchecum's analysis was simplistic at best and deliberately dishonest at worst. Most of those identified as having no children in the school, for example, were former students who spoke from personal experience about the school's importance. Only 29 of the 146 signers were listed as having children in public schools, and a mere 4 had children in other boarding schools. Three were listed as refusing to send their children to Rainy Mountain. Overall, Stinchecum's analysis of the petitioner's signers did not reveal any legitimate complaints.

On the matter of an independent review from the Board of Indian Commissioners, Stinchecum noted that Warren K. Moorehead of the board had in fact visited the agency. However, Stinchecum did not believe that Moorehead had an accurate understanding of the situation, and he described Moorehead's opinions as "of really no value." Moorehead had not actually visited the school, Stinchecum claimed, and "in fact knows nothing whatever concerning the matter other than the fact the Indians oppose the closing of the school at this time." Moorehead's report notwithstanding, the agent believed the decision to close the school was sound, and Stinchecum concluded that he would be "much disappointed to know the Office reaches any other conclusion."[24]

The Indian Office responded to the petition with the same explanations that it had given all other interested parties. In late February the assistant commissioner replied in writing that it was the "settled policy" of the government to place Indian children in public schools where it was possible to do so. This was done out of a concern for economy and because it represented the "best interests of the Indian children." Furthermore, records showed that a "large percentage" of the district's children had access to public schools, a debatable assumption, especially in light of what "access" really meant. Finally, Rainy Mountain was in the poorest condition of the agency's boarding schools and would require "a great deal of money to put it in good condition." The letter gave no indication that the tribe's protest had produced any reconsideration of the matter.[25]

Having rebuffed the Kiowas, the Indian Office still had to deal with resistance from white school officials and parents. Their anger was no less real than that of the Kiowas; ironically, many of the same fears expressed by the Kiowas lay at the heart of the whites' protest. Like the Kiowas, local whites were not very enthusiastic about having their children in the same schools as Indian children. It was not their fault that Rainy Mountain had fallen on hard times, they said, and they were not inclined to suffer because of that. And at least one citizen saw sinister events unfolding. J. W. Dellinger of Gotebo wrote somewhat breathlessly to Representative McClintic in January 1920 and called his attention to "a rumor now agitating our people recently." The government, according to Dellinger, had "sold all the Indian School property to the Catholic Church and hereafter they will be conducted under that denomination." It was his duty, Dellinger continued, to inform McClintic that "against such action all the citizenry of this country enter their solemn protest right now."[26]

If the rest of the area's whites failed to see a papist plot unfolding before their very eyes, they at least saw something they did not like and did not intend to tolerate. Mr. J. M. Rule, president and manager of the Hobart Democrat-Chief, began the attack with a letter to Senator Owen in mid-February 1920. A thinly veiled tirade against allowing Indian children to attend public schools, the letter revealed sentiments typical of many area whites. "This school is necessary for the proper . . . education of the Indian children," wrote Rule, "who pick up their education slowly and cannot be given proper attention by instructors in the public schools." The citizens of Hobart were unanimously in favor of keeping Rainy Mountain open, he concluded, and Rule was sure that Owen would lend his valuable assistance in seeing that Rainy Mountain survived.[27]

Mrs. J. F. Baldridge, chairman of the Kiowa County American

Red Cross (she used its official letterhead to write to Senator Owen), was even more direct. Her group's reasons for opposing the school's closing were twofold. First, the local schools were already crowded beyond capacity, so closing Rainy Mountain would only encumber an already overburdened school system. Second, and more important, Kiowa children were not ready to enter public schools. "The Indian standard of living is centuries behind that of the ordinary American," she wrote. The Indian child did not know how "to keep clean, how to eat at a table, how to sleep in a bed, or even how to wear citizen's clothing." Although schools like Rainy Mountain worked diligently to give Indian children instruction in these and other areas, the process was slow and fraught with dangers. "The Indian child is a menace to all of his associates until he has been taught the laws of hygiene and clean living," she continued, and that could only occur in an Indian boarding school. If Rainy Mountain closed, Kiowa children would lose their only chance "to learn how to live in a clean, sanitary way."[28] Baldridge's narrow, provincial world view was typical, and it reflected the mean-spirited and patronizing attitude that dominated neighboring communities.

The superintendent of the Hobart public schools, Dr. F. A. Balyeat, took his turn next in a late February letter to Senator Owen. Echoing Mrs. Baldridge, Balyeat confirmed for the senator that the Hobart schools were badly overcrowded and thus unable to accommodate any more students. Moreover, it was his opinion as a professional educator that Indian children were unfit for public classrooms anyway. "It has been the experience of our teachers," he wrote, "that the Indians cannot be started in school . . . without crippling the work of the room and greatly retarding the progress of the Indians." He observed that most of the Kiowa children spoke little or no English and suffered badly in comparison to their more accomplished white counterparts. Indian children responded "very reluctantly" to public school methods of instruction; his school was not equipped to provide the special environment that Indians needed. Even if he had the staff and was willing to accept such a task (and he was not), here was a fact that no school could undo: "We submit that the Indian is greatly handicapped by this futile attempt to civilize him by trying to get him to learn what he cannot understand."[29]

Even if Indian children were capable of learning at the same pace as whites (and Balyeat clearly believed they were not), they would not be welcome. Balyeat told the senator that "with few exceptions the Indian children who attended the Hobart Schools are unwelcome and repulsive to the whites." Because Indian children were almost always dirty and bred disease, he continued, they were unable to mix comfortably with whites. Teachers occasionally refused to accept rooms that had Kiowa children in them. After careful consideration Balyeat concluded that Indian children would be a menace to the safety and progress of his schools. He closed by observing that he had lived among Indians since his boyhood and did not, of course, wish to see them deprived of their schooling. By the same token, as something of a local authority on the matter he did not wish to see them mixed in among his system's students, and he encouraged Owen to prevent the closing of Rainy Mountain.[30]

Interestingly, Balyeat expressed a different opinion of the episode forty years later. In his history of Kiowa County schools, Balyeat recalled that Rainy Mountain was "well staffed and equipped" and that its closing had not caused any particular problems or adjustments. "Schools of Kiowa County responded to the change in proportion to the number of Indian children available," he reported. "Slowly but steadily these pupils attended better, became better integrated, and added justification to the policies of the Bureau of Indian Affairs."[31]

A flood of complaints similar to those made by Balyeat and others eventually reached the Indian Office. Most of them were grounded in the belief that Indians were unfit and unsuited for schooling in the public system. From the Chamber of Commerce in Mountain View came the revelation that "sixty percent of the Indian children have trachoma and are not in condition to be placed in public schools. Will not take much more than regular amount to run school and put in fairly good repair." The president of the school board at Mountain View noted that all of the local public schools were badly overcrowded. "White people protest against Indian children attending schools to which they pay no taxes. Unsanitary Indian children not desired in public schools." The Hobart Commercial Club struck a pose of righteous indignation: "We have lived in this country too long for a new comer from the extreme east . . . not experienced with the Indian to make us submit to any such [change]." The club generously offered to host a tour of the school's grounds for the Indian Office "so they can see actual conditions. School has approximately 150 students, some of them wearing blankets. Believe expense in 1920 would not exceed 1919."[32]

The Gotebo Chamber of Commerce noted that a recent fact-finding visit to the Rainy Mountain campus left members convinced that a "very small amount of money will be needed for repairs. . . . The Superintendent of the Indian Agency at Anadarko has never seen fit to spend any reasonable amount for repairs." Absorbing Kiowa children into the white schools was characterized as "a big mistake." The chamber also belittled the commissioner's estimate for repairs as an uninformed exaggeration. Why, any "reasonable man," it said, could see that something like four thousand dollars would put the school in good order. The Bank of Gotebo agreed, described Sell's estimate of forty thousand dollars as "ridiculous," and suggested that five thousand dollars would be sufficient. The Farmer's and Merchant's National Bank of Hobart added its opinion by noting that Rainy Mountain was "the only school in the country that can afford necessary facilities for Indian children."[33]

Of course this was the kind of argument that the Indian Office did not want to hear. Stinchecum, caught in the middle, quickly attempted to soften the impact of such protests by drafting a letter to Sells in mid-March. As to the concern about the health of Rainy Mountain's pupils, he assured the commissioner that this was an infrequent problem. "As a rule our

Indians are fairly tidy," he wrote, "and are at all times in reasonably presentable condition." On the whole he believed they
would blend nicely with white school children. Recent protests,
he was certain, were merely attempts to influence the commissioner's office. Stinchecum argued that for every case in which
an Indian child had been found unsuitable for schooling because
of health reasons or disciplinary problems, he could just as
easily find one involving a white child. And on the "one or two
occasions" when investigation had revealed problems, every
necessary step had been taken to remedy the situation. As to
the issue of Indian children being unwanted in the public
schools, he told Sells that "as a mater of fact, our pupils have
been, in nearly every case, actually welcomed as public school
pupils."[34]

Surviving documents and reports suggest that there was a
measure of truth to the points being raised by both camps.
Although there was undoubtedly opposition to enrolling Indians in the public schools, it is equally clear that in some cases
the children were treated reasonably well. A 1913 report from
one government inspector, for example, revealed that the thirteen Comanche pupils at Mountain View School (about twelve
miles east of Rainy Mountain) were doing about as well as their
white counterparts. When compared with whites in "aptness,
application, and advancement," the report graded the Indian
students as "Good." At nearby Bunker Hill School, where
eleven Kiowa children were enrolled, the results of a similar
comparison yielded scores of "Fair" in all categories. The same
was true for the two Apache children enrolled at Cache Creek,
not far from Lawton. A December 1913 issue of Home and
School, a newsletter of current events published by the Red
Stone Mission in Anadarko, noted that several school districts
had large numbers of Indian students, all of whom "are doing
well in their work. Other districts report Indian children also.
It is time that our districts wake up to the fact that the Indian
children are here and must have attention. The average Indian

boy or girl will compare very favorably with the average white boy or girl."[35]

Others came to the defense of Indian schools and students. The redoubtable Mary Clouse wrote a stinging report in March 1920 that criticized those who objected to enrolling Indian children in public schools: "Called on teachers of three white schools where Indians living in Rainy Mountain district attend school with the white children. Received good reports. Some of the patrons class Indians with negroes and object to the children attending our public schools. Such people ought never to have moved to Okla. This country was promised to the Indians to be there's [sic] so long as water ran or grass grew." Yet Clouse was keenly aware of the stakes and conceded that for the time being Rainy Mountain should remain open. "There are so few district schools that they would be overcrowded. To send our children to Ft. Sill or Riverside will be detrimental to the parents who will spend too much time camping near these schools." Clouse also decried the discrimination that Kiowa children regularly suffered, a fact she repeatedly reported to Stinchecum, who just as repeatedly ignored it. In late 1917, for example, she noted that local white teachers openly favored white students and condoned the intimidation and physical abuse meted out to Indian children. As a result of such circumstances, and out of simple necessity, Clouse concluded that Rainy Mountain ought to remain open.[36]

As the spring of 1920 came and went, however, it became clear that appeals to keep the school open would fail. In May, Stinchecum informed Sells that the permanent closing had been set for June 30. After that time only a modest work party would be needed to harvest the school's small crops, look after the buildings, and "close up affairs generally." After a muted farewell ceremony in late June, at which former students offered emotional testimonials, the children went home for the last time. The staff closed and locked the buildings and shipped most of the beds, mattresses, laundry equipment, and dry goods to the agency's other schools. As for the school itself, the Indian Office hoped to sell most or all of it to the highest bidder. With buildings, tools, supplies, and land appraised at more than ninety-eight thousand dollars, the government considered Rainy Mountain more valuable on the auction block than as an Indian school.[37]

A solution appeared in late summer when several civic groups approached the Indian Office about transforming Rainy Mountain into a sanatorium for tubercular veterans. At the end of June the chairman of the Oklahoma City chapter of the Red Cross; the presidents of the city's Lion's Club, Kiwanis Club, YMCA, and Chamber of Commerce; the chairman of the Soldiers' Welfare Committee; and the chaplain of the American Legion Post wired a telegram to Senator Owen urging him to arrange the transfer of the school to the Public Health Service for use as a tuberculosis treatment center. "Not a single bed in the state of Oklahoma available for a tubercular soldier," went their message. "All men are sent outside of the state and suffer from homesickness and do not recover as they would in Oklahoma City. Have a heart."[38]

Similar pleas went to Representative Ferris, who along with Owen forwarded the messages to the Indian Office. Commissioner Sells responded that he would take the matter under consideration and wired Owen that he had in fact already tendered the offer to Public Health. If it wanted the school, Sells indicated he would approve the action. By the summer of 1920 even Mary Clouse spoke in favor of turning the campus into a hospital. But she argued that the school ought to be used as "a T.B. hospital for Indians." This, she continued, "would be a fitting end to a school that has done much good to these Indians."[39]

On August 6, Sells wired the adjutant of the Charles B. Burke American Legion Post in Madill, Oklahoma, to inform him that the Public Health Service "has my consent to use Rainy Mountain School as hospital [for] ex-soldiers. Understand Surgeon General has matter under consideration." At the end of the month he sent a similar message to the adjutant of the Dobb-Frazier American Legion Post in Duncan. "This Office has already consented to the use of the plant for hospital purposes," wrote Assistant Commissioner E. B. Meritt, "and understands that the United States Public Health Service . . . has the matter under advisement." Anticipating the arrival of a physician to administer the hospital at Rainy Mountain, Stinchecum made plans to ready several campus buildings for immediate use.[40]

In late October, however, Meritt ordered Stinchecum to hold further action at the school in abeyance. Apparently, Public Health officials were still debating whether to use the Rainy Mountain site. At the end of the month the Surgeon General's office informed the Indian Office that it would not take Rainy Mountain after all. The school's isolation and remoteness rendered it impractical, and the Surgeon General was of the opinion that "climatically and structurally it is not adapted to the purposes for which the Public Health Service are in need."[41] Rainy Mountain would not have a second life.

From 1910 until its closing in 1920, Rainy Mountain's fortunes steadily declined. The shifting priorities of the Progressive Era meant that schools everywhere suffered the effects of willfully limited programs. That narrowing view of education's role, buttressed by Rainy Mountain's continuing poor circumstances, marked the school as an easy target for elimination. It might have survived longer had policy makers been more optimistic in their evaluation of Indian education; they were not, and Rainy Mountain proved helpless in the face of that fact.

In the fall of 1920, Rainy Mountain sat empty and unused for the first time in twenty-seven years. But for a brief stint as a work camp during the New Deal, it never again opened. The main buildings fell rapidly into disrepair, and fire destroyed the barn and various outbuildings. Other major structures collapsed, and the basement of the 1915 classroom building became a garbage dump. Local Kiowas eventually dismantled the boys' dormitory, the oldest and most distinctive structure on the campus, and used the stones for construction at the nearby Rainy Mountain Baptist Mission. In time ranchers opened the grounds to cattle, and the campus slowly disappeared beneath the grass of the Oklahoma prairie.

8

Conclusion
"Who Am I? I Am a Kiowa"
The Legacy of Rainy Mountain

As Parker McKenzie wandered across the ruins of the Rainy Mountain campus that August afternoon in the summer of 1990, he suddenly came across the school's old concrete flagpole base, which was hidden in the grass. McKenzie did not see it until he stepped on it. Looking down to see what he had found, he said, "How about that," immediately snapped to attention, and placed his hand over his heart, a lesson learned at Rainy Mountain almost a century before. A moment later he resumed our conversation about his life as a young boy on the Kiowa-Comanche-Apache Reservation. The contradiction of those two experiences struck me with considerable force. An hour earlier McKenzie had been giving me driving directions in the Kiowa language with careful explanations about differences in tense, inflection, and tone. He talked easily of this Indian family or that Indian family and of the survival of various Kiowa cultural traditions. At the nearby Rainy Mountain Church cemetery he gave me a lesson in Kiowa genealogy and carefully pointed out the graves of former students. Finding the flagpole base, however, took him back to a time and place that stood in stark relief to all that he had been so busily telling and showing me. Indeed, that earlier era had been intended to prevent conversations like the one we were having from ever occurring.

Like many former students, McKenzie is an example of how the boarding schools simultaneously failed and succeeded. They failed inasmuch as they did not destroy Kiowa identity

or culture. Cutting children's hair, dressing them in new clothing, and teaching them to farm, bake, or sew did not necessarily
transform identity. Given the circumstances at Rainy Mountain it was unlikely that such a transformation could have been
achieved anyway. Yet the school succeeded in important ways,
another contradiction considering the conditions that usually
prevailed. Hundreds of young Kiowas went through the place
and gained invaluable experience and skills that they used after
leaving school. Fluency in English, for example, was a critical
factor. Most students left the school with varying levels of
proficiency, but with enough knowledge to survive. The vocational instruction they received likewise made it possible for
them to make their way in the world that lay outside the
campus. It was not a perfect preparation, and it was not what
they deserved, but it helped to ease the transition from the life
their parents had led to the very different one that they faced.

The irony is that most students began new lives by combining
two worlds. And it is here that the contradictory nature of
schools such as Rainy Mountain is most clearly revealed. It
was possible—indeed it was necessary—to join different worlds
together to keep Kiowa identity viable. Thus the seeming incon-
gruity of going to boarding school and staying Indian was not
so much a conundrum as it was a fact of life. Kiowas had
changed many times during their history; the boarding schools
were only the latest in a long series of events. Learning English,
for example, or a trade made it possible to function in the
modern world, but not at the cost of losing important cultural
foundations. Indeed, it was the maintenance of their cultural
base that enabled many Kiowas to endure the world around
them. Cora Dunn was mistaken in her belief that she could
change them forever. She might mold them into English-speak-
ing Christians, but she could not transform them into exact
replicas of Anglo-America.

In later life former students revealed the limits of change.
James Silverhorn went through the boarding schools but remained closely associated with important tribal institutions.

He joined the Native American Church about 1932, for example, and assumed prominence as one of its leaders in the Kiowa community. As an adult he kept four of the Kiowa sacred medicine bundles. Former Rainy Mountain student Fred Bigman also joined the Native American Church and like many other former students used it as an avenue to maintain his culture. One Kiowa man, a Fort Sill graduate who served in the military for nearly thirty years, came home to Oklahoma at his retirement and became a stalwart in the Native American Church and powwow communities. When asked if the schools ever took his cultural identity away, he replied, "They couldn't, I didn't let that happen. People are all the time asking me who I am. Who am I? I am a *Kiowa*." McKenzie remembered that "many families encouraged their offspring to carry on Kiowa traditions as a matter of tribal identity. Such encouragement could not be thought of as hindrances to their education. They presumably saw it to be better as two persons instead of one."[1]

There are many ways to understand the determination of Kiowas to survive the transforming experience of Rainy Mountain. To stand in nearby Carnegie Park on the Fourth of July is to appreciate that legacy with a special immediacy and intensity. There, one can see and hear the living embodiment of what it meant for those children to hold on to the songs, language, and rituals that made them Kiowa. The Gourd Clan, an especially influential group in contemporary Kiowa culture, holds its annual dance on the Fourth and uses the occasion to make a deliberate and stunning statement about the continuing vitality of tribal identity. Numerous public statements are made, and homage is paid to those people who simply refused to give up their identity. This means acknowledging the generations who went through the schools in the early twentieth century.[2]

The pattern is unmistakably clear; former boarding school students retained crucial elements of Kiowa culture, combined them with what they learned at the schools, and went on with their lives. Frederick Hoxie attributes this partially to the fact that the decision to scale back the Indian school system during the Progressive Era gave Indians breathing room. By retreating from an assimilationist agenda, in which every detail was vital, to one that accepted limited possibilities for Indians, the government ironically removed important impediments to preserving culture. According to Hoxie, the irony is that by doing so the government encouraged, even allowed, a plural society to emerge in Indian communities. Sally McBeth concurs. In her examination of western Oklahoma tribes and reservation boarding schools, McBeth finds that "the very segregationist and assimilationist beginnings of the Oklahoma boarding schools effectively, if inadvertently, seem to have fostered the formation of an Indian identity." Indeed, one of McBeth's consultants told her "the boarding schools have their strong points and their weak points. We endure over the years despite the bad experiences, and we get stronger on account of them."[3]

Other important changes helped as well. During the 1930s the "evolutionary assimilation" of John Collier's Indian New Deal recognized the vitality of native culture and officially forbade its destruction. Collier emphasized the usefulness of cultural diversity and allowed students to retain their tribal heritage. Except for the termination era of the 1950s, forced assimilation would never again figure in the bureau's official policies. The Indian schools survived, but by World War II they had begun to move away from the inflexible standards of an earlier era. Native cultures were nurtured and the schools became important sources for protecting and transmitting tribal traditions.

For all of his eccentricities and ill-conceived plans, Collier nonetheless helped to establish an environment that encouraged Indians to take back their culture and reclaim their heritage. The foundation established in part by boarding school students like those from Rainy Mountain flourished partly as the result of Collier's effort to redirect policy. Having survived the severe trial of the reservation era, former students retained a core of values, actions, and practices that helped ensure cultural identity; in the decades to come it would be easier to ensure the survival of that knowledge.[4]

Rainy Mountain School can now barely be seen from the road. The mountain is there, an enduring landmark representing what N. Scott Momaday says is "a landscape that is incomparable, a time that is gone forever, and the human spirit, which endures."[5] The campus, however, is largely gone, save for the ruins of a few buildings. Its outlines are faintly visible from the top of the mountain, but unless one knew with certainty what had once existed there, it is impossible to recognize the campus of a reservation boarding school. Yet Rainy Mountain remains a powerful force for the Kiowa people. Most living Kiowas have relatives who attended the school, roamed its campus, and felt its forces—good and bad. Kiowas visit the mountain regularly to walk the grounds, cut sage for ceremonial use, or stop at the nearby mission and cemetery. For many of them the trip is akin to a pilgrimage; the combination of the mountain's historic cultural importance and of the school's role in their lives and in the lives of their kinsmen is palpable. Visitors to Rainy Mountain invariably talk about the school and what it must have been like for the grandparents, great-aunts, cousins, nephews, or friends who went there. And they always speak with reverence about those people and about what happened a century ago in this lonely corner of a vast reservation.

A trip to the school in May 1994 with the granddaughter of two former students reminded me of its indelible presence. Lingering at the top of the mountain, taking in its broad vista, she told me that coming to Rainy Mountain was important because she knows her grandparents "were here. They were *here*. And they're still here. I know my grandfather came to this spot where I'm standing, because he buried his marbles here one time so that the older kids wouldn't take them." She dug her shoe into the soil and wished quietly that she could find the marbles. "The marbles are here, somewhere," she said. "And so is he. When I come here I know he's here."

The Kiowa people have never forgotten this place, and they venerate the memory of relatives who went to the Rainy Mountain Boarding School. It is a memory that celebrates a survival during a troubling time as well as the precious cost of that survival. And those who go to the mountain today understand the advice given to me when I made my first trip to that tumbledown campus and its slowly disappearing buildings: "Walk quietly at that place, son," an elderly Kiowa man told me, "because the souls of those small children are still there."

Notes

PREFACE

1. Cora Dunn to William A. Jones, September 4, 1899, Rainy Mountain School Files, Records of the Kiowa Agency, Indian Archives Division, Oklahoma Historical Society, Oklahoma City.

2. *Annual Report of the Commissioner of Indian Affairs*, 1896, p. 1016; Frederick Hoxie, *A Final Promise: The Campaign to Assimilate the Indians, 1880–1920*, 190.

3. C. V. Stinchecum to Mary Clouse, April 12, 1918, Field Matron's Files, Microfilm KA 74, Records of the Kiowa Agency, Indian Archives Division, Oklahoma Historical Society, Oklahoma City.

Employing what Milton M. Gordon called the idea of "Anglo-conformity," policy makers looked to the immigrant experience as the model for "the complete renunciation of . . . ancestral culture in favor of the behavior and values of the Anglo-Saxon core group" (*Assimilation in American Life: The Role of Race, Religion, and National Origins*, 85).

4. Willard Rollings, "In Search of Multisided Frontiers: Recent Writing on the History of the Southern Plains," in *New Directions in American Indian History*, ed. Colin Calloway, 89.

5. Margaret Connell Szasz, *Education and the American Indian: The Road to Self-Determination since 1928*; Margaret Connell Szasz, *Indian Education in the American Colonies, 1607–1783*; Hoxie, *Final Promise*.

6. David W. Adams, "The Federal Indian Boarding School: A Study in Environment and Response, 1879–1918" (Ed.D. diss., Indiana University, 1975); Sally J. McBeth, *Ethnic Identity and the Boarding School Experience of West-Central Oklahoma American Indians*; Henrietta Mann, "Cheyenne-Arapaho Education, 1871–1982" (Ph.D. diss., University of New Mexico, 1982).

7. Robert Trennert, *The Phoenix Indian School: Forced Assimilation in Arizona, 1891–1935*; Basil H. Johnston, *Indian School Days*; Devon Mihesuah, *Cultivating the Rosebuds: The Education of Women at the Cherokee Female Seminary, 1851–1909*; K. Tsianina Lomawaima, *They Called It Prairie Light: The Story of Chilocco Indian School*; Michael C. Coleman, *American Indian Children at School, 1850–1930*. See also David W. Adams, *Education for Extinc-*

tion: *American Indians and the Boarding School Experience, 1875–1928,* which is forthcoming as this manuscript goes to press.

8. Robert Utley, *The Indian Frontier of the American West, 1846–1890,* 140.

9. N. Scott Momaday, *The Way to Rainy Mountain,* 4.

CHAPTER 1

1. Robert M. Utley, *The Last Days of the Sioux Nation,* 37; Francis Paul Prucha, *American Indian Policy in Crisis: Christian Reformers and the Indian, 1865–1900,* 265. There are few comprehensive histories of Indian education. The standard surveys include Evelyn C. Adams, *American Indian Education: Government Schools and Economic Progress;* Estelle Fuchs and Robert J. Havighurst, *To Live on This Earth: American Indian Education;* and David H. DeJong, *Promises of the Past: A History of Indian Education.* Other important studies are those of Margaret Connell Szasz: *Indian Education in the American Colonies, 1607–1783,* and *Education and the American Indian: The Road to Self-Determination since 1928.*

2. *Annual Report of the Commissioner of Indian Affairs* (hereafter cited as *ARCIA*), 1873, p. 377; Frederick Hoxie, *A Final Promise: The Campaign to Assimilate the Indians, 1880–1920,* 190. A fine discussion of the larger issues affecting Indian education between 1880 and 1900 is in David W. Adams, "Fundamental Considerations: The Deep Meaning of Native American Schooling, 1880–1900," *Harvard Educational Review* 58:1 (February 1988): 1–28.

3. Robert S. Walker, *Torchlights to the Cherokees: The Brainerd Mission,* 22; Francis Paul Prucha, *The Great Father: The United States Government and the American Indians,* I:136, 147. For discussions of the formative era in policy making, see also Francis Paul Prucha, *American Indian Policy in the Formative Years: The Indian Trade and Intercourse Acts, 1790–1834,* and Reginald Horsman, *Expansion and American Indian Policy, 1783–1812.* An excellent assessment of the decision to civilize Indians is Herman J. Viola, "From Civilization to Removal: Early American Indian Policy," in *Indian-White Relations: A Persistent Paradox,* ed. Jane F. Smith and Robert M. Kvasnicka, 45–56. The best summary of Indian schooling in the formative period is Szasz, *Indian Education.* Szasz comments that Indian education "lay at the cutting edge of cultural interaction in the sixteenth and seventeenth centuries. A number of colonial Euroamericans and Indians deemed Indian schooling as the ultimate tool for achieving cultural change among Indian people" (4). See also Henry Warner Bowden, "Missions in the Nineteenth Century (1803–90)," *American Indians and Christian Missions: Studies in Cultural Conflict,* chap. 6; and Robert F. Berkhofer, Jr., *Salvation and the Savage: An Analysis of Protestant Missions and American Indian Response, 1787–1862,* especially chap. 1, "The Grand Object."

There are, of course, interpretations that take a less optimistic stance. See, for example, Francis Jennings, *The Invasion of America: Indians, Colonialism and the Cant of Conquest,* and the most famous of all, Dee Brown, *Bury My Heart at Wounded Knee: An Indian History of the American West.*

4. *ARCIA,* 1866, pp. 20–21. For a useful summary of the Indian school

system's growth after 1830, see Ronald Satz, "Civilizing the Indians," in *American Indian Policy in the Jacksonian Era*, chap. 9.

5. *ARCIA*, 1879, p. 73.

6. S. C. Armstrong, "Education of the Indian," *Journal of Proceedings and Addresses of the Annual Meeting of the National Educational Association*, 1884, p. 177; A. L. Riggs, "Education of the Indian," ibid., 181.

7. *ARCIA*, 1892, p. 55; Richard Henry Pratt, "Industrial Training As Applied to Indian Schools," *Journal of Proceedings and Addresses of the Annual Meeting of the National Education Association*, 1895, p. 764.

8. Morgan, "The Education of American Indians," *Education* 10 (September 1889): 247. This essay was a recapitulation of the remarks he made at the 1889 Lake Mohonk Conference; *ARCIA*, 1885, p. 14.

9. Prucha, *American Indian Policy in Crisis*, 292.

10. Richard Henry Pratt, *Battlefield and Classroom: Four Decades with the American Indian, 1867–1904*, 335.

11. Armstrong, "Education of the Indian," 179.

12. *Annual Report of the Secretary of the Interior* (hereafter cited as *ARSI*), 1877, p. xi–xiii; 1879, pp. 10–11; *ARCIA*, 1880, pp. 7–10. Prucha summarizes the issues in *American Indian Policy in Crisis*, 265–91. See also Theodore Fischbacher, *A Study of the Role of the Federal Government in the Education of the American Indian*, 125–31.

13. *ARSI*, 1880, p. 8; *ARCIA*, 1880, pp. 85–86.

14. Prucha, *American Indian Policy in Crisis*, 293 (see 293–304 for a summary of Morgan's career); *ARCIA*, 1889, pp. 3–4, 302. See also Dorothy W. Hewes, "Those First Good Years of Indian Education: 1894 to 1898," *American Indian Culture and Research Journal* 5, no. 2 (1981): 63–82.

15. Lake Mohonk Conference Proceedings in *ARCIA*, 1889, pp. 16–17.

16. Thomas J. Morgan, *Studies in Pedagogy*, 327–28, 348–50; *ARCIA*, 1889, pp. 3–4.

17. *ARCIA*, 1891, pp. 3–8. Unless otherwise noted, all citations in the following paragraphs come from this source. Lake Mohonk Conference Proceedings cited in *ARCIA*, 1889, pp. 16–17.

18. Ibid., 1899, pp. 4–5.

19. Morgan to Secretary of the Interior, November 30, 1892, in Prucha, *American Indian Policy in Crisis*, 314–15.

20. *ARCIA*, 1890, p. xvi.

21. Lake Mohonk Conference Proceedings in ibid., 1885, pp. 94–95.

22. *ARCIA*, 1895, pp. 3, 16; 1898, pp. 2, 8; *Annual Report of the Board of Indian Commissioners* in ibid., 1900, p. 707.

23. *ARCIA*, 1899, p. 7; 1901, pp. 9, 20.

24. Ibid., 1881, pp. 1–2.

25. Ibid., 1903, pp. 2–3.

26. *Annual Report of the Board of Indian Commissioners* in ibid., 1901, pp. 809–10.

27. Frances C. Sparhawk, "The Indian Question," *Education* 7 (September 1886): 50–51.

28. For discussions of the reservation system and its civilizing programs,

see Robert A. Trennert, *Alternative To Extinction: Federal Indian Policy and the Beginnings of the Reservation System, 1846–1851;* Alban W. Hoopes, *Indian Affairs and Their Administration, with Special Reference to the Far West, 1849–1860;* Robert W. Wooster, *The Military and United States Indian Policy, 1865–1903;* Utley, *Last Days of the Sioux Nation,* especially chap. 3, "The New Life"; Robert H. Keller, Jr., *American Protestantism and United States Indian Policy, 1869–1892.*

29. *ARCIA,* 1897, p. 11; 1898, p. 13.

30. Ibid., 1897, p. 11; 1895, p. 9; 1896, p. 13; Sister Macaria Murphy, "The Day School; the Gradual Uplifter of the Tribe," *Journal of Proceedings and Addresses of the Annual Meeting of the National Educational Association,* 1901, p. 913; C. C. Covey, "The Reservation Day School Should Be the Prime Factor in Indian Education," *Journal of Proceedings and Addresses of the Annual Meeting of the National Education Association,* 1901, p. 901.

31. Morgan quoted in Prucha, *American Indian Policy in Crisis,* 301; *ARSI,* 1880, pp. 7–8.

32. Bruce David Forbes, "John Jasper Methvin: Methodist 'Missionary to the Western Tribes' (Oklahoma)," in *Churchmen and the Western Indians, 1820–1920,* ed. Clyde Milner and Floyd A. O'Neil, 56.

33. *ARCIA,* 1899, p. 10.

34. Ibid., 1881, p. 27.

35. Ibid., 1896, pp. 12–13; 1898, pp. 10–11.

36. Ibid., 1911, p. 190.

37. These schools are discussed at greater length in the next chapter.

38. The best source remains Pratt, *Battlefield and Classroom.* See also Elaine G. Eastman, *Pratt: The Red Man's Moses.* Prucha has a lengthy bibliography in *American Indian Policy in Crisis,* 272, at n. 16. *ARCIA,* 1895, p. 6; 1899, p. 10. By far the best study other than Pratt's of an off-reservation boarding school is Robert Trennert, *The Phoenix Indian School: Forced Assimilation in Arizona, 1891–1935.* Tsianina Lomawaima, *They Called It Prairie Light: The Story of Chilocco Indian School* is also revealing, especially the sections on student life. For a recent study of the Hampton experiment, see Donal F. Lindsey, *Indians at Hampton Institute, 1873–1923.*

39. *ARCIA,* 1898, p. 9; 1902, p. 32. On the outing system, see Robert Trennert, "From Carlisle to Phoenix: The Rise and Fall of the Indian Outing System, 1878–1930," *Pacific Historical Review* 52 (August 1983): 267–91.

40. Lake Mohonk Conference Proceedings in *ARCIA,* 1889, p. 23. See also Irving G. Hendrick, "The Federal Campaign for the Admission of Indian Children into Public Schools, 1890–1934," *American Indian Culture and Research Journal,* 5, no. 3 (1981): 13–32.

41. *ARCIA,* 1899, pp. 14–15; 1898, p. 14; Hendrick, "Indian Admission to Public Schools," 21; Hoxie, *Final Promise,* 207–208.

42. C. F. Kelsey to Calvin H. Asbury, October 14, 1917, cited in Hendrick, "Indian Admission to Public Schools," 23.

43. *ARCIA,* 1910, p. 5; 1912, pp. 37, 187; 1921, pp. 7, 54.

44. Ibid., 1899, pp. 560–61; 1912, p. 187; 1921, p. 54.

45. Hoxie, *Final Promise*, 254. Hoxie's statistics are compiled from *ARCIA* between 1902 and 1920.

CHAPTER 2

1. Richard White, *It's Your Misfortune and None of My Own: A New History of the American West*, 3. I follow Donald Worster's lead in calling the Southern Plains a "vast austerity." See his comments in *Dust Bowl: The Southern Plains in the 1930s*, 3–4.

2. Population estimates are from James Mooney, "Calendar History of the Kiowa Indians," in *Seventeenth Annual Report, Bureau of American Ethnology*, 235–37. The best summary of the effort to bring Kiowas and Comanches onto the reservation is William T. Hagan, *United States–Comanche Relations: The Reservation Years*, especially chaps. 1–3. For other assessments of the region's military history, see William H. Leckie, *The Military Conquest of the Southern Plains*; Wilbur S. Nye, *Carbine and Lance: The Story of Old Fort Sill*; Nye, *Plains Indian Raiders: The Final Phases of Warfare from the Arkansas to the Red River*; Rupert N. Richardson, *The Comanche Barrier to South Plains Settlement*; Robert Wooster, *The Military and United States Indian Policy, 1865–1903*, especially chap. 5, " 'To Conquer A Lasting Peace': The Frontier, 1869–1877"; and Robert Utley, *The Indian Frontier of the American West, 1846–1890*, especially chap. 6, "Wars of the Peace Policy, 1869–1886."

3. The best description of the negotiations remains Douglas Jones, *The Treaty of Medicine Lodge*. An excellent summary of the issues may be found in Hagan, *United States–Comanche Relations*, 1–43, on which I have relied heavily, and Grant Foreman, "Historical Background of the Kiowa-Comanche Reservation," *Chronicles of Oklahoma* 19 (June 1941): 129–40. See also Mildred Mayhall, *The Kiowas*, but note that her account is quite poor. Provisions of the treaty are in Charles J. Kappler, *Indian Affairs: Laws and Treaties* II: 977–84.

4. Hagan, *United States–Comanche Relations*, 29–31, 42–43. A similar argument appears in Robert H. Keller, Jr., *American Protestantism and United States Indian Policy, 1869–82*. "Government practice," he writes, "regardless of policy, depended on white society, promoted white expansion, reflected white values, and protected white frontiersmen. The government ultimately was committed to its own citizens, to settlers, to white taxpayers and voters," 11.

5. Lawrie Tatum, *Our Red Brothers and the Peace Policy of President Ulysses S. Grant*, 106; Ida Cleo Moore, "Schools and Education among the Kiowa and Comanche Indians, 1870–1940" (M.A. thesis, University of Oklahoma, 1940), 15.

6. On the Quaker administration of the agency, see Lee Cutler, "Lawrie Tatum and the Kiowa Agency, 1869–1873," *Arizona and the West* 13 (Autumn 1971): 221–44; Burritt M. Hiatt, "James M. Haworth, Quaker Indian Agent," *Bulletin of the Friends Historical Association* 74 (Autumn 1958): 80–93; Aubrey L. Steele, "Quaker Control of the Kiowa-Comanche Agency," (M.A. thesis, University of Oklahoma, 1938); Aubrey L. Steele, "The Beginning of Quaker

Administration of Indian Affairs in Oklahoma," *Chronicles of Oklahoma* 17 (March 1939): 364–92; Aubrey L. Steele, "Lawrie Tatum's Indian Policy," *Chronicles of Oklahoma* 22 (Spring 1944): 83–98; T. Ashley Zwink, "On the White Man's Road: Lawrie Tatum and the Formative Years of the Kiowa Agency, 1869–1873," *Chronicles of Oklahoma* 56 (Winter 1978–79): 431–41. For a good summary see Keller, *American Protestantism*, 132–39.

7. Population statistics are from Tatum's annual report in *ARCIA*, 1870, p. 728; Hagan, "The Reservation Policy: Two Little and Too Late," in *Indian-White Relations: A Persistent Paradox*, ed. Jane F. Smith and Robert M. Kvasnicka, 160.

8. Tatum, *Our Red Brothers*, 10; Hagan, *United States–Comanche Relations*, 61–63.

9. *Annual Report of the Commissioner of Indian Affairs* (hereafter cited as *ARCIA*), 1872, p. 396. This amounted to what Keller describes as a policy devoted to three contradictory ends: "Protecting Indian rights, promoting westward expansion, and protecting American citizens." (*American Protestantism*, 11.)

10. Hagan, *United States–Comanche Relations*, 158.

11. *ARCIA*, 1870, p. 725.

12. James M. Kyle, "How Shall the Indians Be Educated?" *North American Review* 159 (November 1894): 437; Heth quoted in Laurence F. Schmeckebier, *The Office of Indian Affairs*, 72; Utley, *Last Days of the Sioux Nation*, 38; Keller, *American Protestantism*, 10.

13. Methvin quoted in John Jasper Methvin, *In the Limelight; or, A History of Anadarko and Vicinity*, 50. See Hagan, "Five Agents in Eight Years," *United States–Comanche Relations*, chap. 8, for a revealing discussion of agents. Speaking at the Lake Mohonk Conference in 1893, Merrill Gates complained that "under the pretentious name of 'home rule' senators and representatives were allowed to dictate the nomination, as agents, of perfectly worthless men." Indian Service appointments, he said, "should cease to be part plunder, awarded to partisan workers to build up party interest" (Annual Report of the Lake Mohonk Conference in *ARCIA*, 1893, no. 1017); Robert Keller properly warns against the temptation to cast all agents as frauds and criminals. Citing William Unrau's work, Keller notes that "what is needed . . . are specific agency studies that carefully examine what actually happened on a reservation apart from the constant accusations and claims of fraud that beset almost every agency." (*American Protestantism*, 248, n.27.) The evidence for the Kiowa-Comanche-Apache Reservation suggests that what Keller labels the "corrupt agent mythology" is, in fact, often accurate.

For a comparison of other agencies, see William Unrau, "The Civilian as Indian Agent: Villian or Victim," *Western Historical Quarterly* 3 (October 1972): 405–20; Unrau, "Indian Agent vs. the Army," *Kansas Historical Quarterly* 30 (Summer 1964): 129–52; John C. Paige, "Wichita Indian Agents, 1857–1869," *Journal of the West* 12 (July 1973): 403–13.

14. N. L. Purnell to Charles Adams, March 11, 1890, Employees' Files, Records of the Kiowa Agency, Indian Archives Division, Oklahoma Historical Society, Oklahoma City (hereafter cited as OHS).

15. J. J. Barett to Frank Baldwin, June 2, 1897; Harry Veidt to Adams, June 22, 1890; Morgan Savage to Adams, January 9, 1891; Mary Shirk to James Randlett, July 3, 1903, Agents and Agency Files, Records of the Kiowa Agency, ibid.

16. Steele, "Beginning of Quaker Administration of Indian Affairs in Oklahoma," 371.

17. George Chandler to George Day, November 18, 1891, Agents and Agency Files, Records of the Kiowa Agency, OHS.

18. *Annual Report of the Central Superintendency* (hereafter cited as *ARCS*), 1870, p. 718; *ARCIA*, 1872, pp. 429, 632. Thirty years later not much seemed to have changed. In an 1899 letter to Kiowa-Comanche Agent James Randlett, Commissioner William A. Jones admitted that "heretofore it has been a source of great annoyance to me personally, and you can imagine what relief it is to me to be able to put it entirely out of my mind" (William A. Jones to Randlett, November 11, 1899, Agents and Agency Files, Records of the Kiowa Agency, OHS).

19. *ARCS*, 1875, p. 768; Field Matron's Weekly Report, March 31, 1897, Field Matron's Files, Records of the Kiowa Agency, Microfilm KA 72, OHS.

20. *ARCS*, 1871, p. 876. For discussions of the Kiowa agency and reservation experience, see Michael D. Mitchell, "Acculturation Problems among the Plains Tribes of the Government Agencies in Western Indian Territory," *Chronicles of Oklahoma* 44 (Autumn 1966): 281–89; Forrest Monahan, "The Kiowa-Comanche Reservation in the 1890s," *Chronicles of Oklahoma* 45 (Winter 1967–68): 451–63; Hugh D. Corwin, "Protestant Mission Work among the Comanches and Kiowas," *Chronicles of Oklahoma* 46 (Spring 1968): 41–57; Martha Buntin, "History of the Kiowa, Comanche, and Wichita Agency," *Panhandle-Plains Historical Review* 4 (Spring 1931): 62–78; William D. Pennington, "Government Policies and Farming on the Kiowa-Comanche Reservation, 1869–1901" (Ph.D. diss., University of Oklahoma, 1972); William Hagan, "Kiowas, Comanches, and Cattlemen," *Pacific Historical Review* 40 (August 1971): 333–55. For a comparison of a neighboring agency and reservation, see Donald Berthrong, *The Cheyenne and Arapaho Ordeal: Reservation and Agency Life in the Indian Territory, 1875–1907*.

21. *ARCS*, 1870, p. 729.

22. Josiah Butler, "Pioneer School Teaching at the Comanche–Kiowa Agency School, 1870–1873," *Chronicles of Oklahoma* 6 (December 1928): 499–500.

23. Ibid., 500. See Butler's report to Tatum, July 27, 1871, Fort Sill School Files, OHS.

24. Thomas C. Battey, *The Life and Adventures of a Quaker among the Indians*, 39. For Tatum's account of the school, see *Our Red Brothers*, 93–106; *ARCIA*, 1870, p. 588.

A good summary of education on the Kiowa-Comanche Reservation may be found in George Posey Wild, "History of Education of Plains Indians of Southwest Oklahoma since the Civil War" (Ph.D. diss., University of Oklahoma, 1941). Although Wild's interpretation of the benefits of education and its success in eradicating what he clearly thought were heathen savage cultural traits is discomforting, his narrative history of the agency's various schools is the most complete ever written.

25. Ruby W. Shannon, *Friends for the Indian: 100 Years of Education at Riverside Indian School*, 3. This is a personal memoir and history of Riverside written by a former teacher.

26. Tatum recorded Battey's sign from the Lord this way: "[On] March 30th, 1872, he distinctly heard the question audibly addressed to him by the Lord 'What if thou should have to go and sojourn in the Kiowa camps?' " (Tatum, *Our Red Brothers*, 101). Moore, "Schools and Education among the Kiowas and Comanches," 16. Battey's account is in *The Life and Adventures of a Quaker among the Indians*, 115–35.

27. Shannon, *Friends for the Indian*, 7–9.

28. *ARCIA*, 1873, p. 588. Tatum's account is in *Our Red Brothers*, 101–106.

29. A. J. Vail, *A Memorial of James M. Haworth*, 87; Wild, "History of the Education of Plains Indians of Southwest Oklahoma since the Civil War," 67–68. Hagan records the decision to create the school board with considerably less enthusiasm than Wild and Vail show. Calling it "a quixotic move that apparently achieved little," Hagan expresses the opinion that Indian parents were not eager to enroll their children in the first place, and he does not believe that the school board improved relations on that matter. See *United States-Comanche Relations*, 134.

30. *ARCIA*, 1876, pp. 398–99; 1875, p. 567; *Annual Report of the Kiowa Agency* (hereafter cited as *ARKA*) in *ARCIA*, 1875, p. 775.

31. *ARKA*, 1877, p. 484; 1880, p. 195; Agent's Reports for 1895, Records of the Kiowa Agency, OHS.

32. *ARKA*, 1885, pp. 311–12; 1877, p. 484.

33. Ibid., 1879, pp. 174–75.

34. Ibid., 1879, pp. 174–75; 1880, p. 197; 1881, pp. 141–42; 1887, pp. 164–65; 1892, pp. 386, 640; Hagan, *United States-Comanche Relations*, 199–200. Wild, "History of Education of Plains Indians," suggests that the primary reason for Comanche obstinacy was that they "objected to their children attending school with the Kiowa" (p. 227). For corroboration, see Agent W. D. Myers's annual report from 1889, when he noted that the Comanches were "still clamorous for a school of their own," an attitude which he attributed to "tribal prejudice" (*ARKA*, 1889, p. 189).

35. *ARKA*, 1882, p. 130; 1884, p. 125; 1885, p. 311.

36. Ibid., 1888, pp. 95, 97; 1889, pp. 188–89.

37. Morgan to Charles Adams, March 28, 1891, Employees' Files, Records of the Kiowa Agency, OHS; Annual Report of the Superintendent of Indian Schools, 48th Cong., 1st sess., 1883. H. Doc. 1, 469.

38. C. F. Larrabee to Lloyd Click, October 11, 1907, Rainy Mountain School Files, Records of the Kiowa Agency, OHS (hereafter cited as RMS, OHS).

39. Supervising Principal, Kiowa Schools, to Mary C. Short, September 12, 1913, RMS, OHS; Cyrus Cook to John Richardson, November 10, 1871; Phebe

Cook to Richardson, February 12, 1872, Church Files, 1870–1925, Records of the Kiowa Agency, OHS.

40. Matthew Wahlstrom to Hunt, October 30, 1879, Church Files, 1870–1925, Records of the Kiowa Agency, OHS.

41. H. S. B. Ashby to Hunt, June 28, 1882; Charles Brown to Hunt, April 2, 1882; Unknown to Hunt, March 27, 1882; W. Officer to Adams, November 1, 1890, Church Files, 1870–1925, Records of the Kiowa Agency, OHS; Shannon, *Friends for the Indian*, 78–79.

42. Hagan, *United States–Comanche Relations*, 195–96; Thomas Jefferson Morgan to George Day, December 16, 1891, and February 6, 1892, Employees' Files, Records of the Kiowa Agency, OHS; Utley, *Last Days of the Sioux Nation*, 38.

43. Quote on schools as asylums from Report of Inspector Armstrong, September 7, 1885, Agents' Reports, Records of the Kiowa Agency, Microfilm KA 14, OHS. This passage rests heavily on the discussion in Hagan, *United States–Comanche Relations*, 195–97.

44. C. C. Painter, *Condition of Indian Affairs in Indian Territory and California*, 39; Wild, "History of the Education of Plains Indians," 86. Hagan, *United States–Comanche Relations*, also has an account of this inspection; see 196.

45. Marital status of employees taken from a list of school employees dated July 12, 1902; James McGregor to Stecker, January 9, 1911, RMS, OHS.

46. The phrase is from a letter from Commissioner of Indian Affairs Robert Valentine to Agent Stecker, January 30, 1909, ibid. This letter concerned complaints about the hiring of a white woman as assistant seamstress at Rainy Mountain at a salary more suited to the pay scale applied to Indians.

47. Jennie Jackson to Randlett, December 28, 1899; Cora Dunn to Randlett, February 19, 1900, ibid.

48. McGregor to Stecker, January 29, 1912, ibid.

49. Report of the Fort Lapwai School, *ARCIA*, 1892, p. 662; Report of the Haskell School, ibid., 1892, pp. 664–65; Annual Report of the Pine Ridge Agency, ibid., 1893, p. 288; Annual Report of the La Pointe Agency, ibid., 1893, p. 348.

50. Annual Report of the Crow Creek Agency, ibid., 1894, p. 277; Report of the Oneida School, ibid., 1994, p. 229.

51. Annual Report of the Rosebud Agency, ibid., pp. 293–98. Emphasis added.

52. Muriel Wright, *A Guide to the Indian Tribes of Oklahoma*, 174. For a summary of the mission schools on the Kiowa-Comanche Agency, see Wild, "History of Education of Plains Indians," 150–90.

53. *ARKA*, 1889, p. 189; 1890, p. 188; William F. Vargas to John Oberly, December 13, 1888; Oberly to W. D. Myers, December 22, 1888; Thomas J. Morgan to George Day, February 3, 1893; 1894 Annual Report of the Mary Gregory Memorial Mission, Kiowa Schools, Records of the Kiowa Agency, Microfilm KA 96, OHS.

54. *ARKA*, 1889, p. 189; 1890, p. 189. The quote on Methvin is from Sidney H. Black and John Younger Bryce, *The History of Methodism in Oklahoma:*

The Story of the Indian Mission Annual Conference of the Methodist Episcopal Church, South I: 237; Hagan, *United States–Comanche Relations,* 199. See also Sidney H. Babcock, "John Jasper Methvin," *Chronicles of Oklahoma* 19 (June 1941): 113–18.

55. Eugenia Mausape interview, September 14, 1967, T-138-A: 27, Doris Duke Oral History Collection, Western History Collections, University of Oklahoma Library Archives, Norman.

56. Methvin's comment about "vile misrepresentations" is in Bruce David Forbes, "John Jasper Methvin: Methodist 'Missionary to the Western Tribes' (Oklahoma)," in *Churchmen and the Western Indians, 1820–1920,* ed. Clyde A. Milner II and Floyd A. O'Neil, 41–73. For comments on the Methvin Institute, consult 55–65.

57. W. W. Carithers to Randlett, March 26, 1905; Thomas J. Morgan to Charles Adams, August 12, September 11, November 5, 1890; Reverend J. S. Morrow to Morgan, May 7, 1891, Kiowa Schools, Records of the Kiowa Agency, Microfilm KA 96, OHS; *ARKA,* 1889, p. 189; 1890, p. 188.

58. *Annual Report of Superintendent of Indian Education* (hereafter cited as *ARSIE*) in *ARCIA,* 1883, p. 475; *ARKA,* 1892, pp. 385, 475; 1880, pp. 364–65; 1897, p. 232.

59. Hagan, *United States–Comanche Relations,* 134; *ARCIA,* 1882, p. 34; *ARSIE,* 1885, pp. 83–84.

60. *ARSIE,* 1883, pp. 475–76; 1885, p. 83.

61. *ARCIA,* 1880, pp. 85–86; 1918, p. 177. The estimate on school children is from Hagan, *United States–Comanche Relations,* 134.

62. For a useful assessment of the Indian Office that helps to explain the administrative lethargy and political limitations of the era, see Leonard D. White, *The Republican Era, 1869–1901: A Study in Administrative History,* especially chap. 9, "The Department of the Interior." White observes that the department had "no semblance of unity" and was charged with so many disparate tasks that it ought to have been called "the Department of the Great Miscellany" (p. 175).

CHAPTER 3

1. *Annual Report of the Kiowa Agency* (hereafter cited as *ARKA*), in *Annual Report of the Commissioner of Indian Affairs* (hereafter cited as *ARCIA*), 1890, pp. 187–88.

2. For representative evaluations of conditions on the reservation see *ARCIA,* 1875, p. 567; 1887, pp. 164–65; *Annual Report of the Central Superintendency,* in ibid., pp. 766, 768, 775; *ARKA,* 1877, p. 484.

3. *ARKA,* 1892, p. 891; Thomas Jefferson Morgan to John Richardson, July 27, 1891; Richardson to Morgan, August 15, 1891; Morgan to George Day, January 14, 1892; Rainy Mountain School Files, Records of the Kiowa Agency, Indian Archives Division, Oklahoma Historical Society, Oklahoma City (hereafter cited as RMS, OHS).

4. Richardson to Morgan, August 15, 1891, ibid.

5. Morgan to Day, August 23, 1891, ibid.

6. Morgan to Day, August 26, 1892; George Moss to Day, May 11, 1892, ibid.

7. Morgan to Day, June 24, November 14, 1892, ibid.

8. Morgan to Moss, June 24, 1892; Day to Morgan, July 19, September 13, 14, 17, 1892; Morgan to Day, November 14, 1892, and February 3, 1893; Pay Voucher for Rainy Mountain School, September 30, 1892, ibid.

9. Richardson to Morgan, November 17, 1892; Morgan to Richardson, October 10, December 8, 1892, ibid.

10. Richardson to Morgan, February 28, 1893; Day to Morgan, February 24, 1893; Morgan to Day, March 10, April 17, 1893, ibid.

11. Acting Commissioner of Indian Affairs to Day, March 9, 1893; Pay Voucher for Rainy Mountain School, March 31, 1893; Cox to Day, March 17, 1893; Cox to D. W. Browning, April 5, 1893, Browning to Day, April 22, 1892, ibid.

12. Inventory list, February 15 and July 1, 1893, ibid.

13. Invoice from F. Barteldes, Lawrence, Kansas, March 25, 1893, ibid.

14. Pay Vouchers for Rainy Mountain School, June 30, September 30, December 31, 1893; Browning to Hugh Brown, October 20, November 24, 1893; Cox to Brown, November 28, 1893, ibid.

15. Browning to Brown, August 21, 1893, ibid.

16. William A. Jones to William Walker, June 15, 1898, Fort Sill School Files, Employee Records, Records of the Kiowa Agency, Indian Archives Division, Oklahoma Historical Society, Oklahoma City.

17. Isabel Crawford, *Kiowa: The History of a Blanket Indian Mission*, iv.

18. Cora Dunn to W. H. Able, November 6, 1894, RMS, OHS.

19. The figure is derived from a 1912 annual statement on government buildings and improvements at the campus. The list, in RMS, OHS, shows these structures: boys' dormitory (1892, $12,000), girls' dormitory (1899, $12,000), superintendent's cottage (1899, $1,200), farmer's cottage (1894, $500), laundry (1894, $2,000), pump house (1900, $400), playroom and lavatory (1896, $400), mess hall (1899, $8,000), stable (1895, $525), and two small stone storage houses (1895, $400 each).

20. Cox to Browning, May 3, 1894; Browning to Nichols, May 16, 1894, RMS, OHS.

21. Figures are derived from weekly supply invoices and quarterly attendance reports that listed all enrolled students by sex, age, and grade.

22. Cora Dunn to Browning, November 6, 1894, RMS, OHS.

23. Cora Dunn to Frank Baldwin, December 13, 1894, ibid.

24. Cora Dunn to Baldwin, August 3, 1897, ibid.

25. Cora Dunn to Baldwin, January 4, 11, 1897; A. M. Dunn to Baldwin, October 1, 1897, ibid.

26. A. M. Dunn to Baldwin, August 23, 1897; Cora Dunn to James Randlett, July 17, 1903, ibid.

27. Cora Dunn to Randlett, February 15, 1904; Cora Dunn to Randlett, March 19, 1905, ibid.

28. A. M. Dunn to Baldwin, August 23, 1897; A. G. Turner to Baldwin, September 24, 1897; William A. Jones to Baldwin, October 26, 1897, ibid.

29. Cora Dunn to John Blackmon, January 6, 1906, ibid.

30. Richardson to Morgan, August 15, 1891, ibid.

31. Morgan to Day, December 8, 1892; Cox to Nichols, July 2, 1894; Cox to Nichols, August 30, 1894, ibid.; Parker McKenzie to Bill Welge, June 6, 1990, in the possession of the author. An undated but early map at the Oklahoma Historical Society clearly indicates a spring south of the school.

32. Dunn to Browning, July 6, 1895, RMS, OHS.

33. Browning to Baldwin, August 3, 1895; Cora Dunn to Browning, August 26, 1895; Browning to Baldwin, September 13, 1895, ibid.

34. Browning to Baldwin, March 28, 1896; Cora Dunn to Browning, March 14, 1896; Voucher to D. Farriss, June 19, 1896; Voucher to J. A. Rose, June 23, 1896; Voucher to Herman Veidt, June 25, 1896; A. M. Dunn to Baldwin, November 12, 1896, ibid.

35. A. M. Dunn to Veidt, December 7, 1896, ibid.

36. A. M. Dunn to Baldwin, March 21, 24, 1897; A. M. Dunn to Baldwin, April 11, May 5, 1897, ibid.

37. Thomas Smith to Baldwin, May 5, 1897; A. M. Dunn to Baldwin, June 2, 6, 1897; Thomas Smith to Baldwin, June 11, 1897, ibid.

38. A. M. Dunn to Baldwin, June 25, 1897; William A. Jones to Baldwin, August 17, 1897, ibid.

39. A. M. Dunn to Baldwin, August 17, October 1, 22, 1897; Jones to Baldwin, December 9, 1897; A. M. Dunn to Baldwin, January 4, 1898, ibid.

40. McKenzie to Welge, June 6, 1990; Cora Dunn to James Randlett, October 19, 1900; Cora Dunn to Jones, March 15, 1901, RMS, OHS. The reservoir remains visible today as a notch in the mountain's south side near the summit. Concrete footings and bits of pumping machinery are still in place. In the winter the trace left by the pipes that snaked down to the campus is clearly visible.

41. Cora Dunn to Randlett, February 8 and September 26, 1900; Cora Dunn to Randlett, May 7, 1902, and July 17, 1903; Randlett to Cora Dunn, September 9, 1903, ibid.

42. This is discussed in greater detail in chapter 6.

43. Cora Dunn to Randlett, August 21, 1903; Invoice of September 1903, RMS, OHS.

44. Cora Dunn to Blackmon, November 23, 1905, and October 3, 1906; Cora Dunn to Charles Ellis, October 29, 1906, ibid.

45. Cora Dunn to Blackmon, February 9, May 23, 1906, ibid.

46. Cora Dunn to S. A. Johnson, November 4, 1895; Cora Dunn to Baldwin, November 27, 1895, ibid.

47. Cora Dunn to Baldwin, November 28, 1894; Cora Dunn to Randlett, December 22, 1899; Cora Dunn to Randlett, April 18, 1905; C. F. Larrabee to Randlett, April 28, 1905; Charles McNichols to Randlett, June 5, 1905, ibid. Employee statistics are derived from the school's quarterly reports.

48. Cora Dunn to Stecker, September 1, 1909, ibid.

49. Cora Dunn to Randlett, March 6, 1902, and February 8, 1903; Cora Dunn to Baldwin, September 4, 1895, ibid.; Sally J. McBeth, *Ethnic Identity and the Boarding School Experience of West-Central Oklahoma American Indians*, 94. Rainy Mountain's problems became so severe in 1898 that the commissioner

authorized criminal proceedings against at least one employee who had left the school and failed to return when promised, an act the commissioner described as "a grave dereliction of duty" (see William A. Jones to W. T. Walker, September 28, 1898, RMS, OHS).

50. Mary Fleeman to Randlett, March 9, 1905; George J. Williams to Baldwin, October 7, 1896, RMS, OHS.

51. C. F. Larrabee to Alice B. Moncure, November 1, 1907; Moncure to Blackmon, November 24, 1907; F. M. Conser to Blackmon, December 7, 1907; Cora Dunn to Blackmon, December 14, 1907, ibid.

52. Cora Dunn to Blackmon, January 18, 1906, ibid.

53. Cora Dunn to Randlett, October 28, 1901, ibid.

54. A. C. Tonner to W. T. Walker, October 22, 1898, ibid.

55. Cora Dunn to Jones, July 6, 1899, ibid.

56. Cora Dunn to Randlett, January 1, 1903; Cora Dunn to Frederick Barbour, April 4, 1903; Cora Dunn to Blackmon, October 18, 1906, ibid.

57. Cora Dunn to Randlett, April 17, 1903; Cora Dunn to Stecker, March 12, 1908, ibid.

CHAPTER 4

1. A recently published collection of essays suggests that scholars remain reluctant to acknowledge an Indian voice. "As with so much of American Indian history," writes Philip Weeks in *The American Indian Experience, a Profile: 1524 to the Present,* "it can best be told from the framework of white history." Incredibly he adds that "it was, and largely is, whites who so influentially and dramatically affected the American Indians, their lives, culture, and history," xi.

In fact, there are important studies that demolish such simplistic and distorted interpretations. Former students have left memoirs that give us an insider's view. Three of the best are Francis LaFlesche, *The Middle Five: Indian Schoolboys of the Omaha Tribe;* Jim Whitewolf, *The Life of a Kiowa-Apache Indian,* especially 83–97, "Going to School"; and Helen Sekaquaptewa, *Me and Mine: The Life Story of Helen Sekaquaptewa as Told to Louise Updall,* especially 91–108, 121–43. See also Robert A. Trennert, Jr., *The Phoenix Indian School: Forced Assimilation in Arizona, 1891–1935,* especially chap. 6; Basil H. Johnston, *Indian School Days;* Sally J. McBeth, *Ethnic Identity and the Boarding School Experience of West-Central Oklahoma American Indians;* Devon A. Mihesuah, *Cultivating the Rosebuds: The Education of Women at the Cherokee Female Seminary, 1851–1909;* K. Tsianina Lomawaima, *They Called It Prairie Light: The Story of Chilocco Indian School;* and Henrietta Mann, "Cheyenne-Arapaho Education, 1871–1982" (Ph.D. diss., University of New Mexico, 1982). Among the very best recent studies is Michael C. Coleman, *American Indian Children at School, 1850–1920.* His use of the autobiographical voice is compelling in its ability to uncover and compare important aspects of the Indian school experience.

2. McBeth's *Ethnic Identity and the Boarding School Experience* relies heavily on oral histories, especially the Doris Duke Collection, and points the

way toward a student-centered discussion of schools on the Kiowa-Comanche-Apache Reservation. Her methodology directly influenced this study.

3. Coleman, *American Indian Children in School*, 197–98.

4. Lomawaima, *They Called It Prairie Light*, xvi. The use of oral accounts continues to trouble some historians, who insist that such sources are unreliable. Indeed, one historian once told me that he refuses to use oral history because "there is nothing a twentieth century Indian can tell me about a nineteenth century Indian."

5. Thomas Jefferson Morgan to George Day, November 14, 1892, Rainy Mountain School Files, Records of the Kiowa Agency, Indian Archives Division, Oklahoma Historical Society, Oklahoma City (hereafter cited as RMS, OHS).

6. Circular 148, April 6, 1885, issued by the Secretary of the Interior to Agents, Census Files, Records of the Kiowa Agency, Microfilm KA 2, Indian Archives Division, Oklahoma Historical Society, Oklahoma City (hereafter cited as OHS).

7. McBeth identifies six reasons for attending the boarding schools: 1. Attendance would enable children to cope more effectively with a changing cultural environment. ("Now," said one Kiowa-Apache man, "we in White man's world. Today. We got to go that way.") 2. Schools provided clothes and other necessities. ("I wanted to go home and be with momma," recalled one former student, "but she said, 'Well, if you come home we'll only be eating one meal a day, and so I think you should go to Riverside.' ") 3. Death of a parent often meant the child was sent away to school. 4. Children went because their friends were there. 5. They went because of difficulty in the public schools and embarrassment over poor performance. 6. They attended for the opportunity to associate with other Indians. McBeth, *Ethnic Identity and the Boarding School*, 108–111. See also Lomawaima, *They Called It Prairie Light*, 32–44.

8. Myrtle Paudlety Ware interview, November 11, 1967, T-76: 2; Annie Bigman interview, June 14, 1971, M-1:3, Doris Duke Oral History Collection, Western History Collections, University of Oklahoma Library Archives, Norman (hereafter cited as DDOH).

9. Guy Quoetone interview, March 23, 1971, T-37:16, ibid.

10. "Happy 90th Birthday Lewis Toyebo, February 28, 1982," commemorative birthday celebration reminiscence in the possession of Mrs. Ruby Williams of Fort Cobb, Oklahoma (hereafter cited as "Lewis Toyebo Birthday"); Cora Dunn to John Blackmon, January 30, 1906, RMS, OHS.

11. Sarah Long Horn interview, June 27, 1967, T-62:6–7, DDOH.

12. Fred Bigman interview, June 14, 1967, T-50:24–26, ibid.

13. James Haumpy interview, July 11, 1967, T-81:6, ibid.

14. Parker McKenzie to the author, August 1, 1990.

15. *Annual Report of the Kiowa Agency* (hereafter cited as *ARKA*) in *Annual Report of the Commissioner of Indian Affairs* (hereafter cited as *ARCIA*), 1896, p. 255; U.S. Congress, Senate, 56th Cong., 1st sess., 1900, S. Doc. 76, Serial 3850, pp. 9–10; Eugenia Mausape interview, T-37:200; Cecil Horse interview, T-27:191–92, DDOH.

16. Bruce David Forbes, "John Jasper Methvin: Methodist 'Missionary to

the Western Tribes' (Oklahoma)," in *Churchmen and the Western Indians, 1820–1920*, ed. Clyde A. Milner II and Floyd A. O'Neil, 64–65; Howard L. Harrod, *Mission among the Blackfeet*, 21.

17. *ARKA*, 1891, p. 351; 1896, p. 254; Big Tree to James Randlett, August 30, 1905, RMS, OHS; Inspection Report of the Kiowa Agency, June 10, 1897, Agents' Reports, Records of the Kiowa Agency, OHS; Whitewolf, *Life of a Kiowa-Apache*, 83.

18. Cora Dunn to Randlett, September 5, 14, 1900; Cora Dunn to John Blackmon, September 2, 1907, RMS, OHS.

19. Cora Dunn to Randlett, September 25, 1899; James McGregor to Charles Eggars, December 29, 1913; Ernest Stecker to McGregor, December 30, 1913; McGregor to Stecker January 5, 1914, ibid.

20. Cora Dunn to Randlett, March 16, 1905; Cora Dunn to John Blackmon, September 11, 28, 1906, ibid.

21. William A. Jones to William T. Walker, October 1, 1898, ibid.; *ARCIA*, 1898, pp. 6–7. It is interesting to note, however, that by the early twentieth century the Indian Office was taking a different approach. In 1918 the Indian Office reminded field matrons that it was official policy to give each child "whose attendance was good, a sum of $25.00" at the close of the year (see J. Prickett to Mary Clouse, August 7, 1918, Field Matron's Files, Records of the Kiowa Agency, Microfilm KA 74, OHS).

22. Cora Dunn to Charles E. Ellis, October 23, 1906; Cora Dunn to Frank Baldwin, April 10, 1895; McGregor to Stecker, December 29, 1913, RMS, OHS.

23. David W. Adams, "Fundamental Considerations: The Deep Meaning of Native American Schooling, 1880–1900," *Harvard Educational Review* 58:1 (February 1988):13–14. Forbes, "John Jasper Methvin," 56.

24. McKenzie to the author, August 1, 1990.

25. Guy Quoetone interview, T-637:17, DDOH. For an interesting comparison, see Jim Whitewolf's account of his first day at the Kiowa School in 1891 in *Life of a Kiowa-Apache*, 83–84.

26. Guy Quoetone interview, T-637:21; Annie Bigman interview, June 15, 1967, T-57:16; Sarah Long Horn interview, June 27, 1967, T-62:9,; Juanita Yeahquo interview, June 21, 1967, M-2:8, DDOH; "Lewis Toyebo Birthday."

27. Powell cited in Francis Paul Prucha, *The Great Father: The United States Government and the American Indians* II: 674; see also Daniel F. Littlefield, Jr., and Lonnie E. Underhill, "Renaming the American Indian, 1890–1913," *American Studies* 12 (Fall 1971): 33–45; "Lewis Toyebo Birthday"; Forbes, "John Jasper Methvin," 56–57. Students also received birthdates. Parker McKenzie remembered that most students were assigned a birthday on either the first or the fifteenth of a particular month.

28. "Lewis Toyebo Birthday"; McKenzie to Randle Hurst, October 23, 1987, in the possession of the author; Myrtle Ware interview, T-76:4, DDOH; Parker McKenzie to Former Rainy Mountain Students, June 14, 1963, photocopy in the possession of the author.

29. William T. Hagan, *United States–Comanche Relations: The Reservation Years*, 198; McKenzie to Hurst, October 23, 1987; McBeth, *Ethnic Identity*

and the Boarding School, 99–100. In 1890 the Indian Office issued "Rules for Indian Schools," which stated that "in play and in work, as far as possible . . . they must be kept entirely apart" (*ARCIA,* 1890, pp. cl–clii).

30. Sarah Longhorn interview, T-62:10; Fred Bigman interview, T-50:24, DDOH.

31. Fred Bigman interview, T-50:24, ibid.; Parker McKenzie, "How Written Kiowa Came Into Being," n.d., manuscript in the possession of the author.

32. McBeth, *Ethnic Identity and the Boarding School,* 102–103.

33. McKenzie to the author, August 1, 1990; McKenzie to Hurst, October 23, 1987.

34. McKenzie to Hurst, October 23, 1987; Juanita Yeahquo interview, M-2:8, DDOH; McBeth, *Ethnic Identity and the Boarding School,* 105.

35. Sarah Long Horn interview, T-62:10; Myrtle Ware interview, T-76:5, DDOH; Whitewolf, *Life of a Kiowa-Apache,* 87–90.

36. Myrtle Ware interview, T-76:10, DDOH; McKenzie to Hurst, October 23, 1987. Parker McKenzie said that during his years at Rainy Mountain, and later at the Phoenix Indian School, he and his fellow Kiowas eagerly sought one another out to practice their language. Although some lost their language, most seemed to retain it. McBeth has written that "the retention of Native languages is relevant to ethnic interests because a language can express a system of social values and lend credence to a social group" (*Ethnic Identity and the Boarding School,* 134–35).

For a similar appraisal see James Merrell, *The Indians' New World: Catawbas and their Neighbors from European Contact through the Era of Removal.* "Language expresses a people's collective consciousness, its own special way of interpreting the world. By itself, then, language is both a vehicle for transmitting the essence of a culture and a powerful tool of socialization in that culture. It leads people to speak—and therefore also to think—according to established formulas. Indians brought up to think Catawba during the mid-nineteenth century were equipped to cross the threshold into the mental world of their ancestors," (262–63).

This sentiment is repeatedly expressed in the Oklahoma Indian community, where many consider the retention of native languages a vital part of contemporary Indian life. "I've given many things up to become a member of this country," one man (who was a boarding school student in the 1930s) told me at a memorial dance for the Kiowa chief Setainte in the summer of 1990. "But I will tell you one thing, there's one thing I'll never give up, and that's my language."

37. R. W. Bishoff to C. V. Stinchecum, March 20, 1918, RMS, OHS.

38. Dorothy W. Hewes, "Those First Good Years of Indian Education: 1894 to 1898," *American Indian Culture and Research Journal* 5, no. 2 (1981): 74.

39. Annie Bigman interview, T-57:18–19; Fred Bigman interview, T-50:27–28, DDOH. One Rainy Mountain student told me that after one student was whipped so savagely that he died, administrators covered up the incident by reporting the death as the result of pneumonia.

40. McBeth, *Ethnic Identity and the Boarding School,* 106–107; Cora Dunn to Baldwin, May 27, 1895, RMS, OHS.

41. Cora Dunn to Randlett, February 13, 1900, RMS, OHS.
42. McBeth, *Ethnic Identity and the Boarding School*, 86–87.
43. James Haumpy interview, T-81:6, DDOH.
44. Nora Cailis to Casper Cailis, January 6, 1916, Field Matron Files, Records of the Kiowa Agency, Microfilm KA 74, OHS.
45. S. W. McMichael Statement, April 14, 1909, from "Report on Case of Miss Arthie Edworthy, Assistant Matron, Rainy Mountain School, April 24, 1909," Establishment or Abolition of Schools, Kiowa Agency Classified Files, 1907–39, Record Group 75, National Archives, Washington, D.C. (hereafter cited as KA, NA).
46. Sydney Holmes Statement, April 14, 1909; Corwin Boake Statement, April 14, 1909; Cecil Horse Statement, April 15, 1909; ibid.
47. Arthur Curtis Statement, April 20, 1909; Louis Toyebo Statement, April 15, 1909; Arthie Edworthy Statement, April 21, 1909, ibid. Cora Dunn to Stecker, April 1, 1909; Descriptive Statement of Changes in School Employees, March 8, 1909; James McGregor to Stecker, July 16, 1910; J. H. Dortch to Stecker, August 3, 1910; C. F. Hauke to Arthie Edworthy, August 8, 1910, RMS, OHS.
Hagan provides several similar examples, one of which involved a young Kiowa widow and a Methodist minister who became romantically involved at the Kiowa School in 1889. After ordering the minister from the agency, Agent W. D. Myers discovered the man at the school again, ordered him jailed for a day and a night, and then had him escorted to the Texas border by the police. When the man pleaded with the agent for permission to marry the Kiowa woman, Myers denounced him as a wretch whose "hypocritical form" had made him a "villain who would under the cloak of religion accomplish the ruin of a woman." Hagan also notes that a teacher and matron at the Kiowa School were forced to resign after he was seen leaving her room in his stocking feet (*United States–Comanche Relations*, 197–98).
48. *ARCIA*, 1895, p. 6.
49. *Annual Report of the Superintendent of Indian Schools* in *ARCIA*, 1902, pp. 420–21.
50. McBeth, *Ethnic Identity and the Boarding School*, 89. Lomawaima makes the revealing argument that not only was the Indian school curriculum poorly administered and planned, but it also "ran counter to developments in mainstream America." The craftsmanship and apprenticeship programs typical of Indian schools were decades out of line with prevailing attitudes in American business and education (see *They Called It Prairie Light*, 65–72). For evaluations of what those attitudes were, see Lawrence Cremin, *American Education: The National Experience, 1783–1876*; Lawrence Cremin, *American Education: The Metropolitan Experience, 1876–1980*, especially chap. 3, "Patterns of Diversity"; Lawrence Cremin, *The Transformation of the School*; Michael Katz, *Class, Bureaucracy, and Schools: The Illusion of Educational Changes in America*, especially chap. 3, "Twentieth-Century School Reform: Notes Toward a History"; Joel Spring, *The American School, 1642–1990: Varieties of Historical Interpretation of the Foundations and Development of American Education*, 2d ed., especially chap. 7, "Schooling and the New Corporate Or-

218 NOTES TO PAGES 113–20

der," and chap. 9, "Meritocracy: The Experts Take Charge"; Rush Welter, *Popular Education and Democratic Thought in America*; and Raymond Callahan, *Education and the Cult of Efficiency*.

51. Rainy Mountain Indian School Calendar, 1913–14, RMS, OHS. This regimen was typical of other schools as well. For a discussion of the similarities at a Choctaw mission school, for example, consult Christopher J. Huggard, "Culture Mixing: Everyday Life on Missions among the Choctaws," *Chronicles of Oklahoma* 70 (Winter 1992–93): 432–49; see also Wilma A. Daddario, " 'They Get Milk Practically Every Day,' The Genoa Indian Industrial School, 1884–1934," *Nebraska History* 73 (Spring 1992): 2–11.

52. Geneve Albright Burford, "Prairie Lore," quoted in "Rainy Mountain School Experiences," *Anadarko Daily News*, August 15–16, 1987, p. 2.

53. Juanita Yeahquo interview, M-2:8, DDOH; "Rules For Indian Schools, 1890," quoted in Francis Paul Prucha, *The Churches and the Indian Schools, 1888–1912*, 161–62; McBeth, *Ethnic Identity and the Boarding School*, 100.

54. Mary Clouse to C. V. Stinchecum, November 3, 1915, Field Matron's Files, Records of the Kiowa Agency, Microfilm KA 74, OHS.

55. See *ARCIA*, 1916, pp. 9–23. Despite the obvious differences between nonreservation schools such as Carlisle and reservation schools such as Rainy Mountain, the same general themes and goals predominated. The central distinctions between the two were scale and intensity. In his work on Indian school girls, Robert Trennert has observed that the guiding principle at nonreservation schools was identical to that at smaller schools: to "transform them into a government version of the ideal American woman." Cora Dunn was trying to do the same thing at Rainy Mountain. Moreover, notes Trennert, Carlisle, Phoenix, and other nonreservation schools "generally failed to attain . . . [their] goals" (Robert Trennert, "Educating Indian Girls at Nonreservation Boarding Schools, 1878–1920," *Western Historical Quarterly* 13 [July 1982]: 169–90).

56. F. H. Abbott to Stecker, February 11, 1911; Quarterly Report for Indian Schools, December 1912; Cato Sells to Stecker, February 15, 1913, RMS, OHS.

57. McKenzie to Hurst, October 23, 1987; McKenzie, "How Written Kiowa Came into Being," n.d., photocopy in the possession of the author; C. F. Hauke to Stecker, March 10, 1915, RMS, OHS.

58. Mary Clouse to C. V. Stinchecum, November 17, 1916; Stinchecum to Clouse, December 15, 1916, Field Matron's Files, Records of the Kiowa Agency, Microfilm KA 74, OHS.

59. McKenzie to the author, August 1, 1990.

60. Fred Bigman interview, T-50:24–25, DDOH.

61. Ethel Howry interview, T-78:154, ibid.

62. Myrtle Ware interview, T-76:7–8, ibid.

63. Juanita Yeahquo interview, M-2:5; Sarah Long Horn interview, T-62:8–9, ibid. Lomawaima makes the same observation in her work on Chilocco.

64. Myrtle Ware interview, T-76:3, 5, DDOH.

65. William Lone Wolf interview, T-42:8, ibid.; McBeth, *Ethnic Identity and the Boarding School*, 92–93; McKenzie to Hurst, October 23, 1987; Whitewolf, *Life of a Kiowa-Apache*, 94.

66. Parker McKenzie interview, Mountain View, Okla., August 1, 1990;
Lillie McCoy to Baldwin, June 3, 1896, RMS, OHS; McBeth, *Ethnic Identity and
the Boarding School*, 97; Lucy Gage, "A Romance of Pioneering," *Chronicles of
Oklahoma* 29 (Summer 1951): 297; Sally Cowgill to John Q. Smith, August
8, 1875, cited in Hagan, *United States–Comanche Relations*, 134–35.

67. Fred Bigman interview, T-50:29; Guy Quoetone interview, T-149: n.p.,
DDOH.

68. McKenzie to the author, August 1, 1990; McKenzie to Mrs. Henry T.
Choquette, April 2, 1965, photocopy in the possession of the author.

69. Juanita Yeahquo interview, M-2:4, DDOH.

70. Parker McKenzie interview, August 1, 1990; Morgan to Indian Agents
and Superintendents of Indian Schools, October 22, 1891; Cora Dunn to Blackmon, December 12, 1905, RMS, OHS.

71. Cora Dunn to Randlett, May 27, June 4, 1905; J. H. Crickenberger to
J. W. Smith, June 20, 1915, ibid.

72. Cora Dunn to Browning, December 19, 1895, ibid.

73. Cora Dunn to B. F. Taylor, November 29, 1897; Cora Dunn to Randlett,
February 25, 1905, ibid.

74. Cora Dunn to Blackmon, April 25, 1907, ibid.; McKenzie to Hurst, October 23, 1987; McKenzie interview, August 1, 1990.

75. Hauke to Stecker, March 10, 1910; Stecker to Hauke, March 14, 1910,
KA, NA.

76. Cora Dunn to Randlett, April 23, 1902, RMS, OHS; "Lewis Toyebo
Birthday."

77. "Development of Extra-Curricular Activities at Rainy Mountain," n.d.,
from a packet compiled for a school reunion in June 1963, photocopy in the
possession of the author; Unknown to McGregor, October 29, 1912; R. W.
Bishoff to Stinchecum, March 16, 1917, RMS, OHS.

78. Rainy Mountain School Songs, ca. 1910–14, photocopies in the possession of the author, courtesy of Parker McKenzie.

79. James Silverhorn interview, September 28, 1967, T-146:4, DDOH.

80. McKenzie to Hurst, October 23, 1987; Whitewolf, *Jim Whitewolf*, 96;
Lomawaima reports that Chilocco boys maintained a skillfully hidden still,
They Called it Prairie Light, pp. 112, 115, 140–45.

81. McKenzie to Hurst, October 23, 1987.

82. Supply invoices, May 25, 1909, and April 25, 1910, RMS, OHS.

83. E. B. Meritt to McGregor, February 21, 1914, ibid.

84. Field Matron's Quarterly Reports: Mary Given, June 30, 1915; Mary
Clouse, July 14, 1915; Anna Heersma, June 30, 1915; Mary Wilkin, July 14,
1915, Field Matron's Files, Records of the Kiowa Agency, Microfilm KA 74,
OHS. In September 1915, Mary Clouse issued a stinging indictment against
what she called the "Dance Element," charging it with corrupting the morals
of the tribe's young people and tearing down the work of the schools. "These
dances are one of the breeding places of illegitimate children," she wrote,
"which is [sic] becoming the shame of the tribe. Lust is on the increase" (Mary
Clouse to Stinchecum, September 15, 1915, ibid.).

85. McKenzie to Hurst, October 23, 1987.
86. Sarah Long Horn interview, T-62:14, DDOH; "Lewis Toyebo Birthday."

CHAPTER 5

1. For an analysis of national trends, consult Lawrence Cremin, *American Education: The Metropolitan Experience, 1876–1980*, especially Part II, "The Progressive Nation"; and Lawrence Cremin, *The Transformation of the School: Progressivism in American Education, 1876–1957*, especially Part I, "The Progressive Impulse in Education, 1876–1917*." Cremin casts Progressive Era education in a generous light, describing it as humane and democratic, saying that it was "a vast humanitarian effort to apply the promise of American life . . . [that] implied the radical faith that culture could be democratized," viii–ix. For less sanguine accounts, see Raymond Callahan, *Education and the Cult of Efficiency*, and Michael B. Katz, *Class, Bureaucracy, and Schools: The Illusion of Educational Change in America*, in which Katz argues that one of the era's most important legacies is that "the government of school systems has continued to rest on a disdain for a large portion of students and their families" (p. 116). Certainly this sentiment can be applied to Indian schools after the turn of the century. See Frederick Hoxie, *A Final Promise: The Campaign to Assimilate the Indians, 1880–1920*, especially chaps. 1–3; Robert Trennert, "Selling Indian Education at World's Fairs and Expositions, 1893–1904," *American Indian Quarterly* 11 (Summer 1987): 217–18.

2. *Annual Report of the Commissioner of Indian Affairs* (hereafter cited as *ARCIA*), 1892, p. 55; 1920, p. 11. The best summary of the issues affecting Indian policy in this period is Hoxie, *A Final Promise*. For similar assessments, see Brian Dippie, *The Vanishing American: White Attitudes and U.S. Indian Policy*, especially 177–243; and Curtis M. Hinsley, Jr., *Savages and Scientists: The Smithsonian Institution and the Development of American Anthropology, 1846–1910*.

Hoxie's thesis is not unchallenged. Francis Paul Prucha believes that elements of continuity dominated the era. "Some social scientists," he writes, "preached a hierarchy of superior and inferior races; but the men who formulated federal Indian policy and programs did not accept such dogmas" (*The Great Father: The United States Government and the American Indians* II: 761). John Berens reached a similar conclusion in his essay on Progressive Indian policy. "Progressive Indian reform" did not exist, he argues, because the era did not bring about significant new directions in policy. "Neither the philosophy nor the programs of Indian reform were new," he writes. What occurred were "moderate changes" (see "Old Campaigners, New Realities: Indian Policy Reform in the Progressive Era, 1900–1912," *Mid-America* 59 [January 1977]: 51–52, 64). I believe the weight of the evidence makes Hoxie's interpretation more persuasive.

3. Robert F. Berkhofer, *The White Man's Indian: Images of the American Indian from Columbus to the Present*, 58–59. See also his comments on " 'Scientific' Racism and Human Diversity in Nineteenth-Century Social Sciences," 55–61. Hoxie charts the shift to racial determinism as coming fairly late in the nineteenth century; others see more continuity from an earlier period.

Berkhofer suggests that by the 1854 publication of *Types of Mankind; or, Ethnological Researchers,* leading voices had already accepted the shift to scientific racism: "The Barbarous races of America," wrote J. C. Nott (by which he meant nonwhites), "are essentially untameable" (*The White Man's Indian,* 58). Alden Vaughan agrees that such changes were already being felt by the 1850s. "By the middle of the nineteenth century," he writes, "the shift in Anglo-American perception had reached its logical conclusion: Indian culture was merely a reflection of primordial shortcomings and impervious to education or missionization." Citing *Types of Mankind,* Vaughan relates one observer's opinion: "It is vain to talk of civilizing [the Indians]. You might as well attempt to change the nature of the buffalo" ("From White Man to Redskin: Changing Anglo-American Perceptions of the American Indian," *American Historical Review* 87 [October 1982]: 953). For an interpretation of the effect of such thinking on Indian policy, see Reginald Horsman, "Scientific Racism and the American Indian in the Mid-Nineteenth Century," *American Quarterly* 27 (May 1975): 152–68.

4. See Dippie, *Vanishing American,* 199–221; Hoxie, *Final Promise,* 83–114. Hoxie's comments on the world's fairs of the era are especially interesting. See also Richard Drinnon, *Facing West: The Metaphysics of Indian Hating and Empire Building.* On Curtis, consult Barbara Davis, *Edward S. Curtis: The Life and Times of A Shadow Catcher.* For the popular imagery of the day, especially as it concerned Indians, see Richard Slotkin, *Gunfighter Nation: The Myth of the Frontier in Twentieth Century America;* and William H. Goetzmann and William N. Goetzmann, *The West of the Imagination,* especially part 5, "Play the Legend," 285–350.

5. Berkhofer, *White Man's Indian,* 101.

6. Goetzmann and Goetzmann, *West of the Imagination,* 216.

7. *Annual Report of the Board of Indian Commissioners,* 59th Cong., 1st sess., 1905, H. Doc. 20, pp. 17–18. This book treats education as an example of the changing values and priorities inside the Indian Office; other issues, however, are equally good barometers of the shift. In addition to assessing education, for example, Hoxie summarizes brilliantly the impact such change had on land policy, citizenship, politics, and public opinion. My analysis rests heavily on his.

Briefer assessments of the period include Berens, "Old Campaigners, New Realities"; Kenneth O'Reilly, "The Progressive Era and New American Indian Policy: The Gospel of Self-Support," *Journal of Historical Studies* 5 (Fall 1981): 35–56; Randolph C. Downes, "A Crusade for Indian Reform, 1922–1934," *Mississippi Valley Historical Review* 32 (December 1945): 331–54.

8. Prucha, *Great Father* II: 772. See also Francis Paul Prucha, "The Decline of the Christian Reformers," in *Indian Policy in the United States: Historical Essays,* ed. Francis Paul Prucha, 252–62.

9. Roosevelt to Lyman Abbott, September 5, 1903, quoted in Hoxie, *Final Promise,* 112.

10. Berens, "Old Campaigners, New Realities," 59–60.

11. *Annual Report of the Board of Indian Commissioners,* in *ARCIA,* 1901, pp. 4–5.

12. *ARCIA*, 1908, p. 11; Irving G. Hendrick, "The Federal Campaign for the Admission of Indian Children into Public Schools, 1890–1934," *American Indian Culture and Research Journal* 5, no. 3 (1981): 20.

13. James H. Kyle, "How Shall the Indian Be Educated?" *North American Review* 159 (November 1894): 443.

14. A. J. Standing, "The Proper Relation between Literary and Industrial Education in Indian Schools," *Journal of Proceedings and Addresses of the Annual Meeting of the National Educational Association*, 1900, pp. 693–94; F. K. Rogers, "The Teaching of Trades to the Indian," ibid., 699. Mooney quoted in L. G. Moses, *The Indian Man: A Biography of James Mooney*, 151.

15. *Annual Report of the Superintendent of Indian Schools* in *ARCIA*, 1902, p. 424; Estelle Reel, untitled comments, *Journal of Proceedings and Addresses of the Annual Meeting of the National Educational Association*, 1905, p. 931; George P. Phenix, "Essential Features in the Education of the Child Race," ibid., 1907, p. 1005.

16. Prucha, *Great Father* II: 826; Hendrick, "The Federal Campaign for the Admission of Indian Children into Public Schools," 20. See also Hoxie, "Redefining Indian Education: Thomas J. Morgan's Program in Disarray," *Arizona and the West* 24 (Spring 1982): 5–18.

17. *ARCIA*, 1900, p. 14. For a brief account of Jones's career, see W. David Baird, "William A. Jones, 1897–1904," in *The Commissioners of Indian Affairs, 1824–1977*, ed. Robert M. Kvasnicka and Herman J. Viola, 211–20.

18. *Annual Report of the Superintendent of Indian Education*, in *ARCIA*, 1902, p. 424; Hoxie, "Redefining Indian Education," 9–16.

19. Reel's comments are from the *ARCIA*, 1901, pp. 418–57 (which contains a summary of the revised course of study), and *Journal of Proceedings and Address of the Annual Meeting of the National Educational Association*, 1905, p. 932. The entire 1901 report was published separately as *Course of Study for the Indian Schools of the United States, Industrial and Literary*; Hoxie, "Redefining Indian Education," 10.

20. *ARCIA*, 1901, p. 39.

21. C. C. Covey, "The Reservation Day School Should Be the Prime Factor in Indian Education," *Journal of Proceedings and Addresses of the Annual Meeting of the National Educational Association*, 1901, p. 901.

22. Calvin W. Woodward, "What Shall Be Taught in an Indian School?" ibid., 906. See also O. H. Bakeless, "The Unification Of Industrial And Academic Features of the Indian Schools," ibid., 902–904, in which Bakeless warned his readers, "We must get rid of the theoretical flavor of the schoolroom and the peculiar tendency on the part of the teacher to want all bright pupils to prepare for the so-called 'professions.'"

23. See Prucha's comments in *Great Father* II: 816–19. In his final annual report, Jones offered what Prucha calls "a very rosy picture of accomplishments and of Indian potential" (*ARCIA*, 1904, pp. 39–49).

24. Leupp's 1907 comments quoted from "Indians and Their Education," *Journal of Proceedings and Addresses of the Annual Meeting of the National Education Association*, 1907, pp. 1015–22. On Leupp, consult Don Parman, "Francis Ellington Leupp, 1905–1909," in *Commissioners of Indian Affairs*, 221–32; Nicah Furman, "Seedtime for Indian Reform: An Evaluation of the

Administration of Commissioner Francis Ellington Leupp," *Red River Valley Historical Review* 2 (Winter 1975): 495–517. See also Leupp's memoir, *The Indian and His Problem*; Prucha has a useful summary in *Great Father* II: 766–69.

Interpretations of Leupp's administration vary. Hoxie associates Leupp with those who took a limited view of the government's responsibilities. Furman, on the other hand, hails Leupp as an inspired and highly qualified administrator whose term "shines as an enlightened beacon in a long night of Indian injustices and abuse" (Furman, "Seedtime for Indian Reform," 499).

25. *ARCIA*, 1905, pp. 8–9; Hoxie, "Redefining Indian Education," 14.
26. *ARCIA*, 1907, pp. 21, 24, 27.
27. Ibid., 20–26.
28. "The Failure of the Educated American Indian," *American Monthly Review of Reviews* 33 (January–June 1906): 629–30. This was a response to Leupp's essay of the same title that appeared in *Appleton's Booklover's Magazine*, May 1906, pp. 594–609.
29. *ARCIA*, 1907, p. 24; Leupp, "Indians and Their Education," 1020–21.
30. Herbert Welsh, "Comment on Thomas Morgan's 'Indian Education,' " *Journal of Social Science* 40 (December 1902): 178. Hoxie, *Final Promise*, has a very good summary of these and other comments (191–94).
31. Charles B. Dyke, "Essential Features in the Education of the Child Races," *Journal of Proceedings and Addresses of the Annual Meeting of the National Educational Association*, 1909, pp. 928–32.
32. Leupp, "Why Booker T. Washington Succeeded in His Lifework," *Outlook* 68 (May 31, 1902): 327.
33. For a summary of Valentine's years as commissioner, see Diane T. Putney, "Robert Grovesnor Valentine, 1909–1912," in *Commissioners of Indian Affairs*, 233–42.
34. *ARCIA*, 1908, p. 44; 1910, pp. 14–15; 1912, pp. 181–93; 1914, p. 136. See Hendrick's discussion in "The Federal Campaign for the Admission of Indian Children into Public Schools," 22–23.
35. *ARCIA*, 1910, p. 16.
36. Ibid., 1911, p. 29; 1912, pp. 38, 41. Leupp quoted in Hoxie, *Final Promise*, 202.
37. For a summary of Sells's administration, see Lawrence C. Kelly, "Cato Sells, 1913–1921," in *Commissioners of Indian Affairs*, 243–50; *ARCIA*, 1915, pp. 4–5; Prucha, *Great Father* II: 829–30.
38. *ARCIA*, 1918, pp. 20, 26.
39. Ibid., 20–21; 1921, p. 5. For Burke's career as commissioner, see Lawrence C. Kelly, "Charles Burke, 1921–1929," in *Commissioners of Indian Affairs*, 251–61.
40. *ARCIA*, 1892, p. 5; 1899, p. 23.
41. Tsianina Lomawaima, "Domesticity in the Federal Indian Schools: The Power of Authority over Mind and Body," *American Ethnologist* 20 (May 1993): 236–37.
42. "Indian Industrial Development," *Outlook* 67 (January 12, 1901): 101–102.
43. Ibid.

44. G. Stanley Hall, "How Far Are the Principles of Education along Indigenous Lines Applicable to American Indians?" *Journal of the Proceedings and Addresses of the Annual Meeting of the National Educational Association*, 1908, p. 1163.

45. S. L. Heeter, "The Teacher's Responsibility to the Indian Child," ibid., 1909, p. 933.

46. Trennert, "Selling Indian Education at World's Fairs and Expositions, 1893–1904," 203–20; quoted passage is at 219–20. See Hoxie, *Final Promise*, 83–94, for an entertaining and informative discussion of world's fairs and the changing nature of government exhibits. Dippie, *Vanishing American*, 199–215.

47. Hoxie regards this as an especially important point; see "Redefining Indian Education," in which he argues that such decisions "may well have saved a number of tribal cultures from extinction" (p. 18). Sally McBeth makes a similar point in her work on the boarding schools; see "Indian Schools and Ethnic Identity: An Example from the Southern Plains Tribes of Oklahoma," *Plains Anthropologist* 28 (Spring 1983): 119–28.

CHAPTER 6

1. Inspection Report of C. L. Ellis, April 24, 1909, Kiowa Agency Classified Files, 1907–39, Establishment or Abolition of Schools, Record Group 75, National Archives, Washington, D.C., (hereafter cited as KA, NA).

2. Lengthy excerpts of the report and Valentine's comments and suggestions are in Robert Valentine to Ernest Stecker, July 7, 1910, Rainy Mountain School Files, Records of the Kiowa Agency, Indian Archives Division, Oklahoma Historical Society, Oklahoma City (hereafter cited as RMS, OHS).

3. Ibid.

4. Ibid.

5. Ibid.

6. Ibid.

7. Ibid. Parker McKenzie remembered that Dunn regularly drove his hogs away from the school to a local farm before inspections. McKenzie also said that Dunn fed his hogs with government corn (McKenzie interview, Mountain View, Okla., August 1, 1990).

8. Valentine to Stecker, July 7, 1910, RMS, OHS; McKenzie to Henry McKenzie, December 15, 1973, in the possession of the author. McKenzie remembered milking cows twice daily but commented, "We never saw no milk, and butter, too, on our tables. Most of it went to the campus quarters of married employees." McKenzie's recollection of meals differed significantly from the comments in McConihe's report. Far from being well fed, McKenzie said, "We were forever hungry" (McKenzie to Randle Hurst, October 23, 1987, in author's possession).

9. Valentine to Stecker, July 7, 1910, RMS, OHS.

10. Ibid.

11. Stecker to Valentine, September 3, 1909, ibid.

12. F. H. Abbott to A. M. Dunn, July 26, 1909; Abbott to Cora Dunn, January 5, 1910, ibid. These letters accepted the couple's resignations.

NOTES TO PAGES 159–67

13. Valentine to H. B. Peairs, April 29, 1910; Peairs to Valentine, May 4, 1910, KA, NA; Valentine to Peairs, May 16, 1910; "Memorandum for Legislative Committee," RMS, OHS.

14. U.S. Congress, House, 61st Cong., 2d sess., H. Doc. 930; U.S. Congress, Senate, 61st Cong., 2d sess., S. Doc. 8390.

15. Stecker to Valentine, August 24, 1910; Dortch to Stecker, September 23, 1910, RMS, OHS; Kiowa-Comanche Agency Annual Report, September 1, 1910, Agents' Reports, Records of the Kiowa Agency, OHS.

16. Parker McKenzie, "Development of Extra-Curricular Activities at Rainy Mountain," n.d., from a packet compiled for a 1963 reunion of former students and staff members. Photocopy in the possession of the author, courtesy of Parker McKenzie.

17. McGregor to Stecker, April 14, 1910, RMS, OHS.

18. Ibid.

19. McGregor to Stecker, October 16, 1910, ibid.

20. C. F. Hauke to Stecker, November 12, 1910, ibid.

21. McGregor to Stecker, November 21, 1910, and Stecker to Valentine, November 25, 1910, ibid. It is worth noting that the original inspection calling for fire equipment occurred on April 7, 1910. Stecker did not request authority to purchase the equipment until May 16, 1910; it was actually ordered in late September and arrived in mid-November, seven months after the matter had first been raised. This kind of administrative foot dragging was typical.

22. Estimate of Needs for Fiscal Year Ending June 30, 1912, ibid.

23. Supervising Principal to Ernest Stecker, March 10, 1913, ibid.

24. The best summary of health issues during the era is Diane T. Putney, "Fighting the Scourge: American Indian Morbidity and Federal Policy, 1897–1928" (Ph.D. diss., Marquette University, 1980); see 141–43 for a general discussion of trachoma. An excellent discussion of the trachoma problem is Robert Trennert, "Indian Sore Eyes: The Federal Campaign to Control Trachoma in the Southwest, 1910–40," *Journal of the Southwest* 32 (Summer 1990): 121–49.

25. McGregor to Dr. Ferdinand Shoemaker, April 18, 1912, RMS, OHS.

26. McGregor to Stecker, December 16, 1912; Stecker to Valentine, December 19, 1912; McGregor to Stecker, August 10, 1912; Valentine to Charles Norton, August 26, 1912, ibid.

27. McGregor to Stecker, April 16, 1913, ibid.

28. Abbott to Stecker, April 19, 1913, ibid. A voucher dated June 30, 1913, indicates an expenditure of sixty dollars for a pump house and concrete reservoir at the school.

29. Lewis G. Lavlin to Sells, December 11, 1913; "Program of Tuberculosis Day," December 7, 1913, ibid. The December 1913 issue of "Home and School," a newsletter of current events published in Anadarko, reported that "the school is thankful to the Indian Office for establishing the position at the school. In addition to treating the pupils, the doctor will render medical aid to the Indians living within a reasonable distance of the school" (KA, NA).

30. "Tuberculosis Day Program," ca. 1915, Undated Files, Riverside School Files, Records of the Kiowa Agency, OHS.

31. Annual Report of the Rainy Mountain School, December 13, 1913, KA, NA; McGregor to Stecker, January 29, 1914, RMS, OHS.

32. Physician's Semi-Annual Report, Rainy Mountain School, December 31, 1916, and March 31, 1917; Stinchecum to Dr. D. V. Hailman, February 9, 1916, RMS, OHS; Jim Whitewolf, *The Life of a Kiowa-Apache Indian*, 92; Field Matron's Weekly Field Reports, May 24, 1919 (Susie Peters), and June 7, 1919 (Allie Brewer), Field Matron's Files, Records of the Kiowa Agency, Microfilm KA 75, OHS.

33. Report on Trachoma at the Fort Sill School, October 2, 1911; Hauke to Stecker, August 1, 1911, Fort Sill Indian School Files, Records of the Kiowa Agency, OHS.

34. Hauke to Stecker, February 13, April 8, 1913; Charles Eggars to Stecker, March 20, 1913, RMS, OHS.

35. McGregor to Stecker, April 2, 1913; Stecker to Valentine, April 14, 1913, ibid.

36. Inspection Report of Kiowa Agency Schools: School Work and Employees, May 1, 1913, KA, NA.

37. McGregor to Stecker, July 31, 1913, RMS, OHS.

38. McGregor to Stecker, September 22, 1913, ibid.

39. Annual Inspection of Rainy Mountain School, December 1913, KA, NA.

40. McGregor to Stecker, March 21, 1914, RMS, OHS.

41. Delos K. Lonewolf, Sherman Chaddlesone, Kiowa Bill, Apeahtone, and Goomdo to Cato Sells, January 23, 1914, KA, NA.

42. E. B. Meritt to Delos K. Lonewolf and members of the Business Committee, February 16, 1914, ibid.

43. "Contract between the United States of America and Herman Pepper and James F. Wass," RMS, OHS; Inspection Report of Kiowa Agency Schools: Academic Training, September 13, 1915, KA, NA; Voucher for 210 opera chairs for "recently completed new school building" at Rainy Mountain, September 21, 1916, RMS, OHS.

44. Parker McKenzie to Bill Welge, January 26, 1987, and June 6, 1990, in author's possession; McKenzie to the author, August 1, 1990; McKenzie to Henry McKenzie, November 15, 1973, in author's possession. McGregor later gained acclaim for his published account of the 1890 Wounded Knee episode. In the early 1970s the highly acclaimed *Memoirs of Chief Red Fox* was revealed to be a plagiarized work based on McGregor's earlier research. His family sued and was awarded damages in an out-of-court settlement.

CHAPTER 7

1. Parker McKenzie interview, Mountain View, Okla., August 1, 1990. Stinchecum, who had a well-deserved reputation as a penny-pincher and disciplinarian, once ordered an agency employee to remit eighteen cents mistakenly allowed on an expense report; on another occasion he ordered several employees to remit seven cents each to balance an agency account. Stinchecum to Anna Heersma et al., June 26, 1915, Field Matron's Files, Records of the Kiowa Agency, Microfilm KA 74, Indian Archives Division, Oklahoma Historical

Society, Oklahoma City; Stinchecum to M. Becker, December 1919, Microfilm KA 75, ibid.

2. J. W. Smith to John Crickenberger, January 27, 1915; Ernest Stecker to Cato Sells, February 27, 1915, Rainy Mountain School Files, Records of the Kiowa Agency, Indian Archives Division, Oklahoma Historical Society, Oklahoma City (hereafter cited as RMS, OHS). Like McGregor's wife before her, Crickenberger's wife accepted a teaching position at the school. On Crickenberger's self-defined role as caretaker, see Crickenberger to J. W. Smith, February 8, 1915, and C. F. Hauke to Stecker, March 10, 1915, ibid.

3. Hauke to Stecker, March 10, 1915, ibid.

4. Crickenberger to Smith, April 1, 1915, ibid. Crickenberger said much the same thing to Cato Sells (see Crickenberger to Sells, April 14, 1915, ibid.).

5. C. V. Stinchecum to Cato Sells, May 24, 1915, ibid.

6. Inspection Report of Kiowa Agency Schools: Course of Study, September 15, 1915, Kiowa Agency Classified Files, 1907–39, Record Group 75, National Archives, Washington, D.C. (hereafter cited as KA, NA).

7. Inspection Report of Kiowa Agency Schools: Course of Study, February 13, 1916; Stinchecum to Sells, August 22, 1916; Sells to Stinchecum, March 28, 1916, ibid.

8. Edgar Allen to Sells, March 16, 1917, ibid.

9. Stinchecum to Sells, January 5, 1917, ibid.

10. Sherman Chaddlesone to Representative Scott Ferris, November 8, 1919, ibid.

11. E. B. Meritt to Stinchecum, September 4, 1919; telegram from Stinchecum to Indian Office, September 8, 1919; Meritt to Stinchecum, September 4, 1919; telegram from Stinchecum to Indian Office, September 8, 1919; Stinchecum to Sells, September 19, 1919, RMS, OHS.

12. Sells to R. S. Russell, February 26, 1920; Russell to Sells, March 8, 1920, KA, NA.

13. Ibid.

14. Field Matron's Weekly Report for September 16, 1915, and Mary Clouse to J. Prickett, September 11, 1917, Field Matron's Files, Records of the Kiowa Agency Microfilm KA 74, OHS.

15. Chaddlesone to Ferris, November 8, 1919, KA, NA.

16. Ibid.

17. Ferris to Sells, November 14, 1919; Meritt to Ferris, November 21, 1919; James McClintic to Sells, January 24, 1920; Meritt to McClintic, January 30, 1920, ibid.

18. Telegrams from Ferris to Franklin Lane, Robert Owen, and Sells, February 3, 1920, ibid.

19. Telegram from Sells to Ferris, February 4, 1920; Owen to Sells, February 3, 1920; Sells to Owen, February 4, 1920, ibid.

20. McClintic to Robert Onco, February 6, 1920; Sells to Owen, March 18, 1920, ibid.

21. Petition of the Kiowa Tribe, January 1920, ibid.

22. Ibid.

23. Stinchecum to Sells, February 18, 1920, ibid.

24. Just before this letter Stinchecum wired the office to say that public schools were available to nearly all of Rainy Mountain's students: "Indian children have as good an opportunity as white children living in the same space. . . . School should by all means be closed" (telegram from Stinchecum to Indian Office, February 5, 1920, ibid.).

25. Meritt to George Hunt, February 20, 1920, ibid.

26. J. W. Dellinger to McClintic, January 20, 1920, ibid.

27. J. M. Rule to Owen, February 13, 1920, ibid.

28. Mrs. J. F. Baldridge to Owen, February 14, 1920, ibid.

29. F. A. Balyeat to Owen, February 16, 1920, ibid.

30. Ibid.

31. F. A. Balyeat, "History of the Public Schools of Kiowa County, Oklahoma," typed manuscript, ca. 1958, Dr. Frank A. Balyeat Collection, Western History Collections, University of Oklahoma Library Archives, Norman.

32. "Rainy Mountain School," n.d., but clearly from spring of 1920, KA, NA. This document is a compilation of comments received in the Indian Office relative to the school's closing.

33. Ibid.

34. Stinchecum to Sells, March 17, 1920, ibid.

35. June 1913 inspection report for Mountain View, Bunker Hill, and Cache Schools, ibid.

36. Field Matron's Weekly Report, March 20, 1920, Field Matron's Files, Records of the Kiowa Agency, Microfilm KA 75, OHS.

37. An inventory and property value list from October 1, 1919, showed buildings valued at $72,385 plus other property (furnishings, desks, tools, and so on) valued at $25,724, RMS, OHS; see also Stinchecum to Sells, May 5, 1920, and Meritt to Stinchecum, June 2, 1920, KA, NA.

38. Telegram from D. I. Johnston et al. to Owen, July 31, 1920; telegram from J. W. Harreld to Sells, July 31, 1920, KA, NA.

39. Telegram from McClintic to Sells, August 3, 1920; telegram from Sells to McClintic, August 3, 1920; telegram from Sells to Harreld, August 1, 1920, ibid.; Field Matron's Weekly Report, June 12, 1920, Field Matron's Files, Records of the Kiowa Agency, Microfilm KA 75, OHS.

40. Telegram from Hill Anglea (?) to Sells, August 6, 1920; telegram from Sells to Anglea, August 6, 1920; J. W. Wilkinson to Sells, August 12, 1920; Meritt to Wilkinson, August 27, 1920; Stinchecum to Sells, October 11, 1920; telegram from Stinchecum to Indian Office, August 1, 1920, KA, NA.

41. Meritt to Stinchecum, October 28, 1920; and Surgeon General to the Commissioner of Indian Affairs, October 29, 1920, ibid.

CHAPTER 8

1. James Silverhorn interview, September 28, 1967, T-146:1; Fred Bigman interview, June 14, 1967, T-50:1, Doris Duke Oral History Collection, Western History Collections, University of Oklahoma Library Archives, Norman (hereafter cited as DDOH); McKenzie to the author, August 1, 1990.

2. See Clyde Ellis, "'Truly Dancing Their Own Way': The Modern Revival and Diffusion of the Gourd Dance," *American Indian Quarterly* 14 (Winter

1990): 19–34; Eric Lassiter, " 'They Left Us These Songs . . . That's All We Got Left Now': The Significance of Music in the Kiowa Gourd Dance and Its Relation to Native American Continuity," in *Native American Values: Survival and Renewal*, ed. Thomas Shirer and Susan M. Branstner, 375–84; and, Luke E. Lassiter, "Towards Understanding the Power of Kiowa Song: A Collaborative Exercise in Meaning," (Ph.D. diss., University of North Carolina at Chapel Hill, 1995). See also Benjamin R. Kracht, "Kiowa Powwows: Continuity in Ritual Practice," *American Indian Quarterly* 18 (Summer 1994): 321–48, but note that his emphasis on Victor Turner's concept of *communitas* rests on highly debatable interpretations.

3. Frederick Hoxie, *A Final Promise: The Campaign to Assimilate the Indian, 1880–1920*, 237–44. Hoxie develops this line of thinking in an essay on the Cheyenne River Lakota (see "From Prison to Homeland: The Cheyenne River Indian Reservation before World War I," *South Dakota History* 10 [Winter 1979]: 1–24; Sally J. McBeth, "Indian Schools and Ethnic Identity: An Example from the Southern Plains Tribes of Oklahoma," *Plains Anthropologist* 28 [Spring 1983]:120, 127). McBeth comments at greater length on this in *Ethnic Identity and the Boarding School Experience of West-Central Oklahoma American Indians*. See also Tsianina Lomawaima, "Domesticity in the Indian Schools: The Power of Authority over Mind and Body," *American Ethnologist* 20 (May 1993): 227–40, and Lomawaima, *They Called it Prairie Light: The Story of Chilocco Indian School.*

Hoxie, McBeth, Lomawaima, Richard White and others (including Thomas Biolsi, see note 4 below) have helped to create a theoretical paradigm that lifts the discussion of culture change and adaptation beyond the limiting confines of assimilation-acculturation models. As James Clifford has observed, "stories of cultural contact and change have been structured by a pervasive dichotomy: absorption by the other or resistance to the other. . . . Yet what if identity is conceived not as [a] boundary to be maintained but as a nexus of relations and transactions actively engaging on a subject? The story or stories of interaction must then be more complex, less linear and teleological," in Richard White, *The Middle Ground: Indians, Empires, and Republics in the Great Lakes Region, 1650–1815*, ix.

4. The literature on the Indian New Deal is copious. The best single source remains Kenneth Philp, *John Collier's Crusade for Indian Reform, 1920–1954*. To say that the Indian New Deal completely turned back the tide of assimilation is, of course, an overstatement. However, it did suggest what Thomas Biolsi has characterized as a change in "*the representation of power*" (emphasis in the original here, and in the passage that follows). In his work on the Lakotas and the New Deal, Biolsi writes, "Let it not be thought that the new discourse, symbols, models, performances, and rituals were 'only symbolic,' without material reality. They had a distinct *materiality* because they opened up political space for Lakota people" (*Organizing the Lakota: The Political Economy of the New Deal on the Pine Ridge and Rosebud Reservations*, 185).

5. N. Scott Momaday, *The Way to Rainy Mountain*, 4.

Bibliography

PRIMARY SOURCES

Manuscripts

Indian Archives Division. Oklahoma Historical Society, Oklahoma City.
  Records of the Kiowa Agency.
    Agents and Agency Files.
    Agents' Reports.
    Census Files.
    Church Files.
    Employees' Files.
    Field Matron's Files.
    Fort Sill School Files.
    Miscellaneous Schools Files.
    Rainy Mountain School Files.
    Riverside School Files.
Record Group 75, Records of the Bureau of Indian Affairs. National Archives, Washington, D.C.
  Records of the Kiowa Agency.
    Kiowa Agency, 1907–39: Classified Files.
Western History Collections. University of Oklahoma Archives, Norman.
  Dr. Frank A. Balyeat Collection.
    "History of the Public Schools of Kiowa County, Oklahoma."
  Doris Duke Oral History Collection.
    Annie Bigman Interview, M-1, June 14, 1967.
    Annie Bigman Interview, T-57, June 15, 1967.
    Fred Bigman Interview, T-50, June 14, 1967.
    James Haumpy Interview, T-81, July 11, 1967.
    Sarah Long Horn Interview, T-62, June 27, 1967.
    Eugenia Mausape Interview, T-138-A, September 14, 1967.
    Guy Quoetone Interview, T-149, September 26, 1967.
    Guy Quoetone Interview, T-637, March 23, 1971.
    James Silverhorn Interview, T-146, September 28, 1967.

Myrtle Paudlety Ware Interview, T-76, November 11, 1967.
William Lone Wolf Interview, T-42, March 31, 1967.
Juanita Yeahquo Interview, M-2, June 21, 1967.

Correspondence

All of the McKenzie letters are in the author's possession, courtesy
of Parker McKenzie.
Parker McKenzie to Flora DeLay, June 7, 1963.
——— to Mrs. Henry T. Choquette, April 2, 1965.
——— to Bill Welge, January 26, 1987; June 6, 1990.
——— to Randle Hurst, October 23, 1987.
——— to the author, July 14, 28, and August 1, 1990.

Interview

Parker McKenzie. With author. Mountain View, Okla. August 1, 1990.

Other Miscellaneous Documents

"Happy 90th Birthday Lewis Toyebo, February 28, 1982," photocopy of
commemorative birthday celebration reminiscence in the author's
possession, courtesy of Ruby Williams, Fort Cobb, Okla.
McKenzie, Parker. "Development of Extra-Curricular Activities at
Rainy Mountain." N.d. Photocopy in the author's possession.
———. "How Written Kiowa Came into Being." N.d. Photocopy in
the author's possession.
Shannon, Ruby. "Friends for the Indians: One Hundred Years of Indian
Education at Riverside School." Bound ms., ca. 1970. Linschied
Library, East Central University, Ada, Okla.

Newspapers

Anadarko Daily News, August 15 and 16, 1987.

Government Documents

Kappler, Charles J. Indian Affairs: Laws and Treaties, 7 vols. Washington, D.C.: Government Printing Office, 1904.
Superintendent of Indian Education. Annual Reports, 1883, 1884,
1885, 1890, 1891, 1895, 1896, 1899, 1902, 1903.
U.S. Commissioner of Indian Affairs. Annual Reports, 1848, 1849,
1863, 1866, 1870–1921.
U.S. Secretary of the Interior. Annual Reports, 1877, 1879, 1880.

SECONDARY SOURCES
Books

Adams, David W. Education for Extinction: American Indians and
the Boarding School Experience, 1875–1928. Lawrence: University
Press of Kansas, 1995.
Adams, Evelyn C. American Indian Education: Government Schools

and Economic Progress. Morningside Heights, N.Y.: King's Crown Press, 1946.

Babcock, Sydney, and John Young Bryce. *The History of Methodism in Oklahoma: The Story of the Indian Mission Annual Conference of the Methodist Episcopal Church, South.* Oklahoma City: the authors, 1935.

Baird, W. David. "William A. Jones, 1897–1904." In *The Commissioners of Indian Affairs, 1824–1977.* Ed. Robert M. Kvasnicka and Herman J. Viola. Lincoln: University of Nebraska Press, 1979.

Battey, Thomas C. *The Life and Adventures of a Quaker among the Indians.* Introduction by Alice Marriott. 1875; reprint, Norman: University of Oklahoma Press, 1968.

Berkhofer, Robert F., Jr. *Salvation and the Savage: An Analysis of Protestant Missions and American Indian Response, 1787–1862.* New York: Atheneum Press, 1976.

———. *The White Man's Indian: Images of the American Indian from Columbus to the Present.* New York: Knopf, 1978.

Berthrong, Donald. *The Cheyenne-Arapaho Ordeal: Agency Life in the Indian Territory, 1875–1907.* Norman: University of Oklahoma Press, 1976.

Biolsi, Thomas. *Organizing the Lakota: The Political Economy of the New Deal on the Pine Ridge and Rosebud Reservations.* Tucson: University of Arizona Press, 1992.

Bowden, Henry Warner. *American Indians and Christian Missions: Studies in Cultural Conflict.* Chicago: University of Chicago Press, 1981.

Brown, Dee. *Bury My Heart at Wounded Knee: An Indian History of the American West.* New York: Holt, Rinehart and Winston, 1970.

Callahan, Raymond. *Education and the Cult of Efficiency.* Chicago: University of Chicago Press, 1962.

Calloway, Colin G. *New Directions in American Indian History.* Norman: University of Oklahoma Press, 1988.

Castile, George Pierre, and Robert L. Bee, eds. *State and Reservation: New Perspectives on Federal Indian Policy.* Tucson: University of Arizona Press, 1992.

Coleman, Michael. *American Indian Children at School, 1850–1930.* Jackson: University Press of Mississippi, 1993.

Crawford, Isabel. *Kiowa: The History of a Blanket Indian Mission.* New York: Fleming H. Revell, 1915.

Cremin, Lawrence. *American Education: The Colonial Experience, 1607–1783.* New York: Harper and Row, 1970.

———. *American Education: The Metropolitan Experience, 1876–1980.* New York: Harper and Row, 1988.

———. *American Education: The National Experience, 1783–1876.* New York: Harper and Row, 1980.

———. *The Transformation of the School: Progressivism in American Education, 1876–1957.* New York: Random House, 1961.

Davis, Barbara. *Edward S. Curtis: The Life and Times of a Shadow Catcher.* San Francisco: Chronicle Books, 1983.

DeJong, David H. *Promises of the Past: A History of Indian Education.* Golden, Colo.: North American Press, 1993.

Dippie, Brian W. *The Vanishing American: White Attitudes and U.S. Indian Policy.* Lawrence: University Press of Kansas, 1982.

Drinnon, Richard. *Facing West: The Metaphysics of Indian Hating.* Minneapolis: University of Minnesota Press, 1980.

Dyer, Thomas G. *Theodore Roosevelt and the Idea of Race.* Baton Rouge: Louisiana State University Press, 1980.

Eastman, Elaine G. *Pratt: The Red Man's Moses.* Norman: University of Oklahoma Press, 1935.

Fischbacher, Theodore. *A Study of the Role of the Federal Government in the Education of the American Indian.* San Francisco: R and E Research Associates, 1974.

Forbes, Bruce David. "John Jasper Methvin: Methodist 'Missionary to the Western Tribes' (Oklahoma)." In *Churchmen and the Western Indians, 1820–1920.* Ed. Clyde A. Milner and Floyd A. O'Neil. Norman: University of Oklahoma Press, 1985: 41–73.

Foster, Morris. *Being Comanche: A Social History of an American Indian Community.* Tucson: University of Arizona Press, 1991.

Fritz, Henry B. *The Movement for Indian Assimilation, 1860–1890.* Philadelphia: University of Pennsylvania Press, 1963.

Fuchs, Estelle, and Robert J. Havighurst. *To Live on This Earth: American Indian Education.* Introduction by Margaret Connell Szasz. 1972; reprint, Albuquerque: University of New Mexico Press, 1983.

Goetzmann, William H., and William N. Goetzmann. *The West of the Imagination.* New York: W. W. Norton, 1986.

Gordon, Milton M. *Assimilation in American Life: The Role of Race, Religion, and Natural Origins.* New York: Oxford University Press, 1964.

Hagan, William T. *United States–Comanche Relations: The Reservation Years.* Norman: University of Oklahoma Press, 1990.

———. "The Reservation Policy: Too Little and Too Late." In *Indian-White Relations: A Persistent Paradox.* Ed. Jane F. Smith and Robert M. Kvasnicka. Washington, D.C.: Howard University Press, 1976.

Harrod, Howard L. *Mission among the Blackfeet.* Norman: University of Oklahoma Press, 1971.

Hinsley, Curtis, Jr. *Savages and Scientists: The Smithsonian Institution and the Development of American Anthropology, 1846–1910.* Washington, DC: Smithsonian Institution Press, 1981.

Hoopes, Alban W. *Indian Affairs and Their Administration, with Special Reference to the Far West, 1849–1860.* Philadelphia: University of Pennsylvania Press, 1932.

Horsman, Reginald. *Expansion and American Indian Policy, 1783–1812.* Norman: University of Oklahoma Press, 1992.

Hoxie, Frederick. *A Final Promise: The Campaign to Assimilate the Indians, 1880–1920.* New York: Cambridge University Press, 1989.
Jennings, Francis. *The Invasion of America: Indians, Colonialism, and the Cant of Conquest.* Chapel Hill: University of North Carolina Press, 1975.
Johnston, Basil H. *Indian School Days.* Norman: University of Oklahoma Press, 1989.
Jones, Douglas. *The Treaty of Medicine Lodge.* Norman: University of Oklahoma Press, 1966.
Katz, Michael. *Class, Bureaucracy, and Schools: The Illusion of Educational Change in America.* Expanded edition. New York: Praeger Publishers, 1975.
Keller, Robert H., Jr. *American Protestantism and United States Indian Policy, 1869–82.* Lincoln: University of Nebraska Press, 1983.
Kelly, Lawrence C. "Cato Sells, 1913–1921." In *The Commissioners of Indian Affairs, 1824–1977.* Ed. Robert M. Kvasnicka and Herman J. Viola. Lincoln: University of Nebraska Press, 1979.
———. "Charles Burke, 1921–1929." In *The Commissioners of Indian Affairs, 1824–1977.* Ed. Robert M. Kvasnicka and Herman J. Viola. Lincoln: University of Nebraska Press, 1979.
Kvasnicka, Robert M., and Herman J. Viola, eds. *The Commissioners of Indian Affairs, 1824–1977.* Lincoln: University of Nebraska Press, 1979.
LaFlesche, Francis. *The Middle Five: Indian Schoolboys of the Omaha Tribe.* 1900; reprint, Madison: University of Wisconsin Press, 1963.
Lassiter, Luke E. " 'They Left Us These Songs . . . That's All We Got Left Now': The Significance of Music in the Kiowa Gourd Dance and Its Relation to Native American Continuity." In *Native American Values: Survival and Renewal. Proceedings from the Third International Native American Studies Conference at Lake Superior State University, October 25–26, 1991.* Ed. Thomas Shirer and Susan M. Branstner. Sault Sainte Marie: Lake Superior State University Press, 1993.
Leckie, William H. *The Military Conquest of the Southern Plains.* Norman: University of Oklahoma Press, 1963.
Leupp, Francis. *The Indian and His Problem.* New York: Charles Scribner, 1910.
Lindsey, Donal. *Indians at Hampton Institute, 1873–1923.* Urbana: University of Illinois Press, 1994.
Lomawaima, K. Tsianina. *They Called It Prairie Light: The Story of Chilocco Indian School.* Lincoln: University of Nebraska Press, 1994.
McBeth, Sally J. *Ethnic Identity and the Boarding School Experience of West-Central Oklahoma American Indians.* Washington, D.C.: University Press of America, 1983.
Mardock, Robert W. *The Reformers and the American Indian.* Columbia: University of Missouri Press, 1971.

Mayhall, Mildred. *The Kiowas.* Norman: University of Oklahoma Press, 1962.

Methvin, John J. *In the Limelight; or, a History of Anadarko and Vicinity.* Anadarko, Okla.: Plummer, 1928.

Merrell, James H. *The Indians' New World: Catawbas and Their Neighbors from European Contact Through the Era of Removal.* Chapel Hill: University of North Carolina Press, 1989.

Mihesuah, Devon A. *Cultivating the Rosebuds: The Education of Women at the Cherokee Female Seminary, 1851–1909.* Urbana: University of Illinois Press, 1993.

Milner, Clyde A., and Floyd A. O'Neil, eds. *Churchmen and the Western Indians, 1820–1920.* Norman: University of Oklahoma Press, 1985.

Momaday, N. Scott. *The Way to Rainy Mountain.* Albuquerque: University of New Mexico Press, 1993.

Mooney, James. "Calendar History of the Kiowa Indians." In *Seventeenth Annual Report of the Bureau of American Ethnology.* Washington, D.C.: Government Printing Office, 1898.

Morgan, Thomas Jefferson. *Studies in Pedagogy.* Boston: Silver and Burdette, 1889.

Moses, L. George. *The Indian Man: A Biography of James Mooney.* Urbana: University of Illinois Press, 1984.

Nye, Wilbur S. *Carbine and Lance: The Story of Old Fort Sill.* Norman: University of Oklahoma Press, 1937.

———. *Plains Indian Raiders: The Final Phases of Warfare from the Arkansas to the Red River.* Norman: University of Oklahoma Press, 1968.

Painter, C. C. *Condition of Indian Affairs in Indian Territory and California.* Philadelphia: Indian Rights Association, 1888.

Parman, Donald. "Francis Ellington Leupp, 1905–1909." In *The Commissioners of Indian Affairs, 1824–1977.* Ed. Robert M. Kvasnicka and Herman J. Viola. Lincoln: University of Nebraska Press, 1979.

Philp, Kenneth. *John Collier's Crusade for Indian Reform, 1920–1954.* Tucson: University of Arizona Press, 1977.

Pratt, Richard Henry. *Battlefield and Classroom: Four Decades with the American Indian, 1867–1904.* Edited and with an introduction by Robert M. Utley. New Haven: Yale University Press, 1964.

Priest, Loring B. *Uncle Sam's Stepchildren: The Reformation of United States Indian Policy, 1865–1887.* New Brunswick: Rutgers University Press, 1942.

Prucha, Francis Paul. *American Indian Policy in Crisis: Christian Reformers and the Indian, 1865–1900.* Norman: University of Oklahoma Press, 1976.

———. *American Indian Policy in the Formative Years: The Indian Trade and Intercourse Acts, 1790–1834.* Cambridge: Harvard University Press, 1962.

————. *The Churches and the Indian Schools, 1888–1912*. Lincoln: University of Nebraska Press, 1979.

————. *The Great Father: The United States Government and the American Indians*, 2 vols. Lincoln: University of Nebraska Press, 1984.

————, ed. *Indian Policy in the United States: Historical Essays*. Lincoln: University of Nebraska Press, 1981.

Prucha, Francis Paul. "The Decline of the Christian Reformers." In *Indian Policy in the United States: Historical Essays*. Ed. Francis Paul Prucha. Lincoln: University of Nebraska Press, 1981.

Putney, Diane T. "Robert Grovesnor Valentine, 1909–1912." In *The Commissioners of Indian Affairs, 1824–1977*. Ed. Robert M. Kvasnicka and Herman J. Viola. Lincoln: University of Nebraska Press, 1979.

Raymond, Dora Neill. *Captain Lee Hall of Texas*. Norman: University of Oklahoma Press, 1940.

Richardson, Rupert N. *The Comanche Barrier to South Plains Settlement*. Glendale: Arthur H. Clark, 1963.

Satz, Ronald. *American Indian Policy in the Jacksonian Era*. Lincoln: University of Nebraska Press, 1975.

Schmeckebier, Laurence. *The Office of Indian Affairs: Its History, Activities, and Organization*. Baltimore: Johns Hopkins University Press, 1927.

Sekaquaptewa, Helen. *Me and Mine: The Story of Helen Sekaquaptewa as Told to Louise Udall*. Tucson: University of Arizona Press, 1969.

Shirer, Thomas, and Susan M. Branstner, eds. *Native American Values: Survival and Renewal. Proceedings from the Third International Native American Studies Conference at Lake Superior State University, October 25–26, 1991*. Sault Sainte Marie: Lake Superior State University Press, 1993.

Slotkin, Richard. *Gunfighter Nation: The Myth of the Frontier in Twentieth Century America*. New York: Harper Collins, 1991.

Smith, Jane F., and Robert M. Kvasnicka, eds. *Indian-White Relations: A Persistent Paradox*. Washington, D.C.: Howard University Press, 1976.

Spring, Joel. *The American School, 1642–1990: Varieties of Historical Interpretation of the Foundations and Development of American Education*. 2d ed. New York: Longman, 1990.

Szasz, Margaret C. *Education and the American Indian: The Road to Self-Determination since 1928*. Albuquerque: University of New Mexico Press, 1977.

————. *Indian Education in the American Colonies, 1607–1783*. Albuquerque: University of New Mexico Press, 1988.

Tatum, Lawrie. *Our Red Brothers and the Peace Policy of President*

Ulysses S. Grant. Foreword by Richard N. Ellis. 1899; reprint, Lincoln: University of Nebraska Press, 1970.

Trennert, Robert. *Alternative to Extinction: Federal Indian Policy and the Beginnings of the Reservation System, 1846–1851.* Philadelphia: Temple University Press, 1975.

———. *The Phoenix Indian School: Forced Assimilation in Arizona, 1891–1935.* Norman: University of Oklahoma Press, 1988.

Utley, Robert M. *The Indian Frontier of the American West, 1846–1890.* Albuquerque: University of New Mexico Press, 1984.

———. *The Last Days of the Sioux Nation.* New Haven: Yale University Press, 1963.

Vail, A. J. *A Memorial of James M. Haworth.* Kansas City: H. N. Farey and Company, 1886.

Viola, Herman J. "From Civilization to Removal: Early American Indian Policy." In *Indian-White Relations: A Persistent Paradox.* Ed. Jane F. Smith and Robert M. Kvasnicka. Washington, D.C.: Howard University Press, 1976.

Walker, Robert. *Torchlights To The Cherokees: The Brainerd Mission.* New York: Macmillan, 1931.

Weeks, Philip, ed. *The American Indian Experience, a Profile: 1524 to the Present.* Arlington Heights, Ill.: Forum Press, 1988.

Welter, Rush. *Popular Education and Democratic Thought in America.* New York: Columbia University Press, 1962.

White, Leonard D. *The Republican Era, 1869–1901: A Study in Administrative History.* New York: Macmillan, 1958.

White, Richard. *It's Your Misfortune and None of My Own: A New History of the American West.* Norman: University of Oklahoma Press, 1991.

———. *The Middle Ground: Indians, Empires, and Republics in the Great Lakes Region. 1650–1815.* New York: Cambridge University Press, 1991.

Whitewolf, Jim. *The Life of a Kiowa-Apache Man.* Edited by Charles Brant. New York: Dover, 1969.

Wooster, Robert. *The Military and United States Indian Policy, 1865–1903.* New Haven: Yale University Press, 1988.

Worster, Donald. *Dust Bowl: The Southern Plains in the 1930s.* New York: Oxford University Press, 1979.

Wright, Muriel. *A Guide to the Indian Tribes of Oklahoma.* Norman: University of Oklahoma Press, 1951.

Articles

Adams, David W. "Fundamental Considerations: The Deep Meaning of Native American Schooling, 1880–1900." *Harvard Educational Review* 58:1 (February 1988): 1–28.

Armstrong, S. C. "Education of the Indian." *Journal of Proceedings and Addresses of the Annual Meeting of the National Educational Association,* 1884, pp. 177–80.

Babcock, Sidney H. "John Jasper Methvin." *Chronicles of Oklahoma* 19 (June 1941): 113–18.

Bakeless, O. H. "The Unification of Industrial and Academic Features of the Indian Schools." *Journal of Proceedings and Addresses of the Annual Meeting of the National Educational Association,* 1901, pp. 902–904.

Baxter, Charles J. Untitled address. *Journal of Proceedings and Addresses of the Annual Meeting of the National Educational Association,* 1905, pp. 927–29.

Berens, John. "Old Campaigners, New Realities: Indian Policy Reform in the Progressive Era, 1900–1912." *Mid-America* 59 (January 1977): 51–64.

Blackmar, F. W. "Indian Education." *Annals of the American Academy of Political and Social Science* 2 (July 1891–June 1892): 813–37.

Buntin, Martha M. "History of the Kiowa, Comanche, and Wichita Agency." *Panhandle-Plains Historical Review* 4 (Spring 1931): 62–78.

Butler, Josiah. "Pioneer School Teaching at the Comanche-Kiowa Agency School, 1870–1873." *Chronicles of Oklahoma* 8 (December 1928): 482–528.

Corwin, Hugh. "Protestant Mission Work among the Comanches and Kiowas." *Chronicles of Oklahoma* 46 (Spring 1968): 41–57.

Covey, C. C. "The Reservation Day School Should Be the Prime Factor in Indian Education." *Journal of Proceedings and Addresses of the Annual Meeting of the National Educational Association,* 1901, pp. 900–901.

Crimmins, M. L., ed. "Colonel Robert E. Lee's Report on Indian Combats in Texas." *Southwestern Historical Quarterly* 39 (July 1935): 21–32.

Cutler, Lee. "Lawrie Tatum and the Kiowa Agency, 1869–1873." *Arizona and the West* 13 (Autumn 1971): 221–44.

Daddario, Wilma A. " 'They Get Milk Practically Every Day,' The Genoa Indian Industrial School, 1884–1934." *Nebraska History* 73 (Spring 1992): 2–11.

Downes, Randolph C. "A Crusade for Indian Reform, 1922–1934." *Mississippi Valley Historical Review* 32 (December 1945): 331–54.

Dyke, Charles Bartlett. "Essential Features in the Education of the Child Races." *Journal of Proceedings and Addresses of the Annual Meeting of the National Educational Association,* 1909, pp. 928–32.

Ellis, Clyde. " 'Truly Dancing Their Own Way': The Modern Revival and Diffusion of the Gourd Dance." *American Indian Quarterly* 14 (Winter 1990): 19–34.

"The Failure of the Educated American Indian." No author. *American Monthly Review of Reviews* 33 (January –June 1906): 629–30.

Foreman, Grant. "Historical Background of the Kiowa-Comanche Reservation." *Chronicles of Oklahoma* 19 (June 1941): 129–40.

Furman, Nicah. "Seedtime for Indian Reform: An Evaluation of the Administration of Commissioner Francis Ellington Leupp." *Red River Valley Historical Review* 2 (Winter 1975): 495–517.

Gage, Lucy. "A Romance of Pioneering." *Chronicles of Oklahoma* 29 (Autumn 1951): 284–313.

Gruber, Jacob. "Ethnographic Salvage and the Shaping of Anthropology." *American Anthropologist* 72 (December 1970): 1289–99.

Hagan, William T. "Kiowas, Comanches, and Cattlemen." *Pacific Historical Review* 40 (August 1971): 333–55.

Hailmann, William N. "The Next Step in the Education of the Indian." *Journal of Proceedings and Addresses of the Annual Meeting of the National Educational Association*, 1895, pp. 80–86.

Hall, G. Stanley. "How Far Are the Principles of Education along Indigenous Lines Applicable to American Indians?" *Journal of Proceedings and Addresses of the Annual Meeting of the National Educational Association*, 1908, pp. 1161–64.

Heeter, S. L. "The Teacher's Responsibility to the Indian Child." *Journal of Proceedings and Addresses of the Annual Meeting of the National Educational Association*, 1909, pp. 932–33.

Hendrick, Irving G. "The Federal Campaign for the Admission of Indian Children into Public Schools, 1890–1934." *American Indian Culture and Research Journal* 5, no. 3 (1981): 13–32.

Herring, Rebecca. "Their Work Was Never Done: Women Missionaries on the Kiowa-Comanche Reservation." *Chronicles of Oklahoma* 64 (Spring 1986): 69–84.

Hewes, Dorothy W. "Those First Good Years of Indian Education: 1894–1898." *American Indian Culture and Research Journal* 5, no. 2 (1981): 63–82.

Hiatt, Burritt M. "James M. Haworth, Quaker Indian Agent." *Bulletin of the Friends Historical Association* 74 (Autumn 1958): 80–93.

Holford, David M. "The Subversion of the Indian Land Allotment System, 1887–1934." *Indian Historian* 8 (Spring 1975): 11–21.

Horsman, Reginald. "Scientific Racism and the American Indian in the Mid-Nineteenth Century," *American Quarterly* 27 (May 1975): 152–68.

Hoxie, Frederick E. "From Prison to Homeland: The Cheyenne River Indian Reservation before World War I," *South Dakota History* 10 (Winter 1979): 1–24.

———. "Redefining Indian Education: Thomas J. Morgan's Program in Disarray." *Arizona and the West* 24 (Spring 1982): 5–18.

Huggard, Christopher J. "Culture Mixing: Everyday Life on Missions among the Choctaws." *Chronicles of Oklahoma* 70 (Winter 1992–93): 432–49.

"Indian Treaties and Councils Affecting Kansas." *Kansas State Historical Society Collections* 16 (Winter 1923–24): 746–72.

Kracht, Benjamin R. "Kiowa Powwows: Continuity in Ritual Practice." *American Indian Quarterly* 18 (Summer 1994): 321–48.

Addresses of the Annual Meeting of the National Educational Association, 1884, pp. 181–83.

Rogers, F. K. "The Teaching of Trades to the Indian." *Journal of Proceedings and Addresses of the Annual Meeting of the National Educational Association,* 1900, pp. 698–701.

Sparhawk, Frances C. "The Indian Question." *Education* 7 (September 1886): 50–57.

Standing, A. J. "The Proper Relation between Literary and Industrial Education in Indian Schools." *Journal of Proceedings and Addresses of the Annual Meeting of the National Educational Association,* 1900, pp. 692–95.

Steele, Aubrey L. "The Beginning of Quaker Administration of Indian Affairs in Oklahoma." *Chronicles of Oklahoma* 17 (December 1939): 364–92.

———. "Lawrie Tatum's Indian Policy." *Chronicles of Oklahoma* 22 (Spring 1944): 83–98.

Trennert, Robert A. "Educating Girls at Nonreservation Boarding Schools, 1878–1920." *Western Historical Quarterly* 13 (July 1982): 169–90.

———. "From Carlisle to Phoenix: The Rise and Fall of the Indian Outing System, 1878–1930." *Pacific Historical Review* 52 (August 1983): 267–91.

———. "Indian Sore Eyes: The Federal Campaign to Control Trachoma in the Southwest, 1910–1940." *Journal of the Southwest* 32 (Summer 1990): 123–49.

———. "Selling Indian Education at World's Fairs and Expositions: 1893–1904." *American Indian Quarterly* 11 (Summer 1987): 203–20.

Unrau, William. "The Civilian as Indian Agent: Villain or Victim?" *Western Historical Quarterly* 3 (October 1972): 405–20.

———. "Indian Agent vs. the Army." *Kansas Historical Quarterly* 30 (Summer 1964): 129–52.

Vaughan, Alden T. "From White Man to Redskin: Changing Anglo-American Perceptions of the American Indian." *American Historical Review* 87 (October 1982): 917–53.

Welsh, Herbert. "Comment on Thomas Morgan's 'Indian Education.' " *Journal of Social Science* 40 (December 1902): 178.

Woodward, Calvin W. "What Shall Be Taught in an Indian School?" *Journal of the Proceedings and Addresses of the Annual Meeting of the National Educational Association,* 1901, pp. 904–909.

Zwink, T. Ashley. "On the White Man's Road: Lawrie Tatum and the Formative Years of the Kiowa Agency, 1869–1873." *Chronicles of Oklahoma* 56 (Winter 1978–79): 431–41.

Dissertations and Theses

Adams, David W. "The Federal Indian Boarding School: A Study in Environment and Response." Ed.D. diss., Indiana University, 1975.

Gilcreast, Everett Arthur. "Richard Henry Pratt and American Indian Policy, 1877–1906: A Study of the Assimilation Movement." Ph.D. diss., Yale University, 1967.

Lassiter, Luke E. "Towards Understanding the Power of Kiowa Song: A Collaborative Exercise in Meaning." Ph.D. diss., University of North Carolina at Chapel Hill, 1995.

Mann, Henrietta. "Cheyenne-Arapaho Education, 1871–1982." Ph.D. diss., University of New Mexico, 1982.

Moore, Ida Cleo. "Schools and Education among the Kiowa and Comanche Indians." M.A. thesis, University of Oklahoma, 1940.

Pennington, William D. "Government Policies and Farming on the Kiowa-Comanche Reservation, 1969–1901." Ph.D. diss., University of Oklahoma, 1972.

Putney, Diane T. "Fighting the Scourge: American Indian Morbidity and Federal Policy, 1897–1928." Ph.D. diss., Marquette University, 1980.

Steele, Aubrey L. "Quaker Control of the Kiowa-Comanche Agency." M.A. thesis, University of Oklahoma, 1938.

Wild, George Posey. "History of Education of Plains Indians of Southwest Oklahoma since the Civil War." Ph.D. diss., University of Oklahoma, 1941.

Index